D1326901

Imperialism as Diaspora

Postcolonialism across the Disciplines 13

Postcolonialism across the Disciplines

Series Editors
Graham Huggan, University of Leeds
Andrew Thompson, University of Exeter

Postcolonialism across the Disciplines showcases alternative directions for postcolonial studies. It is in part an attempt to counteract the dominance in colonial and postcolonial studies of one particular discipline – English literary/cultural studies – and to make the case for a combination of disciplinary knowledges as the basis for contemporary postcolonial critique. Edited by leading scholars, the series aims to be a seminal contribution to the field, spanning the traditional range of disciplines represented in postcolonial studies but also those less acknowledged. It will also embrace new critical paradigms and examine the relationship between the transnational/cultural, the global and the postcolonial.

Imperialism as Diaspora

Race, Sexuality, and History
in Anglo-India

**Ralph Crane
and
Radhika Mohanram**

Liverpool University Press

First published 2013 by
Liverpool University Press
4 Cambridge Street
Liverpool L69 7ZU

British Library Cataloguing-in-Publication data
A British Library CIP record is available

ISBN 978-1-84631-896-2 cased

Typeset in Amerigo by Carnegie Book Production, Lancaster
Printed and bound by CPI Group (UK) Ltd, Croydon CR0 4YY

Contents

List of Illustrations   vi

Acknowledgements   viii

Introduction: Race, Gender, and Diaspora: Explorations
    of Anglo-India   1

1 Masculinity Forged Under Siege: The Indian Mutiny of 1857   22

2 The Terrains of Identity: Mimicry and the Great Game   55

3 The Missionary's Position: Love and Passion in Anglo-India   83

4 The Laws of Desire: Intimacy and Agency in Anglo-India   108

Epilogue: Imperialism as Diaspora   136

Bibliography   139
Index   147

List of Illustrations

1. Coat of arms of the Old East India Company, used from 1600 to 1709. Reproduced with permission of the Guildhall Library, City of London/Bridgeman Art Library.   6

2. *Robert Clive and Mir Jafar after the Battle of Plassey, 1757*, by Francis Hayman. Oil on canvas, circa 1760. Reproduced with permission of the National Portrait Gallery, London.   7

3. *The Capture of Delhi*, engraved by Bequet Freres, published by W. Morier, Paris, 1858 (coloured litho), after Rene de Moraine (fl. 1858). Reproduced with permission of the National Army Museum, London/Bridgeman Art Library.   25

4. *Miss Wheeler defending herself against the sepoys at Cawnpore*. From Charles Ball's *The History of the Indian Mutiny* (1858). Reproduced with permission of the Bridgeman Art Library.   26

5. *The Relief of Lucknow*, by Thomas Jones Barker. Oil on canvas, 1859. Reproduced with permission of the National Portrait Gallery, London.   28

6. *The British Lion's Vengeance on the Bengal Tiger*, by John Tenniel, *Punch*, 22 August 1857. Reproduced with permission of *Punch* Ltd., www.punch.co.uk.   32

7. *In Memoriam: Henry Havelock*, by Joseph Noel Paton. Oil on panel, 1858. Private collection.   34

8. *The Remnants of an Army*, by Lady Elizabeth Butler. Oil on canvas, 1879. Reproduced with permission of the Tate Gallery, London.   57

9. *Save Me From My Friends*, *Punch*, 30 November 1878. Reproduced with permission of *Punch* Ltd., www.punch.co.uk.   58

10. 'Our Missionary', in George Francklin Atkinson, *'Curry and Rice,'
    on Forty Plates; Or The Ingredients of Social Life at 'Our Station' in
    India*. London: Day, 1859. Reproduced from the collection of the
    Australian National Library.   89

11. *The Palmer Family*, by Francesco Renaldi. Oil on canvas, 1786.
    Reproduced with permission of The British Library Board (Foster
    597).   111

12. *Sir David Ochterlony in Indian Dress and Smoking a Hookah and
    Watching a Nautch in his House in Delhi*, by an anonymous artist
    working in the Delhi style. Watercolour, circa 1820. Reproduced
    by permission of The British Library Board (Add.Or.2).   112

Acknowledgements

The research and writing of this book was expedited by several grants and periods of study leave. We would like to thank the British Academy for the award of a grant in 2007, which funded Ralph Crane's visit to Cardiff and enabled us to begin work on this project. We would also like to thank the University of Tasmania for the award of a visiting scholarship in 2011, which funded Radhika Mohanram's visit to Hobart and provided us with the opportunity to revise the manuscript. We would also like to express our gratitude to the University of Tasmania and Cardiff University for granting us periods of study leave, during which the bulk of the research and writing was carried out, and for providing financial assistance to cover the cost of permission fees to reproduce the illustrations. The Centre for Colonialism and Its Aftermath at the University of Tasmania provided project funding for the index.

We appreciate the assistance provided by staff in the British Library's Asian and African Studies reading room and by Rachel Adams in the document delivery section of the University of Tasmania's Morris Miller Library.

Earlier versions of the discussions of Charles Pearce's *Love Besieged*, A.E.W. Mason's *The Broken Road*, Margaret Wilson's *Daughters of India*, and Maud Diver's *Lilamani* have appeared in our co-authored introductions to the Oxford University Press (India) editions of those novels, edited by Ralph Crane.

INTRODUCTION

Race, Gender, and Diaspora: Explorations of Anglo-India

This book is a response to a series of questions: how does living elsewhere, making a home overseas, being powerful and wealthy in another country, belonging to the foreign minority, but wielding incredible power and authority over the native majority, living your day-to-day reality in this new space, imagining it to be your new home, interacting daily in a hierarchically superior position with most people, eating different foods, living in a different climate, different housing, and wearing different clothes, and moving up the social ladder, in comparison to where you came from, change you, as well as impact on your writing? Do you unlearn your previous self? Do you redefine this new self? How does being cut off from the site of your racial and national history, while acting in its name, impact on the way in which you constitute yourself? Is there a seamless continuum between the nation of origin (Britain) and the colony (India), in which the minority functions as the hegemonic group? Or is there a transformation of the self, caused by the displacements, discontinuities, and discomforts that permeate the compromises of everyday life?

These questions have, in turn, generated a further set of questions. Do geographical movements affect social structures and relationships? Specifically, do they affect the discursive constructions of race, gender, and sexuality? Is the comprehension of gender learned at 'home' pertinent to new spaces, new climes, and new situations? If gender is redefined and reanimated, what does it do to the experience of sexuality? How do you prevent yourself from feeling sexually attracted to the other, when you grow up together and they surround you, take care of you, and are present within your home? How are sexuality and intimacy experienced, then?

In the broadest sense, how do political and historical transformations impact on issues of race, gender, and identity in Anglo-India? It is these questions that have initiated and directed our reading of Anglo-India, premised on issues of diaspora, nostalgia, fear, and restlessness, as much as on power, aggression, colonialism, racial hierarchies, and gender difference. This introduction consists of two parts: first, Anglo-Indian identity is interpreted as diasporic; second, the impact of the diasporic status on questions of sexuality, gender, and intimacy is examined. Building on this scaffolding, the book as a whole presents a postcolonial reading of the fictions of Anglo-India, rather than a reading of British imperialism per se. It is a reading that emerges from historical certainty and knowledge of the end of the British Raj; we read these texts from within a postcolonial framework, a postcolonialism that makes its way after feminism, after the onset of post-structuralism – with its focus on otherness, ambivalence, and hybridity – after the certainty of globalization, after the attempts to understand multiculturalism, after the witnessing of the rise of China as the new superpower, after the coinage of the term 'the Asian century' and, indeed, with an awareness that India has turned to America, not Britain, as its new progenitor in spirit, teaching it to be global. It is a postcolonial reading that is influenced by the theorizing of global movements of people, both rich and poor, as well as by theories of the body within discourses of gender, race, diaspora, and sexuality, and similarly that of identity – in particular, diasporic identity.

Our focus on Anglo-Indian emotions and their link to their subjectivity is particularly apposite, as recent scholarship on the effects of racial formations gesture towards the melancholia that imbues the racialized subject. Elsewhere, Radhika Mohanram explores whiteness as partaking in the structures of melancholia.[1] The melancholic subject's response to the loss of another (object) as continuous and ongoing is the cornerstone, not only of Freud's theory on melancholia, but is also central to an understanding of his essay 'The Ego and the Id'. What is of importance to this study is how the loss of 'Britain' is rewritten and manifested, both bodily and through the economy of emotions by the Anglo-Indian.

This focus on emotions is directly linked to the diasporic condition. How does this refocusing on Anglo-Indians as diasporic shift our perspective on their identification? In 'Reflections on Exile', Edward Said suggests that the migrant has a 'discontinuous state of being':

> The exile knows that in a secular and contingent world, homes are always provisional. Borders and barriers which enclose us within the safety of familiar territory, can also become prisons, and are often defended beyond reason or necessity. Exiles cross borders, break barriers of thought and experience. (185)

The exile's discontinuous state of being suggests the opposite of having a sedentary, rooted identity; it offers an alternative way of feeling at home in the world. Cosmopolitanism did not only eventuate in postmodernity; colonialism

---

1 See Radhika Mohanram, *Imperial White: Race, Diaspora, and the British Empire*, 122–48.

also provided the opportunity for a cosmopolitan existence. The large-scale movement of Europeans to non-European spaces and non-Europeans to Anglo-Euro-American spaces has contributed to a hybrid way of thinking. In 'The Imam and the Indian', Amitav Ghosh compares the traditional, rural village in the Nile Delta to an airline transit lounge; even villagers, he suggests, can have a history of restlessness and movement (5–6). This discontinuous state of being demands that an alternative mode of understanding of being, bodies, and history be recognized – one that is not fixed, but rather one that is open to revision. For the diasporic individual, according to Iain Chambers, '[h]istory is harvested and collected, to be assembled, made to speak, re-membered, re-read and rewritten, and language comes alive in transit, in interpretation' (3). This form of reading history, generally considered as championing a sedentarist mode of thinking, demands sensitivity to movement, ambivalence, and becoming, with a focus on the processes by which bodies and identities dissolve and transmute into something different. Histories are carried in one's body; historical transformations are also bodily transformations. For the diasporic, knowledge is the sum total of movement. The past is a reconfigured country, a figment of reconstituted memory. Identity is both discontinuous and multiple.

Other theorists who celebrate the radical potential that diaspora offers are Daniel Boyarin and Jonathan Boyarin, who, in their well-cited article on diaspora and Jewish identity, indicate that the two different routes through which group identity is constituted are those of common genealogical origin or common geographical origin. For Boyarin and Boyarin, these two routes are often conflated or racial belonging is often intertwined with the notion of autochthony, which results in the problematizing of immigrant populations. This conflation also results in the renunciation of all difference, so that there is a univocal discourse around the idea of belonging. Further, a social hierarchy also develops, which is inherent to ideas of sameness that are present within group identity. Boyarin and Boyarin offer a different route through which group identity can be imagined by positing a Jewish identity that partakes in a bodily sense of a community, while simultaneously refuting any natural connection between people and place. They valorize diasporic identity, because it is 'a disaggregated identity. Jewishness disrupts the very categories of identity because it is not national, not genealogical, not religious, but all of these in dialectical tension with one another' (721). It is along these same lines that Yasmin Hussain writes:

> Diasporas emerge out of migrations of collectivities and are places of long-term, if not permanent, community formation. [These individual and collective memories] over time become reconfigured and reassembled according to the historical circumstances in which they have been situated. Therefore, should origins be treated in essentialist terms or as a matter of historical displacements? (7)

Whilst there is an idealization of diaspora as cosmopolitan and hybrid, offering multiple identities and allegiances, Khachig Tololyan raises an important and often ignored issue in the theorizing of diaspora – the trajectory of power of the state or nation in the formation of the diasporic subject. In general, the theorizing of diaspora valorizes its ability to disrupt binaries of race or space, such as black/white, West/East or colonizer/colonized (see Braziel and Mannur 4). But what if the diasporic subject reinforces and, in fact, *invents* these binarisms, as in the case of Anglo-India? Anglo-Indians were specifically implicated in British imperial power and constructed in opposition to the colonized Indian subject. In 'Geography, Literature and Migration', Paul White suggests that migration challenges earlier self-perceptions of the migrant. Indeed, in Anglo-India, the incoming British transform into a whiteness that can only be meaningful within an Indian colonial context. Racial hierarchies must be invented and universalized to rationalize colonialism. In fact, one could say that the racializing of the body can be seen also to be caused through movement and migration. The Anglo-Indian racial 'otherness' in India was quickly projected onto the native, as Gayatri Spivak would suggest, 'worlding *their own world*, which is far from mere uninscribed earth, anew, by obliging *them* to domesticate the alien as Master' (211). In *Imperial Bodies*, E.M. Collingham describes the transformation of British bodies from the first half to the second half of the nineteenth century, when a new bodily form emerged, which represented the changing politics of Anglo-India. For Collingham, the improved links between all of the various pockets of British settlements, as well as improved communications between England and India, resulted in the Anglicizing of the Anglo-Indian (50). In an embodiment of changing political relations, the migrant British transmuted from an Indianized body with a love for flamboyant colours and lighter clothing that typified the seventeenth and eighteenth centuries to one that deliberately fashioned itself as Anglicized in the nineteenth century. The increase of the imperial presence in India after the 1857 Mutiny also meant that Anglo-Indian clothes reflected an elaborate symbolism. To emphasize the Anglo- part of Anglo-India meant a growing disregard for the climatic realities of India: civilian British officials had to wear a black suit, notwithstanding its inappropriateness in the heat of India; women wore heavier clothes in winter, imported from Britain, even though it was not really necessary in an Indian winter. Collingham suggests that the sobriety of clothing amongst Anglo-Indian men and women was a 'distancing function ... signifying a retreat into the body but also into Britishness to the exclusion of the Orient' (65).

But was this transformation in Anglo-Indian appearance only to reiterate and align themselves with their counterparts in metropolitan Britain? Did it *only* have a distancing function? Indeed, it is a characteristic of migrant life to recreate various elements from the old country, so that they function as a talisman of great symbolic significance. Wearing black in Anglo-India was a ritual exhumation of their past life in Britain. This excess of inappropriate black clothing, the excess of sobriety in Anglo-Indian colours, also reflects the anxiety of unravelling identity, a deliberate attempt to *appear* British, even if life around them was Indian, so as to embody an imperial difference. And it is this ambivalence at the heart of their bodies' meanings – an ambivalence that emerges from having become homogenously white with a seeming disregard for class and regional distinctions amongst each other; from attempting to be European whilst living in non-European locales; from their bodies signifying their multiple identities, while verbally espousing a singular British identity that further categorized them as migrants – that functions as the starting point of our work.

Whilst the topic of diaspora in contemporary scholarship is associated more often with globalization that has led to striking changes in local, regional, and national practices, previous forms of diaspora share some of the same characteristics, such as hyphenated identities and multinational attachments. For Vijay Mishra, the old and new forms of diaspora cohere around the notion of home. Not only does the diasporic individual long for home, but the reiteration of home is a salutary lesson, for 'diasporic discourse of the homeland is … a kind of return of the repressed for the nation-state itself', as it needs 'diasporas to remind it of what the idea of homeland is' (424). Indeed, it is the desire to return to the homeland that is generally regarded as providing the principle of diasporic identity. Yet even within the context of the loss and alienation that shaped Anglo-Indian attitudes to ruling India, there were also complex attachments, not only to the place of origin, but also to the place of domicile. Rudyard Kipling's work on India, especially in *Kim* (1901), scrambles notions of home and belonging: is India home or Britain (or England or Ireland, for that matter)? One can posit that this ambivalence of where one belongs, which marks Kipling's work on India, is reproduced in the representation of Kim. Thus, home and away are placed in creative tension in this novel, affirming what Avtar Brah states as 'inscribing a homing desire while simultaneously critiquing discourses of fixed origins' (193).

The British in India

Who were the Anglo-Indians? The pre-history of the Anglo-Indians, the beginning of England's shared history with the Indian subcontinent, can arguably be said to have commenced with the charter granted to the 'Governor and Company of Merchants of London trading into the East Indies' by Queen Elizabeth I on 31 December 1600, although, as Philip Lawson points out in *The East India Company: A History*, 'England's interest in the trade of the East began a century before the founding of the East India Company' (7). The Royal Charter set a course that, over the next 250 years, would see the Honourable East India Company – colloquially known as 'John Company' and 'Kampani Bahadur' – 'rise to paramount power in the subcontinent and … lay the foundations for the magnificent imperial structure of the British Raj' (Judd 6).

Figure 1. Coat of arms of the Old East India Company, used from 1600 to 1709. Reproduced with permission of the Guildhall Library, City of London/ Bridgeman Art Library.

The nature of 'the magnificent imperial structure of the British Raj' will be unpacked over the course of this study.

The Company's first factory was set up in Surat in 1612. During the rest of the seventeenth century and despite upheaval in Britain, trade with India flourished under the stable rule of the Mughal emperors, and the company's representatives established a chain of trading posts or factories around the coastline of the subcontinent. Pepper and spices were procured from the Malabar Coast, cotton cloth produced by Indian weavers was obtained from various parts of the subcontinent, Madras supplied sugar, and Bengal traded in silk and saltpetre. In return, England exported various metals, tapestries, mechanical novelties, and, most importantly, silver bullion. This whole

Figure 2. *Robert Clive and Mir Jafar after the Battle of Plassey, 1757*, by Francis Hayman. Oil on canvas, circa 1760. Reproduced with permission of the National Portrait Gallery, London.

commercial operation, rivalled in size only by the Dutch East India Company, was run out of London by twenty-four directors, elected annually by approximately 3,000 shareholders (Moorhouse 25–33; Lawson 18–85). By the end of the seventeenth century, the Company had established three Presidencies – Madras, Bombay, and Bengal – each of which traded independently and reported directly to London.

The next stage of Britain's colonization of India occurred during the first half of the eighteenth century, when, as Geoffrey Moorhouse notes, '[a]lthough conquest was still far from the Company's thoughts, there was a conscious attempt to transplant familiar institutions to this developing colony in the East' (34). As law courts and other civic institutions were established in each of the three Presidencies, the rule of the Mughals and Hindu princes began to give way to the rule of the British. The second half of the eighteenth century saw a growing appetite for conquest and a taste for the additional rewards brought about by the exercise of power. Indeed, Robert Clive's victory in the Battle of Plassey and the subjugation of Bengal in 1757 has been seen by many historians as the real beginning of the British Empire in India – the moment when British influence gave way to British rule. With Mir Jafar in place as a puppet ruler in Bengal, the future Nabobs (the name given to the Anglo-Indians who returned to Britain with vast wealth) began the plunder of the country that would mark the rest of British rule. As Moorhouse puts it:

> From this point, although no-one recognized it for the moment, there was no going back to the notion of East India Company chain stores around the margins of the country, which is what the Directors had been carefully building for nearly 150 years and what they still wished for in Leadenhall Street. From now on the British were in the position of rulers and would only expand from a provincial to an imperial dimension. (47–48)

The governors of the Company settlements became governors of provinces, many in the service of the Company became administrators, and large armies of Indian sepoys were recruited to protect and extend the Company's territories. And while, in the late eighteenth century, men like Warren Hastings, the Governor of Bengal from 1772 to 1785, took an Orientalist approach to his role, by the end of the century, such views were giving way to the belief that India needed the firm hand of British rule in order to prosper. At the end of the century, the imperialist Richard Wellesley, the Earl of Mornington (later the Marquess Wellesley and the older brother of the Duke of Wellington), who served as Governor-General of Bengal from 1798 to 1805, 'inaugurated twenty years of military activity that made the Company by 1818 master of India' (Metcalf and Metcalf 67). But even as the Company's military grip tightened, its control was loosened in other ways, as a consequence of three specific conditions set out in the renewal of the Company's charter in 1813. The new India Act ended the Company's monopoly on Indian trade, ordered that £10,000 should be spent on education, and required that the Church of England be established in India (Moorhouse 86). In the decades which followed, India opened up to evangelicals and to political and social reformers. As Thomas Metcalf notes in *Ideologies of the Raj*, for people like James Mill (father of John Stuart Mill), Indians were a 'rude' people, who had made 'but a few of the earliest steps in the progress to civilization'. For Mill, India existed in 'a hideous state of society', inferior even to that of the European feudal age (Metcalf 30). Mill, along with other liberal and utilitarian reformers like Jeremy Bentham, would have approved that such practices as suttee, thuggee, and female infanticide were outlawed, and educational policies designed to Christianize and Westernize Indians were introduced, which would have a lasting effect on the subcontinent.

The pattern was clear: Britain would fashion India along Western lines, and no ground would be given to Indian culture or customs. Lord William Bentinck, Governor-General of India from 1828 to 1835, clearly recognized the error of this in a speech he delivered to the British Parliament, following his return home from India:

> In many respects the Mohammedans surpassed our rule; they settled in the countries which they conquered; they intermixed and intermarried with the natives; they admitted them to all privileges; the interests and

sympathies of the conquerors and conquered became identified. Our policy has been the reverse of this; cold, selfish and unfeeling; the iron hand of power on the one side, monopoly and exclusion on the other. (quoted in Moorhouse 94)

But by then, policy in India was being moulded by men like Sir Thomas Babington Macaulay, whose infamous 1835 'Minute on Indian Education' advocated an Anglicist, rather than Orientalist, approach to education in India. Reminding ourselves of the pre-history of the Anglo-Indian is important, as it suggests how the policies and politics in India inevitably affected their diasporic identity as imperial.

The large-scale conquest of India in the first half of the nineteenth century was in itself perhaps of less consequence than the attacks on Indian culture and customs during the same period, and it was the pace of these latter changes that made the uprising of 1857 almost inevitable. And, as Moorhouse notes, '[t]he big puzzle about the Mutiny – and it has never been satisfactorily explained – is why it was restricted to a comparatively small area of the subcontinent' (106). What is clearer is that the mistakes that led to the so-called greased cartridges affair, which finally ignited the revolt, would probably not have been made fifty years earlier, before evangelical Protestantism had driven a wedge between the two races (see, for example, Saul David 72–74).

Following the Indian Mutiny of 1857 to 1958, the rule of India passed from the East India Company to the Crown and the period that we now refer to as the British Raj officially began. The Governor-General was also now the Viceroy, and the power he exercised in India was far greater than that exercised by the Prime Minister in Britain. The only checks on the Viceroy were provided by his Executive Council and the Legislative Council, and their roles were little more than advisory ones. India was now subjected to greater military and political control than ever before, exercised by a ruling elite that was increasingly segregated from the population over which it ruled and, as Indrani Sen notes at the outset of *Woman and Empire*,

> [i]n many ways the second half of the nineteenth century was particularly important with regards to the question of gender in British India. The events of the Rebellion of 1857 had culturally foregrounded the white woman – a trend further strengthened by the arrival of English women in India in large numbers around mid-century onwards. (1)

The presence of white women in India was not new. In the late eighteenth century, women started coming out to India in search of husbands; in the early decades of the nineteenth century, a few women, such as Fanny Parkes and Emily Eden, accompanied husbands or brothers to India. However, the rise of the Memsahib in the second half of the nineteenth century was to alter again the fabric of Anglo-Indian society, as the domestic life of the British community became, in Pat Barr's words, 'more self-sufficient and elaborate' (144) and the cantonments and civil lines where they lived were increasingly demarcated from the bazaars and native towns of the subcontinent. The memsahibs celebrated British festivals, attempted to reproduce British gardens in an unforgiving landscape, and, whenever possible, purchased goods from European stores. In *Imperial White*, Radhika Mohanram has argued for the location of white women within imperialism in an atemporality, functioning to provide a sense of home, timelessness, and England – itself a feature of diasporic identity.

There was, however, less call on the army than the civil service in the maintenance of British power during the second half of the nineteenth century, although the regular military skirmishes on the North West Frontier were to become the source of the tales of derring-do, which feature so large in the mythology of British India and Anglo-Indian fiction.

Anglo-Indian

In *Sahibs, Nabobs and Boxwallahs: A Dictionary of the Words of Anglo-India*, Ivor Lewis outlines the shifting meaning of the term Anglo-Indian: 'It first denoted a person of "pure" British descent resident or born in India, but in 1911 the Government of India decided to substitute this term for "Eurasian" as the official one for persons of mixed descent' (51). He adds that: 'It also refers to anything composed of English and Indian elements, to terms adopted by English from Indian languages, and to literature about India written by British authors in English' (51). His definition is entirely in accord with the entry in the *Oxford English Dictionary*:

> A. *adj*. Of, pertaining to, or characteristic of India under British rule, or the English in India. B. *n*. a. A person of British birth resident, or once resident, in India. b. A Eurasian of India.

The *OED* further informs us that the first recorded use of the term was in John Malcolm's *The Political History of India, 1784–1823* (1826) and clearly documents the shift in meaning after 1911.

In keeping with this earlier meaning, we will use the term Anglo-Indian literature throughout this study to describe the body of literature about India written by British authors. This is in keeping with Bhupal Singh's early, but nevertheless still useful, definition of the genre in the opening paragraph of his 1934 study, *A Survey of Anglo-Indian Fiction*:

> The phrase 'Anglo-Indian fiction' may be used in a broad or narrow sense. Broadly speaking it includes any novel dealing with India which is written in English. Strictly speaking it means fiction mainly describing the life of Englishmen in India. In a still narrower sense it may be taken to mean novels dealing with the life of Eurasians, who now prefer to be called Anglo-Indians. (1)

In this book, our focus will be on fiction dealing with the English in

India, rather than with mixed-race characters. Writing over fifty years later, M.K. Naik's definition of the genre is consistent with Singh's:

> Anglo-Indian fiction may broadly be defined as fiction by British writers in which generally a British or occidental protagonist operates mostly in an Indian setting (though the scene may shift to England occasionally), and interacts with Indian and other British or occidental characters. (3)

Naik's definition appears to exclude the work of non-British occidental writers from the canon of Anglo-Indian fiction, but, in practice, he includes the work of Canadian writer Sara Jeanette Duncan (Mrs Everard Cotes) and American writers Louis Bromfield and Margaret Wilson in his study. While they may not strictly be Anglo-Indian authors, these and other non-British novelists of the Raj (from Canada, America, and a little later from Australia and New Zealand) have made a significant contribution to the body of Anglo-Indian fiction. Duncan is the author of six significant Anglo-Indian works, including *The Simple Adventures of a Memsahib* (1893), *The Pool in the Desert* (1903), and *The Burnt Offering* (1909). Bromfield, the author of over thirty best-selling works, wrote two novels set in India after visiting the subcontinent in 1933: *The Rains Came* (1937) and *Night in Bombay* (1940), the former being made into a successful Hollywood movie starring Tyrone Power in 1939. Wilson, who spent time in India as a missionary, published short fiction and two novels set in India, *Daughters of India* (1928) and *Trousers of Taffeta* (1929). We have included a discussion of Margaret Wilson's *Daughters of India* in this study, both because it is a fine missionary novel and also to allow a non-British Anglo-Indian perspective to be introduced.

The 1857 Mutiny and Gendered Anglo-Indian Identity

It is the fine balance between the citing of home – Britain – and the critiquing discourses of fixed origins that we feel is central to the production of a gendered, white Anglo-Indian identity in India. Diaspora theory, for the most part, is predicated on an *ungendered* notion of the diasporic, as if both genders were affected in identical ways. Within a postcolonial framework, however, there is a tendency to gender the colonial process itself, by suggesting a feminization of colonial spaces. In this, the white colonizer is the only masculine form. The implications of this assumption are problematic, because, in this line of reasoning, both colonizing and colonized women are deprived of a proper structural position that they can occupy within a gendered colonial discourse, since both positions of masculinity and femininity are occupied by men from the two groups.

We contend that the emergence of a specifically gendered Anglo-Indian identity was made possible through a break, a rupture, caused by the 1857 Mutiny. The history of British India has always retroactively reclaimed events as far back as the eighteenth century (the Battle of Plassey, for instance) to perceive the beginnings of imperialism. Such a retroactive move locates Britain as moving towards fulfilling its imperial destiny as a global power. Whilst we do not disagree with such readings, we wish to disturb them. We suggest that the movement of the British in India, from being traders to becoming an imperial power, was more discontinuous and uneven than the gradual unfolding of a smooth imperial narrative. The 1857 Mutiny, grounded in its specificity, led to the shaping and contouring of a white Anglo-Indian gendered identity – imperialistic and imperious, a cover for its sense of vulnerability and an awareness of being vastly outnumbered by the natives; masculinized, but with an underlying sense of how quickly Anglo-Indian bodies could be annihilated, violated, mutilated, rendered passive, and feminized. In 'The Diasporic Imaginary', Brian Axel defines his term as 'a process of identification generative of diasporic subjects' (412), and, indeed, Anglo-Indian identity lends itself to such a process. A highly gendered process, Anglo-Indian identity is revealed to be a negotiation between temporality and corporeality, (British) nationalism and imperialism, as brought forth by the 1857 Mutiny.

In *Critical Events: An Anthropological Perspective of Contemporary India*, Veena Das suggests that the occurrence of certain events in the history of a nation 'institutes a new modality of historical action which was not inscribed in the inventory of that situation' and redefines categories (5). Thus, in her reading, the 1947 partition of India, which was particularly detrimental to women and children, re-organized the family and community by giving greater agency to the state. Such re-organization affected the legal status of women and children and altered concepts of Indian femininity and sexuality. In the context of Anglo-India, we argue that the 1857 Mutiny was a critical event that completely transformed British identity in India. If earlier Anglo-Indians saw themselves as employees of the East India Company in India to further trade, this critical event transformed them into servants of the imperial machine. What was new was that the demands of the Empire intersected with racial discourse to create a unique interpretation of events, identity, and sense of destiny. This critical event inserted a new public discourse on Anglo-Indian women and children, in which the agency was held by the Empire and a militaristic masculinity. 'Cawnpore' as a signifier connoted new and threatening meanings to the very presence of Anglo-Indians, which transformed their attitude to India and Indians and shaped an emergent identity into being.

Such a reading of the 1857 Mutiny as a critical event is in continuum with Linda Colley's thesis in *Britons*. For Colley, the span of 130 years between 1707, when the Act of Union joined Scotland with England and Wales, and 1837, when the Victorian period was formally inaugurated, was crucial to the forging of a British national identity. Colley contends that enmity with France, along with a strong sense of Protestantism, amalgamated to form a strong British national identity and suggests that 'Britishness was superimposed over an array of internal differences in response to contact with the Other, and above all in response to conflict with the Other' (6). Indeed the 1857 Mutiny reminded the Anglo-Indians of the stock from which they emerged – shaped by the enmity with, and threat from, the Other, along with the strong sense of destiny that a chosen people would have. As Colley explains, '[s]uffering and recurrent exposure to danger were a sign of grace; and, if met with fortitude and faith, the indispensable prelude to victory under God' (28). While Colley focuses on European history – particularly Britain's engagement with Catholic France – for the forging of Protestantism in Britain, Peter van der Veer asserts that nineteenth-century Protestantism had been formed during the 'transformation of the modern world in which colonial interactions had been crucial' (11). Read together, Colley and van der Veer inform our readings of the cultural history of Anglo-India in general and Mutiny fiction in particular.

While our purpose here is only to delve into the cultural history of the Mutiny and show its connection to a diasporic sensibility, in the chapter on Mutiny fiction we develop this notion of the Mutiny as a critical event and discuss the causes and history of the mutiny at length. We suggest that three different sites – Delhi, Lucknow, and Cawnpore – were central to the shaping of Anglo-Indian history and led to the gendering of Anglo-Indian identity. These moments and sites are by no means insignificant. As Collingham notes, a tour of mutiny sites 'almost took on the character of a pilgrimage' (113) for future generations of Anglo-Indians. In fact, as Stephen J. Heathorn points out, Thomas Cook – founder of the travel agency – 'visited the "Mutiny" cities himself, and thereafter arranged tours of India that included Cawnpore on the itinerary, and commissioned guidebooks to northern India that paid special attention to the memorial sites.' As recently as 2007, 150 years after the Mutiny, a three-week group tour, led by the historian Rosie Llewellyn-Jones, re-enacted this pilgrimage. In doing so, the party of approximately twenty, including descendants of Generals Sir Henry Havelock, Sir Hugh Rose, and Sir Henry Lawrence – who helped to suppress the Mutiny – re-memorialized this significant moment in Anglo-Indian history. Their presence in India caused mass protest, indicating that the memories of 1857 remain significant for both contemporary Indians and British alike.

The fateful events in Cawnpore (Kanpur) provided a stark contrast to those that were played out in Delhi. Cawnpore, a cantonment city located on the Ganges River, consisted of hundreds of bungalows, which were occupied by British officers in 1857; the British part of the city further consisted of barracks for troops, separate bazaars for each regiment, a church, a theatre, and a café (see Blunt 411). When the Mutiny spread to Cawnpore, the British population lived under siege at the cantonment – an important trope for the production of a besieged white identity. Eventually, General Wheeler, who commanded the cantonment, made arrangements with the mutineers to evacuate the besieged city. However, the departing British were instead attacked, and over 200 women and children captured, imprisoned, and eventually killed on 15 July 1857, ahead of the impending arrival of the British relief forces. It took over a month for this news to filter through to Britain and a further three weeks before it could be confirmed.

The scenes that greeted the soldiers when they arrived in Cawnpore were horrific. Eyewitness accounts state that the bodies of the women had been stripped of their clothes before they were murdered and thrown into the well, and the children – some who were still alive – had been thrown into the well on top of their mother's bodies. The repetition of these horrific descriptions circulated in India, Britain, and throughout the Empire. Eventually, the building in which the women and children had been imprisoned and murdered – the Bibighar – was converted into a shrine and museum to be visited by the British. On display as relics were the remnants of the belongings of the dead women and children. Alison Blunt states:

> the remnants and relics described and often collected by British soldiers visiting the Bibighar memorialized the loss of British women who had been killed at Cawnpore and descriptions of their hair and blood represented their fate in viscerally embodied ways. (414)

British soldiers inscribed the walls of the Bibighar as a memorial to the hapless victims. These images, drawings, references, markings on the wall, and legends of Cawnpore were an aesthetizing of violence and functioned as a form of what Cynthia Keppley Mahmood labels 'massacre art' (189), which not only cried for revenge, but also cohered with a specific Anglo-Indian identity, serving as its point of origin – white women and children needing white men and the might of imperial rule to protect them.

How, then, do the images of these women and children work within the dynamics of diasporic identity and the re-imagination of gender? How do massacre art and the aesthetizing of suffering become aligned with imperial identity? We suggest that there are two distinct steps to the argument that makes visible the interpellation of an Anglo-Indian identity. First, there must be a shift in the comprehension of diaspora from its references and connection to the place of origin to one shaped by violation, retaliation, a focus on multiple sites and the affect evoked by the violence. The repeated images from Cawnpore resuscitate – even in 2007, as Rosie Llewellyn-Jones's group realized – a comprehension of racial difference, which places the Mutiny at its originary moment. The constant references to the women and children of Cawnpore allow it to function at a subterranean level to produce a sense of racialized memory and intrudes on every disturbance that imperial rule in India encountered. The memories of the Cawnpore victims derive only in one part from their gruesome death; they also derive from the constant evocation of this history in visual and textual histories. The formation of Anglo-Indian identity requires an understanding of the role of violence and lies at the intersection of imperialism and a sense of belonging and entitlement on the one hand and the vulnerability of young and gendered bodies on the other. The significance of the evocation of Cawnpore lies in its reference to the monstrous, treacherous Other – the Indian mutineers. The images of the Bibighar and the atrocities that occurred therein is a substitution for the images of the history of treachery, the history of vulnerability, and the constant threat and fear of being grossly outnumbered. Through a process of displacement, the women and children of the Bibighar stand in for all Anglo-Indians, both male and female. The violated bodies of the Anglo-Indian women and children, in this instance, also become a sign of the fragility of the Anglo-Indian grip on India – a fragility that had to be constantly erased from view.

Second, Cawnpore as signifier also links vulnerable bodies with imperial governance. The violation of vulnerable bodies of women and children enact a drama of contestation between civilized, imperial governance and the murderous, uncivilized behaviour of the mutinying Indians. The savage, indigenous Indians needed the civilizing, diasporic imperial governance of the British. The fear of vulnerability, of having easily annihilated bodies, produces its object, the white body, distinctly Anglo-Indian and belonging to India with a right to its governance, able to bring order to its chaos, whilst also referring to a powerful elsewhere – Britain and its imperial might. Further, the battered bodies of Anglo-Indians that were thrown down the well at Cawnpore produce an image of the Indian mutineer as rapist and baby killer. Indeed, as a number of feminist scholars, including Jenny Sharpe and Alison Blunt, have suggested, the myth of Judith Wheeler is directly connected to the representation of the mutineer as rapist. General Wheeler's daughter and one of the victims of Cawnpore, Judith Wheeler, was purported to have been kidnapped by an Indian cavalryman. Later, she was to have killed him and his family for the dishonour she had suffered. Furthermore, she is said to have died by throwing herself down the well behind his house (Blunt 413). Out of the myth of Judith Wheeler and other Cawnpore victims arises a sense of an Anglo-Indian gendered identity, as well as a sense of normative and sanctioned heterosexuality; Anglo-Indian women for Anglo-Indian men. As Mrinalini Sinha suggests in *Colonial Masculinity*, '[p]erceptions of real and imaginary assaults by native men on white women became the pretext for the terrible vengeance that Anglo-Indians wreaked on the native population after the defeat of the rebellion' (47). Indeed, miscegenation is anathema, not just for its race-mixing, but because it is a strike against the legitimacy of the Empire, which can be maintained only through the whiteness of Anglo-Indian bodies. As Ann Stoler claims in *Carnal Knowledge and Imperial Power*, the 'micromanagement of sexual arrangements and affective attachments was … critical to the making of colonial categories and deemed … important to the distinctions between ruler and ruled' (8). The fear of rape and miscegenation contours Anglo-Indian identity and is at the core of its production of a sexed body.

The violated body of Cawnpore is remade as non-violate in Delhi. Indeed, the significance of Cawnpore cannot be viewed in isolation, but must be juxtaposed against the images of Lucknow and Delhi, in that, collectively, they refer to the whiteness and mightiness of Anglo-Indian bodies. Whereas Cawnpore was the site of the white female body defiled, Lucknow was the site of the white female body protected. Delhi, in turn, provided the iconic site of the white masculine body returning order to the Empire. We suggest that the juxtaposition of Cawnpore with Lucknow and Delhi makes visible the containment of anxieties through the production of the masculine Anglo-Indian body. This shift in emphasis, from Cawnpore to Lucknow to Delhi, permits Anglo-Indian identity to rewrite itself as permanent and re-imagine itself as entitled. This new gendered identity legitimises the harsh retaliation for Cawnpore and silences the indigenous history of the Mutiny.

What we have been arguing here, following Brian Axel's fascinating work on the diasporic imaginary, is that Anglo-Indian identity is diasporic, predicated on the gendering of the body and through emotions of fear, anxiety, and the self-justification of retribution. The oscillation between imperial right and the vulnerable body is at the core of the diasporic imaginary in Anglo-India. The vulnerable, white, feminized body of Cawnpore is the body under erasure, yet it provides the very scaffolding upon which Anglo-Indian identity is constructed. In its place is erected the complete body – white, male, tough, and impossible to violate. This body is Anglo-Indian; it is the imperious body that overcomes and overwhelms the indigenous in India.

These historical transformations are mirrored in Anglo-Indian fiction, specifically in the body of work that has become popularly known as 'Mutiny fiction'. In the years following the Mutiny, Anglo-Indian novelists created multiple versions of events – particularly surrounding the Siege of Lucknow and the horrific events at Cawnpore – that idealized the British and vilified the mutineers and which would dominate fictional representations of the Mutiny for the next century. However, as Christopher Herbert makes clear, citing as an example T. Henry Kavanagh's 1860 memoir *How I Won the Victoria Cross*, non-fictional records of events published in the decades immediately following the Mutiny were far more critical of the British imperial enterprise in India in the years leading up to the rebellion (12) than their romanticized fictional counterparts.

Anglo-Indian Fiction

As Kate Teltscher shows in *India Inscribed*, there is a long history of British writing on India, including travel literature and missionary letters. Alongside these genres, military memoirs and scholarly accounts of Indian history and culture flourished in the eighteenth century. The first Anglo-Indian novel, *The Disinterested Nabob*, was published anonymously in 1785. It was followed by Phebe Gibbes's *Hartly House, Calcutta*, published anonymously in 1789, and Elizabeth Hamilton's *Translations of the Letters of a Hindoo Rajah* in 1796.[2]

---

2 See Phebe Gibbes, *Hartly House, Calcutta*, ed. Michael J. Franklin (New Delhi: Oxford University Press, 2007); and Elizabeth Hamilton, *Translations of the Letters of a Hindoo Rajah*, ed. Pamela Perkins and Shannon Russell (Peterborough: Broadview, 1999).

Literary texts about India began to be published in large numbers in the 1830s, when literary columns began to appear in daily papers (which were published in the Presidency towns – Calcutta, Bombay, and Madras – as well as in the hill stations) and Anglo-Indian weeklies. These often took the form of short prose narratives, which set out to describe colonial life in India, in order to consolidate the imperial agenda. They included historical tales, in which British rule replaces an older, corrupt system of Indian rule; love stories, which describe a young married couple overcoming the difficulties of life in India or an interracial marriage, which invariably fails; crime stories, in which native villains are brought to book through the diligent work of a British official; missionary tales, in which a Hindu girl recognizes the evil of her religion and converts to Christianity; and sketches, which range from descriptions of the macabre customs of native life to the landscape. However, it was the novel that became by far the most popular form of Anglo-Indian literature in the nineteenth century.

In 1827, Sir Walter Scott published *The Surgeon's Daughter*, and, in 1838, William Makepeace Thackeray's *The Tremendous Adventures of Major Gahagan* was published. According to Oaten, however, 'Meadows Taylor was the first great name in the history of Anglo-Indian fiction' (146). The publication of *Confessions of a Thug* in 1839 caused a sensation in both Britain and India, and Taylor went on to cement his reputation with *Tipoo Sultan: A Tale of the Mysore War* (1840), *Tara: A Maratta Tale* (1863), *Ralph Darnell* (1865), *Seeta* (1872), and *A Noble Queen: A Romance of Indian History* (1878). In the middle of the century, William Delafield Arnold – the brother of Matthew Arnold – published *Oakfield, or Fellowship in the East* (1853), regarded by Saros Cowasjee as 'the single most important work of the pre-Kipling era' (x). Between *Oakfield* and the work of the more famous writers of the late nineteenth century, Sir Henry Stuart Cunningham's *The Chronicles of Dustypore* (1875) and Sir George Tomkyns Chesney's *The Dilemma: A Tale of the Mutiny* (1876) stand out from a great deal of rather indifferent fiction. For many critics, including Oaten and Cowasjee, Kipling's *Plain Tales from the Hills* (1888) marks the real beginning of Anglo-Indian fiction, while *Kim* (1901) marks the high point of the genre. Apart from Kipling, the principal fiction writers of the last decades of the nineteenth century and the early twentieth century (1880 to 1910) – referred to by Allen J. Greenberger as 'the Era of Confidence' in *The British Image of India* – are all women; they include Flora Annie Steel, 'the greatest novelist, in the strictest sense of the word, of whom Anglo-Indian literature can boast' (Oaten 159), Maud Diver, Alice Perrin, Bithia M. Croker, and Sara Jeanette Duncan (Mrs Everard Cotes). Between 1910 and Independence in 1947, the major fiction writers included Edmund Candler, whose novel *Siri Ram – Revolutionist* (1912) portrayed a nationalist figure for the first time; Edward Thompson; Dennis Kincaid; E.M. Forster, whose *A Passage to India* (1923) has functioned as an *ur-text* for all Anglo-Indian (and, to some extent, Indian) writers who have followed him; Christine Weston, and Rumer Godden. Perhaps surprisingly, the genre of Anglo-Indian fiction has survived Independence, with scores of Raj fictions being published since 1947. Prominent amongst post-imperial Anglo-Indian writers are John Masters and M.M. Kaye, whose works display a strong Raj nostalgia; Ruth Prawer Jhabvala; J.G. Farrell; and Paul Scott, whose epic Raj quartet, *The Jewel in the Crown* (1966), *The Day of the Scorpion* (1968), *The Towers of Silence* (1971), *A Division of the Spoils* (1975), and its postscript, *Staying On* (1977), has earned him a revered place in the Anglo-Indian pantheon.

As early as 1855, *The Calcutta Review* was calling for a study of the growing body of Anglo-Indian literature:

> Gradually, year by year, the ranks of our Anglo-Indian writers swell, and new works are thrown with eager anxiety on the wide sea of literature and authorship. We have often wished that a full list of them all could be made out and continually supplemented as occasion required. A dictionary of Anglo-Indian writers, or a history of Anglo-Indian literature, would form a subject of immense interest and instruction, not merely to the griffin or the *littérateur*, who makes India and Indians his interested or idle study, but to the student who wishes to turn over a new page in the history of the human mind and the English language and thought in a country where circumstances, associations, and ties are so very different from those of every other land. (quoted in Oaten n.p.)

The first such work was Edward Farley Oaten's *A Sketch of Anglo-Indian Literature* (1908), which was supplemented a quarter of a century later by Bhupal Singh's *A Survey of Anglo-Indian Fiction* (1934). These pioneering studies were followed by further book-length surveys, which collectively mapped the field and confirmed the view expressed in L.S.S. O'Malley's *Modern India and the West* that 'Anglo-Indian literature is really a subject in itself' (552): Allen J. Greenberger's *The British Image of India: A Study in the Literature of Imperialism* (1969), Brijen K. Gupta's *India in English Fiction, 1800–1970: An Annotated Bibliography* (1973), Rashna B. Singh's *The Imperishable Empire: A Study of British Fiction on India* (1988), M.K. Naik's *Mirror on the Wall: Images of India and the Englishman in Anglo-Indian Fiction* (1991), and Sujit Mukherjee's *Forster and Further: The Tradition of Anglo-Indian Fiction* (1993). Other significant studies include Benita Parry's *Delusions and Discoveries: Studies on India in the British Imagination 1880–1930* (1972), Shamsul Islam's *Chronicles of the Raj: A Study of Literary Reaction to the Imperial Idea towards the End of the Raj* (1979), David Rubin's *After the Raj: British Novels of India Since 1947* (1986), Richard Cronin's *Imagining India* (1989), Ralph Crane's *Inventing India: A History of India in English Language Fiction* (1992), Saros Cowasjee's *Studies in Indian and Anglo-Indian Fiction* (1993), and, more recently, Gautam Chakravarty's excellent work, *The Indian Mutiny and the British Imagination* (2005).

Significantly, most of these studies focus on Anglo-Indian fiction, which, as M.K. Naik observes, 'during the half-century after Bhupal Singh's survey appeared ... has gone from strength to strength, though Anglo-Indian poetry and drama have virtually died out' (x). The present study, too, will focus on the work of selected Anglo-Indian novelists, including lesser-known writers, such as Charles Pearce, Victoria Cross, and Margaret Wilson; writers who were well-known in their day, but whose star has since waned, such as Flora Annie Steel, A.E.W. Mason, Maud Diver, and Alice Perrin; along with the most famous and enduring Anglo-Indian writer, Rudyard Kipling.

Anglo-Indian Fiction as Diaspora Writing

This work consists of four substantial chapters, which, we believe, capture the central preoccupations, attitudes, behaviours, discourses, and themes that cohere around the Anglo-Indian and their diasporic formations. The chapters thematically oscillate around the Mutiny, a sense of duty, the missionary, and interracial love. All of our readings are located within the cultural history of the Anglo-Indian that shaped the theme explored in each chapter. We felt the need to explore the cultural history, because we wanted to tether these texts to their contexts and the material concerns and preoccupations of the Anglo-Indian, which were not exactly the same as those of the British at home. The Anglo-Indians were on the front line of the Empire, greatly outnumbered by the Indians, yet imposing their imperial will over them. Their daily negotiation of power and danger was transformative and marked their fictional and other cultural productions as an extension of their diasporic identity. Thus, this work covers the narratives and artistic endeavours that shaped and governed gendered Anglo-Indian identity and their everyday lives, the danger, intimacy, desire and domesticity, religious feelings and a sense of destiny, imperial rule as a duty and as monastic, and the anxieties and threats of miscegenation. We want to emphasize that these constructions are cultural productions of a people in a diaspora.

Chapter One reads Mutiny fiction to suggest that this critical event re-interpolated the Anglo-Indians, both racially and in terms of gender. In *White*, Richard Dyer suggests that the 1857 Mutiny, along with the Morant Bay Rebellion and the American Civil War, deeply affected Anglo-American white identity, and, indeed, our reading suggests that the threat that the Indians and the mutineers posed profoundly affected the Anglo-Indian sense of embodiment and concretized perceptions of gender relations in India, which had an impact in Britain as well. We argue that the new masculinity that Anglo-Indian men embodied was a direct result of both the violence and their diasporic condition.

Chapters Two and Three contain the narratives of duty, by which Anglo-India rationalized its imperialistic manoeuvres: Anglo-India as steward, maintaining and protecting India for its indigenous inhabitants, and as the civilizing mission bringing Christianity to heathen Indians. Chapter Two is set within the discourse of the danger that Russia posed to British interests in Afghanistan and the North West Frontier Province, and the Great Game played out in South Asia as two European powers jostled for power. Our discussion of the Great Game is framed by a detailed examination of imperial history of the 1830s and 1840s and the activities of a few individuals – Arthur Conolly, Alexander Burnes, and James Abbott, amongst others – who were the first players of the Great Game. The two works discussed in this chapter, A.E.W. Mason's *The Broken Road* (1907) and Kipling's *Kim*, contain the slippages within the racial hierarchy of Anglo-India, which was established and enhanced through the Mutiny. Both novels interrogate the hierarchy between black and white by eliding the differences between the two and the tragedy, waste, and impossibility of maintaining these hierarchies. *The Broken Road*, in particular, locates Britain's Great Game with Russia in India as a sacrifice – what young men have to sacrifice for the sake of the Empire. White masculinity, in this novel, is tethered to sacrifice, a sense of duty, utter loneliness, and a life without women or joy. An asexual commitment to duty becomes a requirement of the white male's diasporic imperial activity.

Whilst Chapter Two focuses on the secular/military side of Anglo-India, Chapter Three explores the part played by religion and the conversion of the natives within imperialism. In this chapter, we analyse Margaret Wilson's *Daughters of India* and Alice Perrin's *Idolatry* (1909), both of which discuss the status of religion within imperialism. Our discussion takes account of the historical transformations that resulted from the rise of evangelical Protestantism following the Napoleonic Wars and how that, in turn, shaped both British and imperial identities in the decades leading up to the Mutiny. While there is a general sense that the church and the military worked in tandem in the colonization of India, the Mutiny had, in fact, fostered an opinion among Anglo-Indians that the threat of religious conversion had initiated the unrest. When India formally became a part of the British Empire in 1858, there was a downgrading of religion in Anglo-India. Yet it was precisely the missionaries and their Christian beliefs that lent a sense of benevolence to an otherwise exploitative Anglo-Indian dominance in India. The sense of morality, justice, and values espoused by the secular members of Anglo-India had as much to do with the Church as Enlightenment principles. Missionary activity, by its very nature, becomes a diasporic activity. Both novels critique imperialism. Further, both novels continue the theme of India as a site of asexuality. Indeed, the first three chapters cohere together to suggest the impossibility of being sexual in India. The final substantial chapter thus proceeds to explore sexuality – a difficult script for Anglo-India – and, in particular, interracial sexuality in Victoria Cross's *Life of My Heart* (1905) and Maud Diver's *Lilamani* (1911). Cross's novel, which has a female Anglo-Indian in love with an Indian, crosses both racial and class boundaries. Diver's novel has a British man in love with an Indian woman and is set in Britain. Our discussion in this chapter traces the history of Anglo-Indian desire and examines the taboos on sexual intimacy between the races. It focuses, in particular, on the way that evangelical Protestantism directed attitudes towards interracial sex in the 1830s and 1840s, as well as the transformations that followed official actions against interracial unions in, for example, the Burma Circular of 1867 and the Crew Circular of 1909.

Finally, this work will attempt to read the relationship between diaspora and imperialism. Diaspora, as a term, is generally reserved for the disenfranchised: the Jewish people exiled from their homeland; the scattering of West Africans through slavery in the Middle Passage; the dispersal of Asians through indenture in the second Middle Passage; or the plight of refugees made homeless and, at times, stateless by war or the redrawing of boundaries on the map. But imperialism not only draws attention to the circuit of power that is inherent to, but occluded by, the notion of diaspora. It also draws together the two terms diaspora and imperialism in new ways. In his essay on the 'Three Meanings of Diaspora', Steven Vertovec enumerates the different characteristics that make diaspora a social form. These characteristics include voluntary migration, conscious maintenance of a collective identity, institutionalizing of exchange and communication beyond territorial states, fostering the feelings of alienation from the host society and economic strategies by pooling resources and investing capital for the betterment of the diasporic group. These characteristics speak directly to Anglo-Indian identities and seem to suggest that imperialism itself is closely related to a diasporic consciousness. The whiteness of the British, the Anglo-Indians, cohered to form a homogenous group, unmarked by class or regional differences. In India, even the colonized Irish became white. In this work, the focus on imperialism reveals its underpinnings as a diasporic formation in India.

What this work offers – both severally and in the sum of its parts – is a more nuanced approach to the understanding of imperial rule in India. Part of this approach is to consider in each chapter how imperial and historical transformations are reflected in the body of Anglo-Indian fiction. Imperialism, while most visible within the context of power and which formed the political economy of Anglo-India, reveals a different image of itself, if read through an alternate economy of emotions and the unmooring that being a member of the diaspora brings. Anglo-Indian fiction reveals a different image of itself, when read against a mix of visual culture and history, as well as other works in the Anglo-Indian canon.

Diaspora, migrancy, homesickness, loneliness, fear, and a heightened sense of danger all produce a different, more complex reading of the Anglo-Indian than the 'bourgeois aristocracy' that straightforward readings of imperialism produce. Our more nuanced reading reveals a ruler who is dependent on the native for far more than his power. The native also offers companionship, a sense of family, security, and being at home, as well as functioning as a source of strength and an abiding reason for Anglo-Indian presence. It is only in this alternate economy of emotions, which runs alongside, but lies outside the politics of race, class, gender, and sexuality, that we can see and begin to understand the contours of everyday Anglo-Indian life and the anxieties involved in being an Anglo-Indian.

CHAPTER 1

Masculinity Forged Under Siege:
The Indian Mutiny of 1857

For 150 years, the dreadful events which took place in parts of northern and central India during 1857 to 1858 have been referred to as the 'Indian Mutiny' within British imperial history and are now ensconced within Indian postcolonial history as the 'First War of Independence'. In keeping with the militaristic nomenclature ('mutiny', 'war'), Anglo-Indian literary representations of the events (which are also variously called the Great Revolt, the Sepoy Mutiny, the Sepoy Rebellion, the Sepoy Revolt, and the Freedom Struggle of 1857)[1] are frequently articulated in terms of masculinity: as the need for British soldier heroes to protect British women from the savagery of Indian men. The politics of the private sphere are used in Mutiny fictions to mask the brutality of colonialism and to demonize the armed uprisings of a colonized people. In his annotated bibliography, *India in English Fiction, 1800–1970*, Brijen Gupta lists more than eighty Mutiny novels published in the ninety years between the uprising of 1857 and Indian Independence in 1947, the majority of which feature the soldier hero defending threatened white British womanhood as their central narrative trope, rather than the politics that instigated this particular historical event.

Mutiny novels were numerous enough and sufficiently popular in the late nineteenth and early twentieth centuries to form a discrete subgenre of the Anglo-Indian novel and imperial adventure story. Indeed, the Victorianist Christopher Herbert argues that 'Mutiny fiction proliferated to the point of becoming a major subcategory of the British novel' (273). As Hilda Gregg observes in 'The Indian Mutiny in Fiction', published in *Blackwood's Edinburgh Magazine* in 1897, '[o]f all the great events of this century, as they are reflected in fiction, the Indian Mutiny has taken the firmest hold on the popular

---

1 For a detailed discussion of the vexed issue of the naming of the conflict, see Christopher Herbert's *War of No Pity*, pp. 7–11.

imagination' (218). Moreover, as Herbert notes, although few of these novels are 'likely to strike readers as particularly distinguished, relative to the high artistic standard of Victorian popular fiction … they are particularly valuable as indices of popular consciousness of the time' (273). The plots of these novels are remarkably similar and, to a large extent, conform to the formula outlined by Shailendra Dhari Singh in *Novels on the Indian Mutiny*:

> The hero, who is an officer, meets the young charming lady, just out from England, or who happens to be in India from before, and falls in love or both come to India in the same ship, and strike a liking on board the ship itself. In India the historical situation is already ripe for mutiny, and the lovers are suddenly pitched into the upheaval. (183)

The signal that '[i]n India the historical situation is already ripe for mutiny' is most often relayed by the mysterious circulation of chapattis (unleavened Indian bread) among the native population, after which, if the novel is a siege novel (as many are), 'the lovers are suddenly pitched into the upheaval' as they and their fellow Europeans (along with 'loyal' Indians) retreat into the Residency of the local Collector, where those that survive endure months of ceaseless fighting and suffer disease and starvation, before finally being rescued by relieving British forces. Throughout the siege, the heroine of the novel, who, in Bhupal Singh's words, is invariably 'spirited, beautiful, courageous, and a good rider' (3), provides both the love interest for the thread of romance that commonly runs through these fictions and functions as the white woman to be protected from the British love rival, if there is one, and, more importantly, from the Indian enemy, who threatens with rape and death. Yet, notwithstanding their predictability, why did Mutiny novels take such a hold on the British popular imagination of the mid-nineteenth century and beyond? And, specifically, what is the relationship between the romance plot and the siege plot in Mutiny novels? First, though, we shall provide a brief narrative of the major causes and events of the so-called Indian Mutiny of 1857.

On 10 May 1857, sepoys (native soldiers) of the 11th and 20th Native Infantry and sowars (native cavalrymen) of the 3rd Light Cavalry in Meerut – an important military station in the Bengal Presidency – mutinied against their British officers and massacred the European residents of the town. This military mutiny was a violent response to a series of grievances, which had been smouldering among the sepoy ranks for many months. The annexation of Oudh (Awadh) under Dalhousie's Doctrine of Lapse in February 1856 had unsettled the high-caste Hindus from that province, who made up one-third of the Bengal Army. The General Service Enlistment Act of 1856, following discontent over postings to Burma, required Indian sepoys to accept service wherever they were sent. Additionally, the poor pay and lack of opportunities for promotion for sepoys were further causes of dissatisfaction. There was also a growing belief that British missionaries were conspiring with officials to convert sepoys to Christianity. But what finally ignited the insurrection in

Meerut in May 1857 – what Barbara Metcalf and Thomas Metcalf usefully label 'the proximate cause' of the Mutiny (100) – was the sepoys' anger over the cartridges which had been issued for use with the new breech-loading Enfield rifles. The sepoys were ordered to bite the tips off the paper cartridges, before inserting them into the barrels of their rifles. It was generally – and accurately – believed that, to make loading easier, these cartridges had been greased with a mixture of animal fats, including beef fat and pork fat, which would defile both Hindus and Muslims. Philip Mason vividly explains the contaminating effect that biting these cartridges would have had on the religious identities of the sepoys:

> On the lips of a Hindu cow's fat would be an abomination for which there is no parallel in European ways of thinking; it was not merely disgusting, as excrement would be; it damned him as well; it was as bad as killing a cow or a Brahman. To a Muslim pig's fat was almost as horrible. (158)

When the sepoys in Meerut refused to bite the cartridges, eighty-five of them were stripped of their uniforms and led off to jail in chains. The next day, as the British officers and their families were preparing for the evening church service, the Mutiny began.

Following the Mutiny in Meerut, the rebels made their way to Delhi, where, on 11 May, they again killed the British officers, their wives, their children, and the native Christians, before proclaiming the reluctant, octogenarian Mughal King of Delhi, Bahadur Shah Zafar II, as the ruler of India (Hindustan). Mutiny novels set in Delhi focus on the British siege of the city and the restoration of British rule. These include James Grant's three-volume novel *First Love and Last Love: A Tale of the Indian Mutiny* (1868), which depicts life in the rebel-held city, as well as in the British encampment; Flora Annie Steel's *On the Face of the Waters* (1896), perhaps the most distinguished Mutiny novel published in the nineteenth century; A.F.P. Harcourt's *Jenetha's Venture: A Tale of the Siege of Delhi* (1899); and the final instalment of Charles E. Pearce's Mutiny triptych, *A Star of the East: A Romance of Delhi* (1912). The storming and capture of Delhi was celebrated as a major victory and duly recorded by many artists of the day. Popular representations include *The Capture of Delhi*, an engraving by Bequet Freres after Rene de Moraine (1858) (see Figure 1), and *The Storming of Delhi*, a line engraving by Thomas H. Sherratt after Matt Somerville Morgan (1859).

As news of the uprising spread, sepoys from other regiments joined the rebels, and further outbreaks occurred in military stations and towns throughout the Bengal Presidency. From Delhi, the rebel force moved to Cawnpore (Kanpur) and, under the leadership of Nana Sahib, laid siege to the British garrison. The events that took place in Cawnpore are the most extreme example of Indian violence and stand out above all others in the British memory of the Mutiny. Cawnpore, as Jane Robinson explains, 'was not merely a matter of military affront: ... It was ... the first time the women of England had ever been slaughtered in the history of battle' (98). After the mutiny of the

PRISE DE DELHI (PAR LES ANGLAIS)

CAPTURE OF DELHI (BY THE ENGLISH)

Figure 3. *The Capture of Delhi*, engraved by Bequet Freres, published by
W. Morier, Paris, 1858 (coloured litho), after Rene de Moraine (fl. 1858).
Reproduced with permission of the National Army Museum, London/
Bridgeman Art Library.

2nd Cavalry regiment on 5 June, the British lived under siege in entrenchments,
until, after eighteen days, General Sir Hugh Wheeler surrendered to Nana
Sahib, who, in return, promised the Europeans safe passage down the river
to Allahabad. Instead, on 27 June 1857, in what became, for Britain, the most
infamous moment of the Mutiny, the party was attacked as it boarded the
boats at Satichaura Ghat; one boat escaped, but was quickly recaptured.
Legend has it that two women, including General Wheeler's daughter, were
abducted.[2] The 210 women and children who survived the massacre at the
ghat (landing point or quay) were imprisoned in the Bibighar (house of

---

2 Two Eurasian girls, Judith Wheeler and Amelia Horne, were believed to have been
carried off by sowars of the 2nd Cavalry. One version of Miss Wheeler's story is
that she killed her captor and his family, before throwing herself down a well;
another version is that she survived and lived as a Muslim woman in Kanpur.
Amelia Horne lived with her captor for several years, either voluntarily or as
his prisoner, before she was allowed to escape. She published two accounts of
her ordeal, first in 1859 and again in 1913. For further details, see Chistopher
Hibbert's *The Great Mutiny*, pp. 194–95.

Figure 4. *Miss Wheeler defending herself against the sepoys at Cawnpore*. From Charles Ball's *The History of the Indian Mutiny* (1858). Reproduced with permission of the Bridgeman Art Library.

women). Then, on 15 July, two days before the rescuing British forces entered Cawnpore, those that had not already died of disease were butchered and their bodies thrown down a nearby well.

The British cultural (and racial) memory of Cawnpore is that of the white woman under threat of rape and murder at the hands of deceptive Indians. Perhaps the best known representation of this trope is the image of *Miss Wheeler defending herself against the sepoys at Cawnpore* (see Figure 4). This famous (though entirely fictional) image depicts Miss Wheeler killing several sepoys, before, it is assumed, killing herself to protect her honour (see Sharpe 71–73). As Andrew Ward points out in *Our Bones are Scattered*, 'her gallant end became a staple of Victorian theatricals and the subject of the most popular of the melodramatic engravings that were collected eventually in Ball's *The History of the Indian Mutiny*' (504). Another popular image was John Tenniel's cartoon *The British Lion's Vengeance on the Bengal Tiger* (see Figure 6), which was published in *Punch* in August 1857, summed up British anger over the Mutiny. For the most part, though, as Alison Blunt explains, in visual representations, 'British women as victims at Cawnpore were imagined only through their violent absence' (415), as in an engraving in the *Bengal Hurkaru* (a daily newspaper for British residents in India) on 25 November 1857, which shows the back of a British soldier looking at the blood-stained interior of the Bibighar. Charles Pearce uses the iconography of the Mutiny in all three of his Mutiny novels to deliberately maintain cultural memory or, what Jenny

Sharpe has called, 'a racial memory of the 1857 uprisings as the barbaric attack of Indian savages on innocent English women and children' (85). In a short Introduction to the second of his triptych of Mutiny novels, *Red Revenge: A Romance of Cawnpore* (1911), Pearce justifies his subject as follows:

> It may seem to some that the story of Cawnpore is one too painful to revive, and if the remembrance meant the horrors alone I should be disposed to agree. But Cawnpore signifies far more than a mere recital of horrors. It stands for all that is noble, heroic, and enduring in the men and women of Great Britain; and as a monumental example of dauntless courage, devotion, and self-sacrifice it cannot be excelled in the world's history. (7)

That 'monumental example' of British courage was celebrated in numerous other textual representations (including popular song) in the second half of the nineteenth century and well into the twentieth. These include Edward Money's *The Wife and the Ward; or, A Life's Error* (1859) and Louis Tracy's *The Red Year: A Story of the Indian Mutiny* (1908); the events are also the subject of Manohar Malgonkar's postcolonial intervention, *The Devil's Wind: Nana Saheb's Story* (1988), which deliberately sets out to balance British portraits of the Nana.

In Lucknow, Sir Henry Lawrence, the Chief Commissioner, gathered the European community and 'loyal' Indian sepoys inside the well-fortified, thirty-three-acre Residency compound. After ninety days, a column of Highlanders under the command of General Sir Henry Havelock and General Sir James Outram fought their way into the Residency, where they, too, were besieged. The garrison survived amidst crumbling buildings and suffering from starvation and disease for five months, before they were finally liberated by Sir Colin Campbell's troops on 17 November 1857. This, rather than the horror of Cawnpore, was the image of the Mutiny that the British would preserve, as J.G. Farrell acknowledges in his post-imperial Mutiny novel *The Siege of Krishnapur* (1973), when his character General Sinclair muses on how the relief of the Krishnapur garrison should be shown to the world:

> Even when allowances were made, the 'heroes of Krishnapur', as he did not doubt they would soon be called, were a pretty rum lot. And he would have to pose for hours, holding a sword and perched on a trestle or wooden horse while some artist-wallah depicted 'The Relief of Krishnapur'! He must remember to insist on being in the foreground, however; then it would not be so bad. With luck this wretched selection of 'heroes' would be given the soft pedal ... an indistinct crowd of corpses and a few grateful faces, cannons and prancing horses would be best. (310–11)

The Siege of Lucknow was considered a high point of British heroism and duly celebrated in the work of artists, poets, and novelists throughout Britain during the remainder of the Victorian period and well into the Edwardian one. Notable amongst these are Abraham Solomon's painting *The Flight from Lucknow* (1858), Frederick Goodall's painting *The Relief of Lucknow (Jessie's Dream)* (1858),

Figure 5. *The Relief of Lucknow*, by Thomas Jones Barker. Oil on canvas,
1859. Reproduced with permission of the National Portrait Gallery, London.

and Thomas Jones Barker's painting *The Relief of Lucknow* (1859) (see Figure 5),
which provides the interdiscursive reference for the Farrell passage quoted
above; Alfred Lord Tennyson's poem 'The Defence of Lucknow' (1879), which
is 'a retrospective commemoration of British fortitude' (Chakravarty 107);
and a host of novels, including H.C. Irwin's *With Sword and Pen* (1904), Charles
E. Pearce's *Love Besieged: A Romance of the Defence of Lucknow* (1909), and, more
recently, J.G. Farrell's Booker Prize-winning novel, *The Siege of Krishnapur*.
Other novels, such as G.A. Henty's *In Times of Peril* (1881), Hume Nisbet's *The
Queen's Desire* (1893), and Frederick P. Gibbon's *The Disputed VC: A Story of the
Indian Mutiny* (1909) (all boys adventure novels) manage to exploit almost all of
the iconic moments and sites of the Mutiny.

In all, fifty-four of the seventy-four regiments of the Bengal Army mutinied
or partially mutinied (David 19). Most of these mutinies were quickly brought
back under control, as was the case with the mutiny of the 55th Native Infantry
stationed at Peshawar. As a warning to others, forty of the sepoys captured by
General Nicholson were sentenced to be blown away from guns. This ghastly
spectacle was witnessed by the whole Peshawar garrison, as well as thousands
of civilian spectators. Each sepoy was tied across the muzzle of a cannon that
had been loaded with powder, but no shot. When the order was given, all forty
cannons were fired simultaneously, blowing the sepoys into oblivion. When
news of the execution reached Britain, it met with the same satisfaction with
which it had been greeted by the Anglo-Indian community in India, as Thomas
Babington Macaulay noted: 'The account of that dreadful military execution
at Peshawar ... was read with delight by people who three weeks ago were
against all capital punishment' (quoted in Hutchins 85). Interestingly though,
as Saul David points out,

it was a punishment first used in India not by the British but by the Moguls; it was regarded by Indian troops as an instantaneous and honourable 'soldier's death' and infinitely preferable to the degradation of death by hanging: and as [Sir John] Lawrence makes clear, it was used not as an act of vengeance but of deterrence, *pour encourager les autres*. (146)

The insurgency was not confined to the military; others, including dispossessed princes, Oudh talukdars (landlords), and peasants, embraced the revolt against British rule. However, the Mutiny was not embraced by the whole population: only three of the twenty-nine native infantry regiments of the Bombay Army mutinied or partially mutinied, and there were no mutinies among the fifty-two native infantry regiments of the Madras Army (David 19); the Sikhs of the recently conquered Punjab remained 'loyal', as did many of the native princes, as well as the Bengali intelligentsia and Bengal's zamindars (Metcalf and Metcalf 101–02). This meant that the uprising was centred on the three northern Indian cities of Delhi, Lucknow, and Cawnpore, where the rebellious sepoys concentrated their efforts, and in central India, where the Maratha leaders – Nana Sahib, Tantia Tope, and the Rani of Jhansi – spearheaded the revolt.

The storming and recapture of Delhi in September 1857 after a long siege was the turning point of the Mutiny. However, it is the massacre at Cawnpore in July 1857 and the successful Relief of Lucknow in November 1857 that became the two iconic sites in the British memory of the Mutiny.

In central India, the fighting continued until the death of the Rani of Jhansi, the fall of Gwalior in June 1858, and the capture and execution of Tantia Tope in April of the following year. Nana Sahib, who, according to Manohar Malgonkar, 'replaced Napoleon Bonaparte as the hate object of a nation' (ix), eluded capture and escaped to the Terai jungles of Nepal, where he is believed to have died of fever in 1859.[3]

While the Mutiny was undoubtedly traumatic for the Anglo-Indian population in India, it was also deeply disturbing for the general public in Britain. It shook their belief, both in their racial superiority and in the Empire. As J.G. Farrell puts it in *The Siege of Krishnapur*, 'India itself was now a different place; the fiction of happy natives being led forward along the road to civilization could no longer be sustained' (225–26). While the fighting continued, explicit and invariably emotive descriptions of the Mutiny kept Britain at once spellbound and horrified. An article published in the *Illustrated London News and Englishwoman's Review* on 26 September 1857, for example, records an eyewitness account of the Bibighar at Cawnpore:

I have been to see the place where the poor women and children were imprisoned and afterwards butchered. It is a small bungalow close to the

---

3 Bahadur Shah Zafar surrendered to the British forces on 21 September 1857. He was eventually put on trial for aiding the mutineers and exiled to Burma, where he died within a few years. For a definitive account of his life and role in the Indian Mutiny, see William Dalrymple's *The Last Mughal*.

road. There were all sorts of articles of women and children's clothing, ladies' hair evidently cut off with a sword, back combs &c. There were also parts of religious books. Where the massacre took place it is covered with blood like a butcher's slaughter house. (quoted in Blunt 414)

Such accounts fuelled cries for vengeance throughout Britain. The prolific Victorian poet Martin Tupper wrote verses demanding the razing of Delhi and the erection of 'groves of gibbets' from which to hang the mutineers, while many in the literate middle classes, including Charles Dickens, wished for revenge (Dawson 94). Their desire for Old Testament retribution – supported by such eminent figures as Lord Shaftesbury, who wrote to Tupper stating that: 'The Sepoys are witnesses against themselves – no evidence is required to establish their guilt' (quoted in Nayar 209–10) – was enacted by General Neill and others. The same September issue of the *Illustrated London News* describes the punishments devised by General Neill at Cawnpore, which, as Alison Blunt observes, 'plumbed new, notorious depths of cruelty' (414):

General Neill was compelling all the high-caste Brahmins who he could capture … to collect the bloody clothes of the victims, and wash up the blood from the floor, a European soldier standing over each with a 'cat', and administering it with vigour … The wretches having been subjected to this degradation, which includes loss of caste, are then hanged, one after the other. The punishment is said to be General Neill's own invention, and its infliction has gained him great credit. (quoted in Blunt 415)

And as Geoffrey Moorhouse writes: 'When Lucknow was finally retaken, sepoys were bayoneted on sight, whether they were armed or not; this was known, among the British troops, as giving them a Cawnpore dinner' (114). Throughout northern India, those suspected of being mutineers were either hanged or blown from the mouths of cannons. However, as Blunt points out, 'the brutality of British soldiers had already reached extreme levels *before* events at Cawnpore had become known' (414, emphasis added). When General Neill reached Allahabad on 11 June, where the 6th Native Infantry had mutinied, troops under his command razed the city and slaughtered 'the inhabitants, old men, women and children as well as those more likely to be active rebels' (Dawson 93).[4] In *The Travels of a Hindu to Various Parts of Bengal and Upper India* (1869), Bholanauth Chunder, a native traveller, records that their corpses hung

by twos and threes from branch and signpost all over town … For three months did dead-carts daily go their rounds from sunrise to sunset, to take down the corpses which hung at the cross-roads and market-places, poisoning the air of the city, and to throw their loathsome burdens into the Ganges. (quoted in Hibbert 202)

4 For a more detailed discussion of Neill's actions at Allahabad, see Hibbert, pp. 200–02.

Yet as Karl Marx reminds us in 'The Revolt in India', published in the *New York Daily Tribune* on 16 September 1857, 'while the cruelties of the English are related as acts of martial vigour, told simply, rapidly, without dwelling on disgusting details, the outrages of the natives, shocking as they are, are still deliberately exaggerated' (Marx and Engels 83).

Although India did not become part of the British Empire until 1858, a year after the onset of the Mutiny – having been ruled prior to 1857 by the East India Company, technically only for the benefit of its shareholders – the suppression of the uprising was perceived by the British public as a 'reconquest' of India, thus endorsing the belief that India had always already belonged to the British. As Francis Hutchins explains, 'India had been in a sense annexed psychologically because of the popular interest which now followed its reconquest. India "belongs to us" Miss [Harriet] Martineau stated confidently, speaking the national mind' (67). Thus, the Mutiny was a significant factor in a rewriting of history and a re-imagining of Britain as a colonial power. The shift in the perception of Britishness and the horrors suffered by the Anglo-Indian civilian population relocated India to a different discursive position, from a space of economic benefits to that of the racial Other, which was the opposite of how the British perceived themselves. Reports of the murder and rape of British women and the slaughter of children obscured the part played by Britain in instigating the Mutiny and shifted the focus to the putative demonic tendencies and treacherous nature of the Indians. For instance, a substantial article entitled 'The Mutinies in India', published in *The Times* stated:

> The history of the world affords no parallel to the terrible massacres which during the last few months have desolated the land. Neither age, sex nor condition has been spared. Children have been compelled to eat the quivering flesh of their murdered parents, after which they were literally *torn asunder* by the laughing fiends who surrounded them. Men in many instances have been mutilated and, being absolutely killed, have had to gaze upon the last dishonour of their wives and daughters previous to being put to death. (9)

Importantly, the Mutiny racialized the Anglo-Indians, as well as the British at home, as cohesively and homogeneously white, unmarked by region or class. The Mutiny created the perception of a seamless continuum between the British domestic population and those who were resident in the far-flung reaches of the Empire. Furthermore, in the aftermath of the Mutiny, Disraeli, the British Prime Minister, extended male suffrage in 1867, changing forever, not only the face of British politics, but also comprehensions of Britishness. In the face of the racialized Other, all British were equal and white together (or at least the men were). As G.O. Trevelyan wrote in *The Competition Wallah* (1864), the Mutiny 'irresistibly reminded us that we were an imperial race, holding our own on a conquered soil by dint of valour and foresight' (quoted in Metcalf 44).

Figure 6. *The British Lion's Vengeance on the Bengal Tiger*, by John Tenniel, *Punch*, 22 August 1857. Reproduced with permission of *Punch* Ltd., www.punch.co.uk.

Mutiny Iconography and Fiction

In this chapter, we will examine two different Mutiny novels, Charles Pearce's *Love Besieged*, first published in 1909, and Flora Annie Steel's 1896 novel, *On the Face of the Waters*, to examine Anglo-Indian identity, its formations of whiteness, and its particular relationship to gendered identity. As is evident, we have selected two Mutiny novels written during the period of British high (or new) imperialism (1870 to 1918)[5] to represent and interpret one of the most important historical events that affected the British almost half a century earlier. Because the two novels were both written during the period of high imperialism, they are, to some extent, inevitably reinventing or re-memorializing the Mutiny from a point forty to fifty years after the events about which they are writing occurred. But it is important to recognize that the two periods – the mid-nineteenth and late nineteenth to early twentieth centuries – are in continuum, as contemporary visual representations of the Mutiny, including Sir John Tenniel's cartoon *The British Lion's Vengeance on the Bengal Tiger* and Sir Joseph Noel Paton's painting *In Memoriam*, aptly demonstrate.

Both of the images, by Tenniel and Paton, capture some of the tensions of race and gender that we explore later in this chapter. John Tenniel's cartoon (see Figure 6) was published across the span of two pages in *Punch* on 22 August

---

5 The dates are those favoured by Elleke Boehmer in *Empire Writing: An Anthology of Colonial Literature 1870–1918*. Eric Hobsbawm prefers more restrictive dates in *The Age of Empire, 1875–1914*.

1857 in the aftermath of a series of eyewitness accounts of the massacre at Cawnpore, which had simultaneously shaken British confidence in its control over India and evoked great anger across Britain. As a cartoonist responding to this crisis of Empire, Tenniel deliberately sets out to influence his viewer, using his cartoon as a tool to fan British public outrage against the sepoys who were held responsible for the fate of British women and children in Cawnpore.

When Joseph Noel Paton's *In Memoriam* was first exhibited at the Royal Academy in 1858, it depicted 'maddened Sepoys, hot after blood … bursting through the door' (quoted in Bayly 241) and was roundly condemned by critics and public alike. In response, Paton revised his work, painting out the murderous sepoys and replacing them with kilted Highlanders. In so doing, he changed the subject of the painting from the ghastly fate of the British women and children at Cawnpore to the altogether more welcome representation of the rescue of British women and children at Lucknow (see Figure 7).

In our reading of the two novels, we want to underscore the centrality of the Mutiny to nineteenth-century British (and Anglo-Indian) identity. Indeed, at least forty Mutiny novels were published during the period of high imperialism – testimony to the enduring importance of the Mutiny in the British imagination. Further, we can see that the continued popularity of Mutiny fiction suggests its function as a parable, for contained within it are the lessons that are relevant to Empire: the fortitude, tenacity, bravery, and overall superiority of the Anglo-Indians that won them India. In *Manliness and Masculinities in Nineteenth-Century Britain*, John Tosh suggests that between 1879 and 1885, the British Empire suffered a series of losses at the hands of the Zulu, Boers, Afghans, and Sudanese, while simultaneously facing renewed violence in Ireland. For Tosh, these losses recalled the threat to the security of the Empire, which the Mutiny had brought about (194). Thus, Mutiny novels of the period of high imperialism seem to function as a root metaphor, providing a way of comprehending contemporary political losses and crises throughout the Empire; contained within them are not only comprehensions of Anglo-Indianness, but also comprehensions of Britishness.

Further, in our analysis of the two texts, we have chosen to examine issues of gender, because, as Joan Scott has indicated in her classic essay 'Gender: A Useful Category of Historical Analysis', the constructions of gender elucidate the many relationships of power represented within society. Also, within the context of colonialism, comprehensions of gender are very closely imbricated with those of nation, class, race, and sexuality. Thus, the repeated references to white women in danger of rape and death as a trope for the Mutiny indicate the importance of the analysis of gender in these fictions. Additionally, we want to focus on the concepts of manliness and femininity, because we feel that the changing concepts of gender relations in nineteenth-century Britain were visible and formed through their various deployments and the tensions that they generated in the colonies. Indeed, the very structure of Mutiny fiction, in which the political/military siege plot is juxtaposed with the romance plot, suggests the close connections between national/imperial

Figure 7. *In Memoriam: Henry Havelock*, by Joseph Noel Paton. Oil on panel,
1858. Private collection.

politics and gender. In other words, Mutiny fiction was not only about the
assertion of British colonialism or Anglo-Indian domination, it was also about
the perpetuation of white superiority in its suggested ending of the happy
coupling of the surviving white hero and heroine.

In this chapter, we will begin our gender analysis with a reading of *Love
Besieged* for its portrayal of an idealized, white, Anglo-Indian masculinity and
the shifts that it underwent during the siege. Indeed, white, Anglo-Indian
masculinity in this novel is forged by the Mutiny. We want to examine,

not only the comprehension of British masculinity that was central to Anglo-Indian formations, but also the part played by Indian masculinity in its representations. By focusing on power relations within gender, we hope to show that they operate as a metaphor for those in the larger political and social arenas. Finally, we have deliberately structured this chapter unchronologically, by concluding it with our analysis of Flora Annie Steel's *On the Face of the Waters*, which was published a decade before *Love Besieged*, because of its feminist overtones and attempt to revise and interrogate conventional comprehensions of patriarchal Anglo-Indian masculinity, as in Pearce's work. In analysing and juxtaposing these two novels, we hope to tease out the close imbrications between gender and racial tensions in nineteenth-century India and Britain and to suggest that imperialism was crucial to the formation of gender relations and representations in Anglo-India.

Love Besieged

Charles Pearce, a newspaper editor and prolific author of popular biographies, wrote a triptych of Mutiny novels between 1909 and 1912: *Love Besieged: A Romance of the Defence of Lucknow*, *Red Revenge: A Romance of Cawnpore*, and *A Star of the East: A Romance of Delhi*. In the Preface to the first of those novels, *Love Besieged*, he exhorts his readers not to forget the events of the Mutiny:

> We in England must never forget the fixed, immutable characteristics of the Indian race. It is well, therefore, that the memory of the past should not be allowed to die out. This end I have had in view in selecting the Siege of Lucknow as the background of a story in which an attempt has been made to picture the circumstances and conditions of the time, the character and methods of the mutineers, the influence of caste, the treachery of which the native is capable and the loyalty which upon occasion he can show, and the heroism, the fortitude, the unflinching devotion of the defenders. (3)

At the same time, he highlights the inscrutability of the native, claiming that '[t]he causes of the disaffection, the identity of the actual leaders, the methods of organisation, are as mysterious now as they were then. Time has done little to add to our knowledge of the native of India' (3). By according a transformative capacity to the Anglo-Indians, while according an unchanging nature to the Indians, Pearce effectively sets up a chiasmus: the Anglo-Indians are complex beings, simultaneously transforming *and* transparent, while in contrast, the Indians are unchanging, but also, paradoxically, unfathomable. In writing this novel, Pearce sets out to comprehend the relationship between the dominant, metropolitan Anglo-Indians and the restless natives, whose secret nature he hopes to lay bare, so that they can be subdued. In his short Preface, he goes on to warn that in the two years preceding the publication of the novel in 1909, 'Western education and training, grafted upon Eastern traditions, custom, character, religion, have introduced fresh dangers, the result of which no man can foresee' (3). The anxiety implicit in the Preface as a whole locates the novel as a parable: what lessons can (or should) be learnt from re-examining the Mutiny sixty years later? Pearce's Preface does not touch upon that which is amply visible to the postcolonial reader: the natives are restless and angry, because power is concentrated in too few hands, and colonialism is intolerable. *Love Besieged* thus takes the status of what Ranajit Guha, in 'The Prose of Counter-Insurgency', calls 'secondary discourse': 'the historical utterance [that] admits of three variations of the past tense … the aorist, the imperfect and the pluperfect, and of course the present is altogether excluded' (130). In Guha's essay, counter-insurgency is the term given to official discourse, and secondary discourse, produced years later, is not substantially different from official discourse, notwithstanding the passage of time, as it is produced from within the same ideological framework. As we shall see, Pearce's readings of events are indeed in a continuum with 1857 British and Anglo-Indian perceptions of the Mutiny.

The novel opens in England in the early months of 1857, where Jean Atherton meets Azimoolah Khan, one of the architects of the Mutiny. Azimoolah pursues Jean in London, but she remains completely unaware of the nature of his interest in her. She arrives in India to join her father, a magistrate in Lucknow, only days before the Mutiny engulfs the city. Evacuated immediately to the Residency, she meets, amongst others in the Anglo-Indian community, two very different men, Dr Lennard and Jack Hawke, as well as the Eurasian woman, Mrs Ross. Dr Lennard and Jack Hawke function as binary opposites. Both are romantically interested in Jean, but while one is open and uncomplicated, the other is moody, socially ostracized, and with a less than honourable past, from which Jean, as a proper young woman, is protected. The travails undergone by the Anglo-Indians in the Residency and the various battles with the mutinous sepoys constitute the bulk of the novel and are described in considerable and accurate detail, but the thread of romance is also highlighted. Dr Lennard dies, hit by a bullet meant for Jean; Jack Hawke's bravery eventually turns the tide for the besieged Anglo-Indians, as well as winning him Jean's love. Mrs Ross is revealed to have a less than savoury character, which is explained away by her being a Eurasian with an Indian grandmother.

In *Love Besieged*, two different traditions in fiction are tightly braided together in the production of the distinctive hero of Mutiny fiction: the imperial adventure tradition of fiction for juveniles, which includes such writers as G.A. Henty,[6] and the imperial romance tradition made popular in the late nineteenth century by H. Rider Haggard and others. Among literary genres, the adventure story captivated its readers by balancing risk and control, juxtaposing the excitement generated in the encounter with the

---

6 G.A. Henty's nine books set in India include *In Time of Peril* (1881) – a juvenile adventure novel that shows the genre at its jingoistic extreme – and the more measured *Rujub, the Juggler* (1895), which is one of the better examples of the Mutiny novel genre.

unknown, alongside the familiarity and comfort of a predictable outcome. This tension between familiar and unfamiliar, chance encounters and human intentions is particularly appropriate for Mutiny fiction, in that the event itself is recorded quite extensively within history and memory. *Love Besieged*, far from being entirely in the realm of the fantastic, is saturated with the actual events of the historical Siege of Lucknow and the presence of historical characters, such as Nana Saheb, Sir Henry Havelock, the architect of the first Relief of Lucknow,[7] and Sir Henry Lawrence, the Chief Commissioner of Oudh, who died during the early days of the siege.

In *Love Besieged*, the Residency becomes the space that initially accommodates competing masculinities and then fazes one out in favour of the other. The text seems to suggest that the galvanizing moment for this discursive shift in the construction of British/Anglo-Indian masculinity is that of the Mutiny. In the opening scenes, in which the Anglo-Indian population flees to the Residency, we see the juxtaposition of Ernest Lennard and Jack Hawke as binary opposites. When Jean meets Ernest, he is described as having 'a refined and intellectual rather than a handsome face' (20). This description is in contrast with Jack, who 'was a handsome fellow whose sunburnt face was burnt to almost the same colour as his tawny hair and moustache' (31). The scandals of his past – gambling, drinking, betting, and, finally, forging someone else's signature to acquire money – is in direct contrast to Lennard's lack of complications. Further, Lennard is also Judge Atherton's first choice for a husband for his daughter Jean, though she turns down his proposal when it comes. Even Jean perceives the two as opposites. At one juncture, she realizes that

> Lennard was the man of thought, Hawke the man of action. If Lennard had brushed away her refusal, she would have liked him better. ... But with Jack Hawke it was different. ... He had told her straight out he loved her and – she had not said no. (162)

Finally, as he leads her to safety, Lennard is killed by a bullet meant for Jean. Even when mortally wounded, he does not cry out and dies without complaint. In short, there is a textual imperative to write Lennard out of the narrative, as if men like him – gentlemanly and soft-spoken – could not possibly survive in a post-Mutiny India. The future and the Empire belonged to men of action, like Jack Hawke.

How are we to read the contrasts that these two men provide? David Newsome suggests that the comprehension of masculinity underwent a metamorphosis in the second half of the nineteenth century: 'To the early Victorian it represented a concern with a successful transition from Christian immaturity to maturity, demonstrated by earnestness, selflessness and integrity; to the late Victorian it stood for neo-Spartan virility as exemplified

---

7 Havelock's bravery was marked by a statue in Trafalgar Square in London, which was paid for by public subscription.

by stoicism, hardiness and endurance' (quoted in Mangan and Walvin 1). Similarly, Jeffrey Weeks notes, in *Sex, Politics and Society*, that 'from the 1860s, there was a new cult of masculinity in the public schools. ... The model of the early public school was the monastery. The model of the later public school was definitely military' (40). Indeed, this emergence of the modern militaristic hero around 1860 reflects the shift in emphasis of bourgeois preoccupations in British cultural history. The dominance and influence of the Evangelicals, particularly the Clapham sect, among the bourgeoisie from the 1790s, with their emphasis on a daily spiritual life and the establishment of the Christian missionary movement that had the duty of Christianizing India, constructed the masculinity of the Christian soldier. Further, the influence and application of Thomas Arnold's principles with their emphasis on spiritual autonomy and intellectual maturity allowed for comprehension of masculinity as a product of will and energy achieved through an inward struggle. Finally, one more factor that contributes to this discursive shift in masculinity can be seen in the increased investment in athletic programmes in public schools by the middle of the century. Schools began to invest heavily in gymnasiums and employ physical education instructors. Team sports also began to be introduced into the school curriculum in the 1860s. As John Tosh explains: 'Team sports trained boys to obey (and later to give) orders; they subordinated the individual to the team effort; and they instilled stoicism in the face of pain and discomfort' (198).

Tosh also suggests that two codes of masculinity were visible in the early and mid-Victorian periods: 'gentlemanliness', which had grown out of a Georgian framework, in which politeness was esteemed above all else, and 'manliness', which favoured such virtues as 'rugged individualism' and which, as a style of masculinity, gained credence as the century progressed, with the burgeoning of the increasingly dominant bourgeoisie. For Tosh, the notion of politeness was the 'faultline' upon which the distinction between the socially exclusive 'gentlemanliness' and the socially inclusive 'manliness', which favoured moral qualities over birth, breeding, and education, could be made (86).

In *Love Besieged*, Lennard can be usefully seen as an example of Tosh's definition of 'gentlemanliness' in his behaviour towards Jean, when, for instance, he accepts her rejection of his proposal without demur. The importance he gives to form is also evident in the fact that, although he is fond of his friend and has stood by him, he does not introduce Jack to Jean when they first meet as he understands that it would be improper for a decent young woman to meet a reprobate like Jack. In fact, the congregated Anglo-Indian community in the Residency, prior to the start of the Mutiny, appear to subscribe to this form of propriety, cutting Jack or simply refusing to acknowledge him (31). Yet as soon as the siege begins, the community's attitude towards Jack shifts as his bravery and ability to take action immediately make him a valuable member of the garrison. The text thus signals the superseding of Lennard's gentlemanliness by Jack's manliness. It is a shift which Dr H.H. Almond – the inspirational headmaster of Loretto School, Scotland's oldest independent school, from 1862 to 1903 – would have applauded. He was of the firm opinion that, in a future Mutiny, the scholar would be of little use, 'it was the man of nerve, high courage and animal spirits' that the Empire needed in times of crisis (quoted in Tosh 198). It is significant that Lennard, as representative of an outdated form of masculinity, dies protecting Jean. But in the harsh reality of the Mutiny, his example of gentlemanliness serves no purpose; without a man to protect her, Jean will inevitably fall victim to the mutineers, as the fate of the women and children at Cawnpore all too vividly confirmed. Jack Hawke, however, as a proponent of the code of manliness, protects Jean *and* survives or protects Jean *because* he survives. Manliness can thus be seen as a particular code of masculinity, which could only be forged under siege.

While an examination of the mid-Victorian period reveals the number of social and cultural shifts that Britain was undergoing, it is necessary also to cite the influence that the image of the soldier-hero had in the discursive shifts that masculinity underwent. The importance of the soldier-hero as a model of masculinity is signalled in *Love Besieged* through the inclusion of two different martial heroes, Sir Henry Havelock and Sir Henry Lawrence. Sir Henry Havelock, the sixty-two-year-old hero of the first Relief of Lucknow, was a practising Baptist, who marks the transition from Christian soldier to the militaristic hero of British cultural history. He was perceived as 'a Christian warrior of the right breed – a man of cool head and resolute heart, who has learned that the religion of war is to strike home and hard, with a single eye to God and his country' (quoted in Marshman 448). Much of Sir Henry Lawrence's career in India was spent away from his regiment, either with the Revenue Survey or the Political Department, but, as David remarks, 'he never forgot his military training' (18). In Andrew Ward's words, he 'was a brave, humane, and prescient civil servant' (79), who, following the annexation of the Punjab in 1849 (which he opposed), governed the new province brilliantly. He was appointed Chief Commissioner of Oudh in March 1857, too late to quell the unrest that he had predicted with extraordinary prescience; as Ward notes: 'As far back as 1843 Lawrence had envisioned a rebel force making quick work of the Company's feeble defences at Delhi' (589, n. 384). His fortitude and ability to strategize and make battle plans are evident in the novel.

In *Love Besieged*, Sir Henry Lawrence and Sir Henry Havelock, as historical figures, clearly belong to the siege/military plot and do not intrude into the romance plot. Yet Sir Henry Lawrence is instrumental in the resurrection of Jack Hawke and his transformation from social outcast to recipient of the Victoria Cross and a happily married man. The chapter entitled 'At Gun Fire', which operates on two distinct levels, furthering both the historical and romance plots, is pivotal in this regard. Sir Henry Lawrence is not involved in the discussion of Jack Hawke's conduct in relation to Edith Ross, the scene which opens the chapter; he 'was apparently either indifferent to this talk or he did not hear it' (37). But when Jack Hawke enters the room, Lawrence calls him over to a seat reserved next to him, so that Jack can brief him on events in the city. Lawrence's public acknowledgement of Jack's value in this time of trouble immediately brings about a change in his social status and underscores the new definition of masculinity – one not fixated upon the past, but defined by actions in the present. That such an endorsement should come from Lawrence is significant; notwithstanding the loss at Chinhut, his ability to strategize is never in question, as his dying words, included in the novel, demonstrate: 'No surrender! Let every man die at his post, but never make terms. God help the poor women and children!' (116).

Sir Henry Havelock is also given a prominent role in the novel. Through his death, we see the way in which Pearce gives equal status to the military and romance plots of the novel. *Love Besieged* concludes with two distinct scenes in the final two paragraphs. The first records the death of Sir Henry Havelock from 'a mortal illness' (215) (malaria) and textually carves out his importance: 'He was carried in the litter in which he died as far as the Alumbagh, where he was buried in the enclosure under a mango-tree, on the bark of which was carved the letter "H"' (215). The second and final paragraph concludes the romance plot, giving the details of Jack's promotion to Major, his V.C., and his marriage to Jean:

> The whirligig of time brings about strange revenges. Jack Hawke, the old scandal forgotten, came to be honoured among the honoured, and it was a proud moment for him when he, Major Hawke, V.C., amid the enthusiastic congratulations of friends and comrades, led from the cathedral church of Calcutta his bonnie Jean. (215)

Significantly, this final paragraph draws together the (fictional) military plot and the romance plot. For his role in the Mutiny, Jack is rewarded with both a Victoria Cross and a wife. The suggestion is that, without the former, the latter would not have been achievable. Jack's manliness both protects and wins his bride. Mutiny iconography and fiction are thus in a seamless discourse with the production of a neo-masculinity.

Graham Dawson posits that Havelock, as a model for the re-imagined masculinity of the British, is tied to the shifts in class hegemony, in that the upward mobility of the bourgeoisie allowed for the emergence of the middle-class, self-made man. The discourse around this re-imagined masculinity is embedded in class and racial specifics. As Dawson explains, according to *The Times*, the achievements of 'impeccably "Anglo-Saxon" heroes' (107), like Havelock, Nicholson, and Neill, who were 'without a single drop of Norman blood in their veins', proved that

> [t]he middle classes now produce that type of mind which may be called the governing one – that character which rules mankind, which accomplishes great objects, which marshals means to ends, gives life to a nation, and produces the great events and the noble achievements of the day. (quoted in Dawson 107)

We want to go further than Dawson to suggest that alongside other such influences, like the growing popularity of public schools, the establishment of gymnasiums, and the needs of the growing Empire, it was specifically the Mutiny that helped precipitate the discursive shift undergone by Anglo-Indian masculinity. Indeed, the close focus that *Love Besieged* places on masculinities and the Mutiny itself seems to suggest the direct connection between the two. In fact, with the exception of Jean and Mrs Ross, the novel barely touches on the women and children who were also besieged in the Residency. Our positing of Indian men as being very important to the construction of British and Anglo-Indian men goes against conventional treatments of the topic, where notions of masculinity are always read through their relationship to femininity. Mid-Victorian comprehensions of gender always locate the discursive shift against the image of women in bourgeois domesticity and as an Angel in the House. Thus, in examinations of mid-Victorian gender, the emphasis is often on the public-private split. Alternatively, representations of a homogenized mid-Victorian masculinity extend the national into the imperialistic; that is, the national is regarded as always already imperialistic. In such a reading, the emphasis on athletic programmes and the development of public schools are perceived as being good for both the country, as well as for its imperialistic ambitions.

Postcolonial readings of nineteenth-century gender relations in India have tended to have a different focus, in that the role of Anglo-India and the politics of colonialism have always been seen as being fundamental to gender constructions. Thus, Gayatri Spivak's famous essay on sati, 'Can the Subaltern Speak?', insists on the changing relationships to power and its impact on Indian men and women in the face of British 'interventions' in misogynistic Indian customs.[8] Partha Chatterjee, in his essay on 'The Nationalist Resolution of the Women's Question', locates the public/private gendered divide in India within the framework of colonialism and colonial relations. In his framework, the paradigmatic relationship between outside (public), Western, masculinity, and another group that consists of the private, traditional, indigenous, and femininity is juxtaposed, thus complicating the concepts of masculinity, femininity, Western, and traditional.

But what if this juxtaposing of masculinity with femininity is just a textual/cultural feint? What if Anglo-Indian masculinity was more closely linked to a colonized masculinity? The role of the Indian in the consolidation of British masculinity is also evident in Macaulay's degenerative description of the Bengali:

> The physical organization of the Bengalee is feeble even to effeminacy. He lives in a constant vapour bath. His pursuits are sedentary, his limbs are delicate, his movements languid. During many ages he has been trampled

8 See also Sangari and Vaid's collection, *Recasting Women*, Radhakrishnan's 'Nationalism, Gender, and the Narrative of Identity', and Katrak's 'Indian Nationalism, Gandhian Satyagraha, and Representations of Female Sexuality'.

upon by men of bolder and more hardy breeds. Courage, independence, veracity are qualities to which his constitution and his situation are equally unfavourable. His mind bears a singular analogy to his body. It is weak even to helplessness, for purposes of manly resistance. ... What the horns are to the buffalo, what the paw is to the tiger, what the sting is to the bee, what beauty, according to the old Greek song, is to woman, deceit is to the Bengalee. (quoted in Edwards 123)

Thus, the Hindu (Bengali) male is depicted as weak, flaccid, unmuscular, and deceitful. In short, he is the opposite of manly, as regards the British comprehension of the term. While Macaulay's description of the Hindu body is constructed through similes, the comparisons and juxtapositions are not coincidental. Among others, the German racial biologist Carl Vogt in the mid-nineteenth century pointed out the resemblances between males of the lower races and the white woman: his pendulous belly was similar to the Caucasian woman, who had given birth to children, and his thin calves and flat thighs were similar to the apes (81). Indeed, Macaulay's reading of the Hindu male body is influenced by racial science of the nineteenth century, when racial biology was also the science of boundaries, and within the development of new knowledge about female anatomy and human nature. Maintaining boundaries was about maintaining power relations – in this instance, maintaining a pseudo-scientific and naturalized hierarchy between the British and the Indian male.

It is within the context of ideology and power relations that Mrinalini Sinha reads the reconstruction of British and Indian masculinity as mutually consti-tutive. Sinha locates the shift in masculinity within the political and economic background of Empire and suggests that Britain's dominant economic and political position within the world was dependent on maintaining control of India, which not only supplied it with raw materials, but also functioned as a 'captive market' for its products. Similarly, India was the site of Britain's overseas investments in agriculture and railways, with its guaranteed rate of profit. Sinha points out that:

Britain's unfavourable balance of trade with the rest of the world – a result of the 'protectionist' policies of many of Britain's trading partners in the second half of the century – was financed through India's export surplus with other countries. The transfer of surplus was managed through the complex system of 'Home Charges' for civil and military expenditures, guaranteed interest on railways, interest on the India Debt accumulating in England, and charges for such 'invisible services' as shipping, insurance, and so on. (3)

It is against this backdrop that she reads India's indigenous educated elite holding high positions and demanding the same privileges that the British enjoyed. The threat that educated Indians posed, along with the Mutiny in 1857, resulted in the reconstitution of British and Indian masculinity (3).

(And it should be remembered that the first Indian universities – in Calcutta, Bombay, and Madras – were founded in the year of the Mutiny.)

Furthermore, in the debates over the Ilbert Bill (1883) and the Age of Consent Act (1891) that preoccupied Anglo-India in the final decades of the nineteenth century, the attributes of Indian sexuality were much discussed. The debates also underscored the lasting consequences of early sexuality amongst Indian men and women. Repeatedly, scientific and medical discourses were invoked to point to the deterioration of the physique of the race, and the effeminate Hindu was perceived to be a direct consequence of early sexual activity among Indians. Further, the effeminacy of Bengali men, as well as the prevalence of diabetes in Bengal, was attributed to their tendency to indulge in the 'disgusting habit' of masturbation (Sinha 158). In short, the shift in masculinity from the monastic to the militaristic man is closely connected to the Mutiny in India. In the new cult of white masculinity, the emphasis was less on spiritual autonomy and intellectual maturity and more on sports, games, and male bonding – qualities deemed necessary in the production of the ideal soldier for the Empire.

We want to suggest that it is not only domestic urgencies that mark British and Anglo-Indian masculinity, but rather that it was determined, too, by the gendering and representation of Indian men. Whereas earlier we discussed the love triangle formed by Jean Atherton, Ernest Lennard, and Jack Hawke, we now want to suggest that there is yet another suitor for Jean, who is not given the same level of attention or status as her other two admirers: Azimoolah Khan, who reappears in the text at various critical moments. He is present in the opening pages of the novel, where the attention that he pays Jean establishes her as a desirable woman. In turn, it is this reading of Jean as desirable that leads us to read Lennard and Jack as two distinct types of men. Azimoolah is then dropped from the narrative and only returns to it when he meets Mrs Ross and agrees to pass on to her the letters which appear to incriminate Jean. Thus, the text seems to suggest that it is Azimoolah who is an impediment in the romance plot, rather than Lennard, and, indeed, Jack is almost deceived by the letters supplied by Azimoolah and planted by Mrs Ross. Finally, towards the end of the novel, Jack meets Azimoolah, his 'confidential native servant in the days of the reckless young officer's prosperity, when he gambled and betted and drank, and went through the whole gamut of Anglo-Indian vice' (72). Jack instantly recognizes him as the 'fiend whose tongue commanded the massacre of the women and children at Cawnpore' (212) and kills him in a moment of retributive fury. In fact, one could argue that it is Azimoolah's deceptive, murderous, lascivious presence that gives meaning to Jack's open and decisive masculinity. Azimoolah functions as the dark Other that re-masculinizes Jack; Azimoolah, rather than Lennard, is Jack's opposite.

But what is invested in such representations? Finally, we want to make one further related point about the role that the women characters play in the novel. In *Love Besieged*, only two women stand out, Jean Atherton and

Edith Ross, who, like Jack and Lennard, function as binary opposites. Jean and Mrs Ross not only represent the innocent young woman from England and the older, hardened, dissipated, bitter widow (respectively), but are also offered up as racial stereotypes. Mrs Ross is tainted for being one-quarter Indian, notwithstanding the fact that she is three-quarters British; regardless of this, the language of degeneration adheres to her figure. Not only is she morally corrupt and instrumental in Jack's earlier disgrace, but, by the end of the novel, she even practices the thuggee method of strangulation when she murders Hasun Khan, who had at one time been a khitmutgar (male servant) in Jack Hawke's service, where he became acquainted with Azimoolah Khan (170). In contrast, Jean is the virginal, sensible young woman that both Anglo-India and Britain needed in the aftermath of the Mutiny. Jean's role, then, is to function as the femininity upon which Jack's masculinity is predicated and, most importantly, to obscure the part that the figure of Azimoolah plays in its narrative and cultural production. Within the white discourse produced by the text, there is an imperative to maintain the delineations between race and gender, especially within the larger framework of degeneracy and a hierarchy of human bodies.

What we have analysed thus far is the relationship between British and Anglo-Indian masculinity and their shifting significations during the nineteenth century. We have suggested that the Mutiny was crucial to this shift, rather than the other way around – the militaristic framework of masculinity that was subscribed to in the second half of the nineteenth century in Britain and Anglo-India was abruptly brought into being around 1857. The valorization of militaristic qualities that came about as a response to the siege informs British comprehensions of manliness as youthful, decisive, determined, bourgeois, and white. In our analysis of *Love Besieged*, we have also suggested that the role played by Indian men, such as Azimoolah Khan, has been occluded from this formation of imperial white masculinity. The narration of gender that circumvents the role of the Indian male renders masculinity to be an entirely white formation. It also allows for white femininity to be posited as the binary opposite of this masculinity, thus making the comprehension of gender itself to be white and imperial. Such a formulation also locates Indian men and women as abject beings, neither subject nor object. Further, this formulation of gender as white also obscures the status of white women, in that they can get interpellated as subjects only within the context of their racialized bodies, not their gender.

On the Face of the Waters

In the final section of this chapter, we will examine Flora Annie Steel's *On the Face of the Waters*, which, in adopting a feminist approach to its subject, attempts to explore the status of Anglo-Indian women. During the concluding moments of this novel, while discussing British responses to the Mutiny and the dangers that the uprising posed to English women, the protagonist, Jim Douglas, exclaims to Hodson, one of the military commanders involved in the Relief of Delhi, 'Is the crisis so desperate that we need to levy the ladies? … Personally I want to leave them out of the question as much as I can. It is their intrusion into it which has done the mischief' (233). For Jim Douglas, the Cawnpore massacre was central to the unfolding of attitudes to the Mutiny, as well as gender roles in Anglo-India. Consequently, we will examine Steel's novel for its complex, alternative approach to gender roles in India, as well as its focus on how Indian and Anglo-Indian femininity are constructed. Further, if *Love Besieged* focuses on white masculinity, we want to suggest that *In the Face of the Waters* examines what white masculinity means to women in India and the narrative roles that are conferred upon both Anglo-Indian, as well as Indian, women. Finally, we will also consider the impact of this racialized heterosexual framework, invoked by the signifier 1857, on the notions of marriage and family.

In *Allegories of Empire*, Jenny Sharpe suggests that *On the Face of the Waters* was written in the wake of the controversy surrounding the Ilbert Bill of 1883 (2). This Bill clarified inconsistencies in the judicial system in India, by granting Indian judges the same jurisdiction as their Anglo-Indian counterparts to try cases involving the white population in rural India. Previously, Anglo-Indians in *mofussils* (rural areas) had the option of being tried in courts in urban areas, which, inevitably, had Anglo-Indian judges presiding over them. The Ilbert Bill, which erased notions of racial superiority (at least among officers of the court), was immensely unpopular with the Anglo-Indian population and resulted in what was deemed a 'white mutiny' (Sinha 40). Protestors likened the Bill to the 1857 Mutiny, as it would give Indian men (the judges) authority and jurisdiction over Anglo-Indian women. Further, it was felt that because 'native officers in the civil service were devoid of both "manly physique" and "manly character" they ought not to be placed in a position of authority over a manly people' (Sinha 41). As a result of the protests, the Bill was subsequently modified in 1884.

If British men were manly, how were British women gendered? What was their relationship to their Anglo-Indian male counterparts? And how were they located in relation to Indian women? *On the Face of the Waters* attempts to give a nuanced understanding of gender in response to these questions, yet, once again, as in *Love Besieged*, the novel does not deal with Indian masculinity at all. Rather, Steel's novel conflates the interrogation of the Mutiny with an interrogation of marriage. It opens with a picture of the failing marriage of Major Erlton and his wife, Kate, on the eve of the Mutiny. Erlton is in love with Alice Gissing, who is also married, and is preparing to leave his wife and abandon his career, in order to be with Alice. We are also introduced early on in the novel to James Grayman (Jim Douglas), who has been ostracized by the Anglo-Indian community and has left the army.

Significantly, the outbreak of violence in Delhi coincides with Kate Erlton's visit to Alice Gissing to discuss the letter that she has received from her husband informing her of his intentions. Their tense discussion is interrupted by 'a child's pitiful scream' (193), and Alice Gissing dies a 'heroic death' (211) at the hands of a mutinous sepoy as she rushes to rescue little Sonny Seymour. Jim Douglas arrives too late to save Alice, but in time to save Kate, who he later rescues a second time. He then hides her in the native quarter of old Delhi, disguised as an Afghan woman, where she is looked after by his servant, Tara – a woman that he had earlier rescued from becoming sati. Eventually, when Jim Douglas fails to return to their rooftop hiding place, Kate, with Tara's help, escapes from the city disguised as a Hindu widow to join the British forces encamped on the ridge outside the city. Major Erlton dies soon after Kate rejoins him, and the novel concludes with the Relief of Delhi and Kate's impending marriage to Jim, whom she has 'rescued' by nursing him back to health. For the Indian Tara, however, whose love for Jim predated Kate's, the only option available is to finally become sati, although Sangeeta Ray, invoking Spivak's 'Can the Subaltern Speak?', argues that she cannot be validated as sati, as her act of suicide 'cannot be "ideologically cathected as 'reward'"'. Ray adds:

> [H]er death is reinscribed by those watching her as yet another fatal accident caused by the mutiny. Steel's final symbolic rendering of the mystery of the mutiny (and all acts committed by the Indians) as the unsolved mystery of the woman 'choosing' to go up in flames stages the power inherent in a literary operation that seeks to provide a hermeneutics of the other by recording the alterity that it encounters in dominant colonial tropes. (87)

On the Face of the Waters attempts to interrogate and reassess the status of Anglo-Indian femininity, which relationship to the Mutiny functions as justification for the excessive retaliations of the military. As Jenny Sharpe suggests: 'The English women's ravaged bodies were the retroactive effect of a terror-inducing spectacle that ushered in a new imperial authority in which a feudal hierarchy was rearticulated as a relationship of race' (81). Indeed, Anglo-Indian women's subjectivity and agency were at best tenuous, given that the majority of those in India were there as the spouses of men in the service of an intensely militaristic, patriarchal Empire. In *Women of the Raj*, Margaret MacMillan claims that 'throughout the period of British rule in India, European men outnumbered European women by about three to one' (16). Lacking equal rights or agency in the nineteenth century, Anglo-Indian women's sense of power could only have been conferred upon them through their heterosexual relations with their own men. Indeed, we can link the unpopularity of the Ilbert Bill to the fact that it was the racial hierarchies and demarcations maintained in India that gave Anglo-Indian women their sense of authority and agency in their relationship with Indian men.

On the Face of the Waters was also written in the wake of intense feminist agitation for the repeal of the Contagious Diseases Acts of 1864, 1866, and 1869. The Contagious Diseases Acts (or the CD Acts, as they were commonly called) legislated that prostitutes could be subject to a pelvic examination on demand of the police, as well as to compulsory quarterly medical examinations. They could also be sent to lock hospitals if they contracted a venereal disease. The unfairness, along with the lack of equality for women, visible in these Acts led to intense agitation from Josephine Butler and the National Ladies Association, which resulted in the repeal of the Contagious Diseases Acts in 1884. It was at this juncture that Butler turned her attention to Indian prostitutes, insisting that they should have rights similar to those of their British counterparts. In *Burdens of History*, Antoinette Burton analyses the relationship between British feminists and Indians of the Victorian period, suggesting that the former had 'culturally specific identities' that consisted of the following characteristics: 'public leadership, national citizenship, and, above all, imperial authority' (100). For the feminists, the way to serve the Empire was through their support and concern for Indian women. Indeed, the Indian patriarchy's misogyny had become a well-established fact since the legislation against sati passed in 1829. Burton proceeds to point out that British Feminists's scrutiny of Indian women located the latter as completely Other. In so doing, any analysis of Indian women was simultaneously a self-aggrandizing move, in that it was accompanied by references to the superior conditions in which British women lived. Burton concludes: 'In an important sense, Indian women were not considered suitable material in and of themselves: they became proper texts, catechisms even, only as they were explained, modified, and put to feminist use' (101). Josephine Butler's work on Indian women stemmed from her Christian beliefs, which provided her with the framework that she needed for her analysis of the plight of Indian women.

It is the imperialist narrativization of history, according to Spivak, that underpins women's rights in nineteenth-century England. In her classic reading of Charlotte Brontë's *Jane Eyre* in *A Critique of Postcolonial Reason*, Spivak points out that the emergence of a feminist individualism in the nineteenth century was enabled precisely by the politics and discourse of imperialism. Her analysis of *Jane Eyre* in *A Critique of Postcolonial Reason* indicates how Jane's growing agency in the novel, which gave it canonical status to Anglo-American feminists, is predicated on the silencing and subsequent death of Bertha Mason, the creole wife of Rochester. Spivak suggests that Jane '[a]s the female individualist, not quite, not-male, articulates herself in shifting relationship to what is at stake, the "native subaltern female" (*within* discourse *as* a signifier) is excluded from any share in this emerging norm' (117). The visibility received by British feminists around their protest against the Contagious Diseases Acts needs to be read in light of the unequal relationships between Indian and British women. Most importantly, the plight of Indian women became the touchstone by which India's ability to self-govern and attain Independence was assessed. The misogyny of Indian men (as seen in the practice of sati) was perceived as evidence of their inability to embrace democracy.

It is necessary to locate *On the Face of the Waters* within the larger context of the Ilbert Bill controversy, as well as imperial feminism's attitudes towards Indian women, for two reasons. First, a significant part of the novel focuses on the relationship between the Englishwoman, Kate, and the Indian woman, Tara. In fact, in certain ways, this relationship dominates the text, eclipsing even those between Kate and Jim or Kate and Alice Gissing. Second, Flora Annie Steel was an active member of the feminist organization, the International Council of Women (ICW). Antoinette Burton records an interesting anecdote about Steel's attendance at an 1899 International Council of Women Congress session. At the meeting, Steel was on the platform with Marie Bhor – an Indian educationalist, who was also studying English literature at Somerville College – and 'several other Indian ladies in native dress'. When the ICW President called on Steel 'to speak for the women of India', she showed no reticence, speaking at length and concluding with the following appeal:

> And so, without the slightest fear, I, representing all those women of the
> East … reach out my hands to the women of the setting sun, knowing that
> by doing so I shall consolidate that vast Indian empire which every English
> man and English woman hopes and prays may last, and hopes and prays that
> upon it the great sun of righteousness and truth and mercy may never set.
> (quoted in Burton 195)

Steel's words suggest that her feminism seems to be always tinged with imperial elitism and that her sense of authority over Indian women is taken for granted. Yet notwithstanding this, *On the Face of the Waters* interrogates the role and status of both Anglo-Indian and Indian women within the Empire in a way that would have been most disturbing to many readers of her generation.

If Mutiny fiction repeatedly reinscribes a certain form of masculinity in British and Anglo-Indian men, so that the repetitive citation establishes the idealized norm, then, in *On the Face of the Waters*, the reader's expectations are immediately subverted by the figure of Jim Douglas. In the novel, Jim's authority over women seems to be established by his constant rescue of them. For instance, he saves Zora, his Indian mistress, from becoming a prostitute; he saves Tara, his housekeeper, from becoming sati; and he saves Kate, on several occasions and on various levels, as, for example, when he acquiesces to her request that he not expose Major Erlton for cheating on the horses, as it would ruin his reputation and therefore their son's future, as well as when he rescues her following the outbreak of the Mutiny. To this extent, the narrative seems to suggest that all three women love him because he has saved their lives, because of his 'manliness'. Yet as the novel unfolds, we become aware that all three of the women are attracted to him, not because he is 'manly', but because he is more like a woman, more like them. Kate is attracted to him initially because he is as much a 'gentleman' as she is a 'lady' (25). Her awareness of him is largely physical, and she notes his 'well-cut mouth' (25), 'the extreme ease and grace of his figure' (25), and his 'fine-cut hands matching the figure' (27). Alice Gissing sees through his Afghan disguise, recognizing him as an Anglo-Indian, and finds him attractive, because, like her, he lives by his wits. Zora and Tara are both attracted to him, because, like them, he is an outcast from his own community.

Indeed, Jim Douglas's masculinity is asserted in the text through his attractiveness to women, rather than his abilities in battle or his homo-social bonding with other Anglo-Indian men. In fact, his use to the military is primarily down to his ability to pass, spy, and provide information – a role that, on its own, does not readily fall within the framework of militaristic masculinity, although, as we have seen with Jack Hawke in Charles Pearce's *Love Besieged*, passing can fall within this framework when it is presented as an extension to more traditional soldiering roles. At critical moments when the narrative could establish him as the idealized male hero, he fails. For instance, he injures his ankle on the way to providing information to Major Erlton that Kate is alive, and, after initially rescuing Kate from the mutinying sepoys, he abandons her for hours, so that, tired of waiting, she eventually attempts to make her own escape (224–27). Similarly, towards the end of the novel, Kate has to save herself once more by hiding in the ceiling and then, later, by making her way to the British camp on her own. Finally, it is Jim Douglas that needs the women to take care of him, when, after he falls ill, both Tara and Kate nurse him back to health.

The idealized masculinity of the Anglo-Indians is encapsulated in Spivak's famous sentence in 'Can the Subaltern Speak?': 'White men are saving brown women from brown men' (297). The reference here is to the abolition of sati by William Bentinck, which established the British as rational, just, modern, law-abiding, and non-misogynistic – in other words, protective and caring of women. Yet *On the Face of the Waters* appears to invert Spivak's formulation to read: 'White men are being saved by brown and white women from brown men.' Spivak points out that '[i]mperialism's image as the establisher of the good society is marked by the espousal of the woman as *object* of protection from her own kind', asking '[h]ow should one examine the dissimulation of patriarchal strategy, which apparently grants the woman free choice as *subject*?' (Spivak 299). Her analysis exposes the ideological framework upon which the discourse around sati was based. For Indian patriarchy, the opportunity to become sati was offered to the grieving widow as a reward; for the British and Anglo-Indians, the law against sati (like imperialism itself) was offered as a social mission (Spivak 301). Neither the British nor Indian patriarchies offered their solutions as a choice to these women. In effect, Indian woman as subaltern could not speak, because there was no discursive position from which she could articulate her choice or preference.

Spivak concentrates on the Indian woman as subaltern, but how does her argument in 'Can the Subaltern Speak?' reverberate through the discursive position occupied by Anglo-Indian women? In some ways, our use of Spivak's article may seem inappropriate, as she clearly defines the subaltern in the text as Indian women. As she pithily puts it: 'if you are poor, black, and female you get it in three ways' (294), and, in Spivak's terms, Anglo-Indian women were neither poor nor black. However, Spivak's focus on sati in 'Can the Subaltern Speak?' is pertinent to Steel's novel as well, in that Tara has earlier been rescued from becoming sati and arguably becomes one by the end of the text; furthermore, Kate, too, enjoined to assume the role of sati by Tara, starts cutting off her hair, so she can emulate one. But most importantly, we want to suggest that the sentence 'White men are saving brown women from brown men' (297), which encapsulates the rescued sati in Spivak's text, is a mirror image of the designation of Anglo-Indian women in need of protection from Indian men during and after the Mutiny, where 'White men are saving white women from brown men.' In fact, for the acquiescence of Anglo-Indian women to be so passively constructed, the horror of sati – what these men do to their own women – is absolutely necessary. The massacre at Cawnpore is underpinned by the horror of sati, in order to valorize Anglo-Indian men as the saviours of all women in India.

Flora Annie Steel's depiction of white and brown women saving white men from brown men thus not only exposes the frailty of white men, but also the slippage through which imperial ideology functions to render these women as passive to gain the ideological acquiescence to their ideological representation as helpless, in order to prop up the militaristic framework of masculinity. The distance between Spivak's sentence and the version generated by Steel's text is the trajectory of what Spivak calls 'the fabrication of repression' (299). Indeed, inspired by Spivak's sentence, we posit that it is imperial patriarchy's construction of the woman's role as passive, thus woman's passivity, thus passivity as feminine, thus the feminine Anglo-Indian's desire, thus Anglo-Indian masculinity as desirable.

Finally, Steel reveals the ideological construction of women by completely conflating the Anglo-Indian woman Kate with the Indian women Zora and Tara. Kate is given Zora's jewellery to wear, notably her bangle, which Jim himself places on her wrist. She is also made to disguise herself as an Indian woman, so that her life can be saved. Thus, Kate looks like Zora, but lives like Tara, even cutting her hair and living for a week as a Hindu woman in Sri Anunda's garden. In the end, it is Tara, seeing the bangle on Kate's wrist, who points out the obvious: 'So the *mem* wears it still. She has not forgotten. Women do not forget, white or black' (376). What women do not forget is their attachment to Anglo-Indian men and the fictions that must be produced to foreground their masculinity. Steel's conclusion to the novel, Tara's suicide and the impending marriage of Kate and Jim in Scotland, disrupts and, ultimately, makes the alternative narrative of the interrogating feminist text vanish completely. The imperative of the Mutiny narrative demands such a closure, yet Steel's narrative, in its moments of exposure, manages to undermine and complicate this subgenre of nineteenth-century British fiction.

The Conclusions of Matrimony

If *Love Besieged* focuses on the Mutiny's role in the reconstruction of matrimony, *On the Face of the Waters* focuses not just on the shaping of femininity, but, in an extension of gender concerns, also on the concepts of family, domesticity, marriage, and intimacy. These topics seem to have no place in conventional treatments of Mutiny fiction, which largely focus on 'empire [as] a site where comradeship was valued [and] domesticity disparaged' (Tosh 200). Yet the significance of marriage, domesticity, and companionship is signalled in *On the Face of the Waters* through the simultaneity of the break-up of Kate's marriage and the outbreak of the Mutiny in an echo of events in Britain: 1857 was not only the year of the Mutiny, but also the year that the Matrimonial Causes Act was debated with great intensity in both Houses of Parliament, before being passed into law on New Year's Day 1858. With the passing of this law, the discursive position of wives became enshrined as individuals in law, whereas previously married women were deemed to be legally represented by their husbands. Indeed, there is a close relationship between the Mutiny and the 1857 Matrimonial Causes Act, insofar as each struck a blow at the unchallenged privileges of white patriarchy in Britain and India.

While the Empire was a site to escape the expense of matrimony and experiment sexually, as Ronald Hyam would have it in *Empire and Sexuality*, domestically, in Victorian Britain, there was a focus on the family, as its stability was perceived as maintaining an orderly nation-state in the face of rapid geographical, as well as class, upheavals during the Industrial Revolution (Stone 146). Leonore Davidoff and Catherine Hall remind us that marriage was a rite of passage to adulthood in the mid-nineteenth century: 'On marriage men assumed economic and jural responsibility for their wives and the expected brood of children. With marriage, women achieved their full adult status' (Davidoff and Hall 322). Davidoff and Hall sketch a picture of mid-nineteenth-century lives in Britain, where the emphasis was firmly on family values and the rise of the middle class. Here, there was a growing delineation between the public and private, with women occupying the latter space. For a man, marriage coincided with new responsibilities in his profession, thus reinforcing the division between public and private or professional and personal spaces (Davidoff and Hall 323). For a man, marriage was supposed to affect and improve his economic, social, spiritual, emotional, and everyday life. For a bourgeois woman, to be a wife and mother was considered to be a focal point and the aim of femininity. Further, with the large number of offspring produced in bourgeois marriages, the mother's role was to provide personal and emotional support to her multiple children. Davidoff and Hall conclude:

> [m]arriage became both symbol and institution of women's containment. It was marriage which would safely domesticate the burgeoning garden flower into an indoor pot plant; the beautiful object potentially open to all men's gaze became the possession of one man when kept within the house like a picture fixed to a wall. (Davidoff and Hall 451)

But how did this structure of matrimony and family work in Anglo-India? In *Empire Families*, Elizabeth Buettner draws a picture of family as a virtual, rather than material, configuration, in that the nuclear family seldom lived together.

If the presence of family was central for nation-state stability, then India became the space where families were ripped asunder. Because the primary signifier was race, rather than class, in Anglo-India, a sense of superior identity could be affirmed only when families sent their children to Britain for their schooling. The principal factors that held a family together in Anglo-India were separation (rather than daily intimacies), longing, and loneliness. The children in this group (Collingham's 'middle-class aristocrats') were sent to boarding schools in Britain, often by the age of five or six, even before they had learnt to read or write, and were looked after by family members – or, in some cases, by strangers – during school holidays. Thus, these children spent their formative years away from their parents, with the concept of Empire and duty parenting them instead. Alternatively, if the mother accompanied her children to Britain during their school years, then the intimacy between spouses was seriously compromised. Thus, anxieties about degeneration, disease, and bodily and racial hierarchies determined the practice of familial intimacies in Anglo-India. Further, these intimacies were mediated, not through the private realm, but through racial hierarchies and ideologies of imperialism.

At the overt level, the political crisis in Anglo-India is equated with the marital crisis. Indeed, *On the Face of the Waters* opens ominously with the threat of both Mutiny and divorce. It follows the format offered by Buettner, in that Major Erlton and Kate have shipped their only son to England for his education, leaving Kate absolutely 'bereft' (31). She displaces the longing that she feels for her son onto Sonny, the three-year-old who lives next door to her. India is presented as a morgue for children, thus denying women their purpose in life: Kate loses her son to England; Alice Gissing's child is dead; and Zora's child, which Jim fathers, is also dead. All of them have an abundance of maternal feelings, but no child to receive them. If the lack of children makes the women excessively and uselessly maternal, fatherhood or fatherly feelings are non-existent in contrast. Jim admits to a sense of relief at his bi-racial child's death, and Erlton seems indifferent to his son. Thus, Empire, or at least Anglo-India, is the site of the breakdown of bourgeois family life. The absence of proper marital relations and the nuclear family under erasure inevitably suggests that India is an unstable political arena. In the end, the novel announces healing in familial relations by positing Kate, Jim, and Sonny in hiding, as a reconfigured nuclear family. Kate's maternal excess is balanced by the presence of the child, and Jim finally takes responsibility for the safety of this family and prepares to marry Kate, rather than merely co-habit with her at the end. Thus, the novel reinstates the centrality of marriage and family, connecting bourgeois life, post-1858, to political stability.

Yet embedded within this conventional discourse of safety and stability through the upholding of familial values lies an alternate one, which seems more in keeping with Steel's cynicism over Mutiny fiction, more in keeping with her feminist feelings generated in the first-wave feminism that saw the Repeal of the Contagious Diseases Acts in Britain and India. In this alternate discourse, which cannot be imagined in Britain, Steel posits and explores the idea of adultery; the domestic crisis can only be played out in the site of the Other. Steel's first chapter, with its apocryphal title 'Going! Going! Gone', depicts not marriage, but the adultery of Alice Gissing and Major Erlton. If marriage is an institution that the state invests in and reveals the private and intimate in the public, then the novel seems to suggest that adultery can be the only outcome in Empire's disinvestment in marriage and family, through the valorization of racial hierarchies, racial purities, and the metropole. By extension, Mutiny itself can be seen as functioning as experimentation, without a proper place (such as a home) or socially sanctioned institutions (such as a marriage), and has to rely on improvization. The aura of uncertainty that adultery can bring hangs over the novel. Indeed, the novel suggests the non-institutionizable relationship as the desirable norm: Alice and Major Erlton, Jim and Zora, Jim and Tara, Jim and Kate. Adultery as the crisis for domesticity becomes a metaphor for the Mutiny: Mutiny as a civil war, Mutiny as a crisis for the Anglo-Indian domestic, the domestication of India, and Mutiny as the feelings of a wife in a bad marriage. Indeed, on the eve of the Mutiny, Britain's relationship with India is akin to an adulterous affair, driven by a desire for the Other and what that Other represents. The novel ends with the 'legitimizing' of Anglo-Indian rule over India and the resubordination of the individualism that illegitimate relationships supposedly represent to the needs of the imperial nation-state. The year 1858 marks the formal inclusion of India as a colony in the British Empire. From the framework of Britain's unsanctioned relationship emerges the clichéd trope of the shotgun wedding, only this time it is the bride (India) who is reluctant.

A final comment to be made in this chapter relates to the cluster of terms – 'masculinity', 'femininity', and 'home' – all of which resignify India differently within an Anglo-Indian diaspora. In this chapter, we have suggested that the 1857 Mutiny was pivotal, not only to the remaking and re-situation of Anglo-Indian masculinity and femininity, but also to an increasingly repressive, militaristic, white patriarchy. Anglo-Indian men and women, dislocated from their national history and relocated within an imperial history, have a different awareness of their bodies, their gender, and their vulnerability, all of which are marked by the events that took place in northern India from 1857 to 1858. We have also tracked the hypermasculinization and the growing dependence of the women who are hyperfeminized, rendered utterly and unexaminably desirable to native men in this new imperial discourse on gender and danger. In *Cartographies of Diaspora: Contesting Identities*, Avtar Brah suggests that no discourse, especially those that are embedded within binaries, exists 'in isolation from others, such as those signifying class, "race", religion or generation. The specificity of each is framed in and through fields of representation of the other' (185). Following Avtar Brah's argument shows us the tight imbrication between all of these terms – 'Mutiny', 'gender', 'home', 'imperialism', 'whiteness', 'diaspora', 'Indian' – each not only functioning within their own discursive field, but also conferring meaning to each other.

For instance, what inflections does the term 'home' carry for a people in the diaspora, who are highly sensitized to the violence and annihilation that surround their everyday life in a space that did not seem to want to be colonized by the Anglo-Indians? In *The Politics of Home*, Rosemary Marangoly George indicates it is a trope for establishing difference, which is built on 'a pattern of select inclusions and exclusions' (2). While home generally refers to a place of safety, shelter, and comfort, for Anglo-Indians during the Mutiny of 1857 to 1858, the term also referred to its antonyms – danger, bodily threat, and fear. It functioned as an uncanny and unhomely space, simultaneously familiar and yet dangerous, surrounded, as it was, by the millions of Indians that the Anglo-Indians governed. Bhabha's words are resonant in this cluster of terms:

> To be unhomed is not to be homeless ... The recesses of the domestic space becomes sites for history's most intricate invasions. In that displacement, the borders between home and world become confused; and uncannily the private and the public become part of each other, forcing upon us a vision that is as divided as it is disorienting. (9)

The Mutiny, then, dematerialized the physical home and rendered it a trope, in that Anglo-Indians began to experience Britain as home and their homes in India only as temporary, notwithstanding the fact that many of them had only ever known India and had never been to Britain. The tight braiding of imperialism and diaspora suggests that their dwellings in India were not apolitical spaces, following common understandings of the public/private split, but were charged with an imperial politics that demanded Anglo-Indians show loyalty to Britain and other the native completely. This loyalty came with its own meanings: it demanded a passivity of their women, post-Cawnpore, in order to emphasize and exaggerate the bravery of Anglo-Indian men. The figure of the Angel in the House took on new political meanings in India, which went beyond those within gender politics. The Residency in Lucknow, where the Anglo-Indians sought shelter, functioned as yet another metaphor, as the new Anglo-Indian woman was further incarcerated within imperial politics and within the discourse of how a 'memsahib' should behave. Meanwhile, in Britain and post-Mutiny, women were fighting for their rights and for the repeal of the Contagious Diseases Acts. First-wave feminism was in its infancy in Britain, but it completely bypassed Anglo-Indian gender politics in India.

Diaspora, then, refers not only to the unmooring of people from their homes, but also refers to the dislocation of signifiers from their signified. Imperialism, gender, and race are all contained within the history of the home in India. In short, while the might of imperialism always contained the fear of Mutiny, diaspora was always at the heart of the Anglo-Indian home.

CHAPTER 2

The Terrains of Identity: Mimicry and the Great Game

Between the end of the Mutiny and the beginning of the twentieth century, from 1858 to 1905, the British Raj in India, according to Denis Judd, was at its zenith (91). In 1858, the rule of India passed from the hands of the Honourable East India Company to those of the British Crown, and, in 1877, Queen Victoria was proclaimed Empress of India, ushering in a renewed belief in the Empire some twenty years after the shock of the Indian Mutiny. This 'era of confidence', as Allen J. Greenberger terms it in *The British Image of India*, is clearly reflected in the literary outpourings of Anglo-India during the final decades of the nineteenth century. Greenberger explains that:

> In order to rule, the novelists believed it was necessary for an individual to be British and to possess certain characteristics which were felt to be natural to that 'race'. The ideal British hero of this 'era of confidence' as well as the protagonist of fiction was brave, forceful, daring, honest, active, and masculine. (11)

In other words, in John Tosh's terms, the British hero exhibits 'manliness' – which David Newsome concludes was 'one of the cardinal Victorian virtues' (195) – rather than 'gentlemanliness'. In the previous chapter, we argued that the re-signification of masculinity was initiated as much by the Mutiny as it was by imperialism and diaspora.

Consequently, the British image of India in popular fiction of the period is of a place ripe with adventure and romance (or perhaps the romance of adventure). Almost all of the novels set in India during the late Victorian period, from 1880 onwards, fall within the tradition of romantic adventure fiction, a form made popular by such writers as G.A. Henty – who, as Nancy Paxton notes, 'developed one of the most influential formulas for the marketing of British history as the raw material for mass-produced adventures for boys' (140): stirring tales of British valour and 'derring-do', populated by dashing young heroes serving the Raj in countless skirmishes in the Punjab or on the Frontier. As Greenberger notes:

> virtually all the novels of this period are set in north-western India – the Punjab, North West Frontier Province, and Himalayan foothills. There are a few cases where the locale is Maharashtra or Burma, but Bengal, Central, and South India are almost completely absent. (35)

Sited as a dangerous zone for its politics and a hostile territory for family life, in direct contrast to Victorian Britain with its emphasis on domesticity and marriage, the Frontier epitomized the camaraderie that a womanless world engendered. For the majority of Anglo-Indian novelists, the north-west was the 'real India' and the preferred setting for Raj novels of romantic adventure, including Henty's *Through Three Campaigns* (1898), Maud Diver's *The Great Amulet* (1914), and Talbot Mundy's *King of the Khyber Rifles: A Romance of Adventure* (1917). In all of these novels, set in a time and place where the threat of war in the north was constant, the author was able to portray his or her British heroes ably performing the ideals of masculine imperialism that had been forged during the Mutiny: defending or extending the borders of British civilization, while simultaneously controlling and subduing the restless natives. Furthermore, the diasporic hypermasculinity in Anglo-India was shaped in this period by an absence of women and through representations of the North West Frontier Province, which was perceived as containing the very essence of the homo-social experience that typified the Empire.

The quest to extend the reach of the British Empire in India was not only prompted by imperial greed, it was also due to political anxiety about its borders, specifically fuelled by the perceived threat of a Russian invasion. In 1839, fearing that the Russians were 'pressing Dost Mohammed for concessions that, if given, would clearly pave the way for the Czar's troops to pour south over the Hindu Kush, as the Mughal invaders had come' (Moorhouse 81), the British invaded Afghanistan. They removed Dost Mohammed, the Amir of Kabul, from his throne and replaced him with a puppet ruler, Shah Suja, under the control of a British Resident. Thus, the Indian subcontinent functioned yet again as a theatre of war between two Western countries jostling for power with each other in non-Western spaces. Under the aegis of colonialism, the posturing of Russia and Britain meant that Indian subcontinental political and social hierarchies underwent sudden radical shifts and breaks. The Afghan tribesmen never accepted the annexation, and sporadic skirmishes continued, until, two years later, Kabul rose against the British with a ferocity that quickly forced them to accept terms. During January 1842, 16,500 people – British men, women, and children, Indian sepoys, and their camp-followers – began their retreat from Kabul through the mountain passes to Jalalabad, ninety miles away. Ten days later, the sole survivor, surgeon William Brydon,[1] reached

---

1 Brydon was wounded in several places, including a serious head wound, which, so it is claimed, but for a copy of *Blackwood's Magazine* stuffed inside his forage-cap,

Figure 8. *The Remnants of an Army*, by Lady Elizabeth Butler. Oil on canvas, 1879. Reproduced with permission of the Tate Gallery, London.

the British fortress at Jalalabad on his dying horse – a moment of imperial nostalgia that was immortalized on canvas by Lady Elizabeth Butler in *The Remnants of an Army* (1879) (see Figure 8).

The following year, in 1843, the British annexed Sind and during 1845 and 1848, again fearing instability in an area close to possible Russian influence, fought two Sikh wars, before finally annexing the Punjab in 1849.

In the second half of the nineteenth century, following the Mutiny, the British fought only three large-scale actions: a second Afghan war from 1878 to 1880; a third Burmese war in 1885; and, in 1897, an extended campaign to restore order on the Frontier, following the uprising (or jihad) in the Swat Valley, led by a charismatic cleric, Hazrat Sadullah Khan, also known as Sar Tor Faqir (the bare-headed faqir) or, as the British preferred to call him, the 'Mad Mullah'.[2]

Politically, the most significant of these was the second Afghan war, which, as Lawrence James observes, '[i]n many respects … resembled the first' (374); few (if any) lessons seem to have been learnt in the intervening forty years. Like the earlier war, the second Afghan war was fuelled by the fear of Russian influence in Afghanistan, and again, as previously, the objective was to secure Afghanistan as a buffer state under the control of a British Resident in Kabul

---

would certainly have killed him. He also survived the Siege of Lucknow during the Indian Mutiny of 1857, although, again, he was severely wounded in the Siege. See his obituary in the *British Medical Journal*, 26 April 1873, p. 480.

2 See Winston S. Churchill, *The Story of the Malakand Field Force: An Episode of Frontier War*; David B. Edwards, 'Mad Mullahs and Englishmen: Discourse in the Colonial Encounter'.

Figure 9. *Save Me From My Friends*, *Punch*, 30 November 1878. Reproduced with permission of *Punch* Ltd., www.punch.co.uk.

(see Figure 9). When the Amir, Shere Ali, refused to accept a British mission, a force of 40,000 soldiers invaded and occupied much of the country. Shere Ali's elder son and successor, Yaqub Khan, signed the Treaty of Gandamak in May 1879, under the terms of which he accepted Louis Cavignari as Resident of Kabul and ceded control of the Khyber Pass and various frontier districts to the British. Cavignari's mission did not last long, however. On 5 September, the Residency was stormed by mutinous Afghan soldiers, and Cavignari and his escort were slaughtered. British troops under the command of General Roberts re-occupied Kabul, and Yaqub Khan was sent into exile. The British considered replacing him with his younger brother, Ayub Khan, but finally installed his nephew, Abdul Rahman Khan, as their puppet Amir. The British withdrawal from Afghanistan, which had been ordered by the new Liberal government, was delayed by an uprising, led by a disgruntled Ayub Khan. The British suffered a serious defeat at Maiwand (where, in Sir Arthur Conan Doyle's first Sherlock Holmes story, *A Study in Scarlet* [1887], Dr Watson tells us he had been wounded) and were besieged at Khandahar, before Roberts, having marched from Kabul with an army of 10,000 men, defeated Ayub Khan's forces to bring the conflict to an end and restore Afghanistan to the neutral buffer state that it had been before the war.

While such large-scale conflicts were few, the North West Frontier was never at peace. The regular skirmishes in the second half of the century, which, as Moorhouse explains, 'were seen by both sides as more of a blood sport than warfare' (105), added to the myth of the Frontier, which was to become the meat of Anglo-Indian adventure fiction in the period of high imperialism,[3] as did the reputation of the Pathan tribesmen as worthy and masculine adversaries. Alongside the constant border skirmishes, the political threat of an Anglo-Russian war was ever-present. After 1880, Russia continued to fight a series of campaigns, which led to the conquest of Turkmenistan and brought the Russian frontier to within 600 miles of British India, prompting the start of what Lawrence James calls '[a] new round in the Great Game' (380).

A vital element of the Great Game, and important in the control of the native population of India, was, of course, knowledge, including topographical knowledge. The mapping of the subcontinent, which began in earnest in 1767 when Lord Clive appointed James Rennell Surveyor-General of Bengal, was an essential part of this accumulation of knowledge about India. In 1783, Rennell produced the first approximately accurate map of India; two decades later, in 1806, William Lambton began triangulating the subcontinent; and in the second half of the nineteenth century, in 1865, Thomas Montgomerie of the Survey of India addressed the vexed problem of mapping the forbidden territory of Tibet, which, like Afghanistan, Kashmir, and Bokhara, was seen as an important buffer between British India and her potentially hostile northern neighbours. As Ian Baucom explains:

> Montgomerie alighted on the solution of training Indians in the use of the compass and sextant, disguising them as pilgrims, equipping them with an array of instruments – including 100- rather than 108-bead rosaries with which they could count off their paces – and sending them across the border to advance the work of the survey. It is among this group of costumed cartographers that Kipling places Kim. (93)

And, as Peter Hopkirk convincingly argues, Kipling also borrowed the idea of code names (C25, R17, and E23) from Montgomerie, as well as the use of disguise (123–26).

In the early decades of the century, long before Montgomerie began to train Indians for the task, British travellers and army officers who were skilled oriental linguists with a taste for adventure explored Afghanistan, Bokhara, and other regions between India and Russia, both openly and secretly, gathering military and topographical information, which would help counter the perceived Russian threat. Their activities and the mapping of the subcontinent, which went hand-in-hand with the espionage, became known as the Great Game – a phrase, according to Hopkirk, that was coined by an early player, Arthur Conolly, an intelligence officer and Captain in the 6th Bengal Light Cavalry, long before it was popularized by Rudyard Kipling in *Kim* (1901) (Hopkirk 1). The historical figures that played the Great Game, including

---

3 The Frontier is also celebrated in poems, such as Kipling's 'The Ballad of East and West', and in numerous boys adventure stories in magazines, such as *Blackwood's Magazine*, *Boy's Own Paper*, and *Chums*, which entertained and inspired the next generation of Empire builders.

Conolly, Alexander 'Bokhara' Burnes, and James Abbott, were apt to ignore facts in favour of rumour; therefore, for much of the century, the threat to India was probably more imagined than real. Conolly, for example, following his travels from Moscow to India between 1829 and 1831, confirmed what many in London and Calcutta feared and perhaps wanted to hear: that it was possible for the Russians to invade India, either in the footsteps of Alexander the Great, through Afghanistan and the Khyber Pass, or via Persia, by way of Herat, Kandahar, and Quetta (James 81).[4] But, as Michael Edwardes reminds us, Russia, in the early decades of the nineteenth century, was hardly on the doorstep of British India: 'Orenburg, the nearest Russian base, was over two thousand miles distant from the most advanced British post (at Ludhiana), and the whole of the Punjab and Afghanistan lay between' (45). Nevertheless, the Game was played with vigour, and it was undoubtedly dangerous. An overconfident Burnes was assassinated by the Afghans at Kabul in 1841, while Conolly was beheaded by the Amir of Bokhara in 1842. James Abbott, the finest of Sir Henry Lawrence's 'Young Men'[5] in Charles Allen's view (206), had more luck. He survived to become Deputy Commissioner for Hazara from 1849 to 1853, before being removed over concerns that he was 'an official with divided loyalties' (Allen 205); the town of Abbottabad, in what is now the North West Frontier Province of Pakistan (and where Osama Bin Laden was hiding before his death in 2011), is named after him.

Though the origins of the Great Game can be traced back to the early decades of the nineteenth century, the phrase is more often associated with the late nineteenth century, which is the setting for Kipling's *Kim* and other popular romantic adventure fictions of the North West Frontier, including A.E.W. Mason's *The Broken Road*, and post-imperial adventure novels, such as John Masters's *The Lotus and the Wind* (1953) and M.M. Kaye's *The Far Pavilions* (1978), both of which are heavily indebted to Kipling's story, and J.G. Farrell's posthumous, unfinished work, *The Hill Station* (1981), which transcends and critiques the traditions of the genre through parody. Crucial to the Great Game at this time were the network of native agents who spied for Colonel Charles Maclean – the Consul-General in Mashad from 1885 to 1891 – and supplied detailed information about Russian troop movements and other activities (James 383–84), just as Mahbub Ali and Hurree Chunder Mookerjee

4 Like many players of the Great Game, Conolly published an account of his travels: *Journey to the North of India through Russia, Persia and Afghanistan.* See also Alexander Burnes, *Travels into Bokhara: Being an Account of a Journey from India to Cabool, Tartary and Persia; also Narrative of a Voyage on the Indus from the Sea to Lahore;* James Abbott, *Narrative of a Journey from Heraut to Khiva, Moscow, and St Petersburgh, during the late Russian Invasion of Khiva.*

5 A group of young officers, including Capt. James Abbot and Lt. John Nicholson, were charged with pacifying the Punjab after the Sikh wars. They worked under the command of Sir Henry Lawrence and, according to Moorhouse, 'exercised their authority with a careful mixture of boyish gusto and mature consideration of local interests' (83).

feed intelligence to Colonel Creighton in *Kim*. However, as James notes, the 'Indian government's intelligence services were never as omniscient as Kipling imagined, and while it did employ some resourceful agents, most of its information came by way of the sort of venal informers Colonel Maclean hired in Mashad' (384).

From the mid-1880s, the intelligence services became increasingly concerned about the threat that the progress of the Russian railway programme offered to the security of British India. Army officers, such as Colonel A. Le Mesurier, posed as travellers and made their way into Central Asia to gather information, which they later published, thus keeping the Great Game in the public consciousness.[6] Just as the skirmishes with the border tribes were more blood sport than warfare, so the Great Game was, in many ways, less about a real threat of Russian expansionism, than a duel between the rival intelligence services, enjoyed by its players and played for its own sake, as Captain Ralph Cobbold understood, when, in *Innermost Asia: Travel and Sport in the Pamirs* (1900), he aptly captures the motivation of the players:

> The British officer, jaded with his work in the heat of the plains, is, like a keen sportsman, prepared to rough with the best. He will willingly for a time do without luxuries, and live, as a Russian officer lives, on what he can get. A month of native chapattis is fully compensated by the mountain air and fine sport available amongst the Himalayas. (quoted in James 387)

This is the historical background of the Great Game that numerous Anglo-Indian novelists, including Kipling and Mason, would draw upon during the period of high imperialism. Maud Diver captures the spirit of this fiction in her description of Sir Henry Forsyth in *The Great Amulet*:

> For all his great brain, he was a man of one idea; and that idea – 'The North safeguarded.' Mere men, himself included, were for him no more than pawns in the great game to be played out between two empires, on the chessboard of Central Asia. (453)

The British hero in these romantic adventure fictions of the North West Frontier invariably has a strong sense of duty to the Empire, which he carries out unflinchingly and with perseverance, whatever the personal cost to himself or to those he loves. Indeed, the North West Frontier Province became the site of his diasporic condition: exiled, isolated, and dutiful. In Talbot Mundy's story 'Hookum Hai', 'duty was the only thing that mattered' in Sergeant Bill Brown's 'scheme of things' (14). At the end of Rudyard Kipling's *Kim*, the eponymous hero must find a road that accommodates both the duty that, as a Sahib, he owes to the Raj and his devotion to the lama that he has served as a faithful chela (or disciple). Similarly, in A.E.W. Mason's *The Broken Road*, the Linforth family believe that it is their duty to push 'the Road' through

---

6 See A. Le Mesurier, *From London to Bokhara and a Ride through Persia*.

the mountains of north-west India to the foothills of the Hindu Kush, even at the cost of three generations of Linforth men.

The notion of duty linked to the administration of the Empire is also closely related to ideas of trusteeship and humanitarianism. A number of historians (Haskell and Laqueur, for example) suggest that a discursive shift around 1750 enabled the production of a humanitarian sensibility in Europe. For Laqueur, this discursive shift coincided with new medical comprehension of the body, which generated a new form of sympathy for the suffering body. For Haskell, it was the Industrial Revolution coupled with capitalism that led to a humanitarian discourse. Within imperialism, trusteeship – belief that the British rulers were actually stewards, guarding and improving the colonies for the indigenous peoples – informed colonial sensibilities. While Edmund Burke urged in 1783 that laws be passed to curb the greed of the British, thus preserving indigenous freedoms, Anglo-Indian administrators in India interpreted the notion of trusteeship as being one which needed the intervention of the British to govern India. The notion of imperial duty was also mixed with ideas about Christianity, humanitarianism, and the anti-slavery movement. The imperial mission was considered to be a noble task, demanding obligations and self-sacrifice. As H.W. Hyatt stated in 1897:

> To us – to us –, and not to others, – a certain definite duty has been assigned. To carry light and civilization into the dark places of the world, to touch the mind of Asia and of Africa with the ethical ideas of Europe; to give to thronging millions, who would otherwise never know peace or security, these first conditions of human advance. (quoted in Eldridge 104)

In this chapter, we will examine Mason's *The Broken Road* and Kipling's *Kim*, both of which are concerned with duty and the need to protect British India (and, by extension, all Indians) from the threat of invasion from the north, from 'the shadow of the Bear ... [which] loomed large on the political horizon'[7] or from the Frontier tribes: it is to this end that Linforth wants to build the 'Road', and Kim plays the 'Great Game'. Like many Anglo-Indian novels of the late nineteenth and early twentieth centuries, both novels are set in northern India at a time, during the late 1880s, when the threat of war with Russia was constant (and published in the first decade of the twentieth century, when fear of war with Russia was again ripe). Yet while both novels have their share of adventure on the Frontier, they are also quite different from other novels that can be grouped under the romantic adventure fiction banner. Mason's *The Broken Road* mixes the devotion to duty of men like Linforth with genuine concern for the effects of educating Indian princes in Britain, rather than in India, while Kipling's *Kim* mixes the intrigues of spying with detailed descriptions of Indian (rather than Anglo-Indian) life, from the bazaars of Lahore to the 'new people and new sights' that Kim and the Lama see 'at every stride' (61) on the Grand Trunk Road.

7 See Maud Diver, 'Light Marching Order', p. 5.

The Broken Road

In his seminal essay 'On Mimicry and Man: The Ambivalence of Colonial Discourse', Homi Bhabha observes that the 'line of descent of the mimic man can be traced through Kipling, Forster, Orwell, Naipaul' (87); in an Anglo-Indian context, that list might be usefully revised to include Mason and Paul Scott. Indeed, Mason's *The Broken Road*, like *Kim*, illustrates clearly Bhabha's explanation of postcolonial mimicry and the inability of the colonial power to completely domesticate the other.

The Broken Road contains two protagonists, Dick Linforth and Shere Ali, who are the same age and whose lives are linked together through signifiers, such as Empire, the 'Road', and Chiltistan. Dick Linforth belongs to a family in which two generations of Linforth men have already dedicated their lives to the building of the Road through Chiltistan in the North West Frontier Province. Shere Ali is the son of the ruler of Chiltistan. Both boys are educated at Eton, followed by Oxford, and are close friends while in England. When Shere Ali has to return to Chiltistan, he realises, for the first time, that, because of his colour, he is considered racially inferior to the British amongst whom he grew up. The rest of the novel unravels around Shere Ali's anger at the loss of his status and his rebellion against his colonial rulers, which leads, finally, to the deployment of Dick Linforth to hunt and capture his friend. The rivalry between the two men that informs the second part of the novel is initiated and emphasized in the first part of the novel, through their shared romantic interest in the central female character, Violet Oliver.

Inevitably, the Anglo-Indian novel focuses on the white protagonist, Dick Linforth, and attempts to valorize him over Shere Ali, by describing him as having '[a] firm chin, a beauty of outline not very common, a certain delicacy of feature and colour' (33), which is in direct contrast to Shere Ali's appearance: 'a certain high pitched intonation of his voice, and an extraordinary skill in the game of polo' (41) and a full lower lip. Thus, the text represents the two men as opposites in appearance (delicate, subtle features versus an excess) as a code for their opposing values and sense of decency. Further, Shere Ali, notwithstanding his privileged background, education, and years spent in England, is portrayed as not being able to be properly English – a failing that becomes visible when he returns to India.

Yet the figure of Shere Ali also functions to exhume the failings of imperialism, in that, notwithstanding its commitment to modernity, which the Road seems to symbolize, and its insistence on English values as being rational and committed to democracy, it is simultaneously portrayed as vicious, political, manipulative, and self-interested. In our analysis of *The Broken Road*, we concentrate on the various narrative strategies that the text attempts to use to co-opt the reader to an Anglo-Indian viewpoint. Reading against this dominant ideology becomes a struggle, because to do so would require the reader to align themselves with a villainous and racially inferior character. Further, the occupation of this reading position as a critic of imperialism is difficult, because there is a seamless discourse that links the machinations of Empire as rightful and virtuous and the narrative development of the plot. However, the curious representation of Shere Ali opens the text up to such an extent, for the reader, that s/he stops reading the novel for its linear unfolding that valorizes imperialism and the character of Linforth, focusing instead on the inequities, prejudices, and various cultural forces that conspire and force Shere Ali to function as a villain. That Shere Ali is meant to be an alternative protagonist – one who functions as a vital critique of imperialism – is evident in the fact that Linforth does not appear in more than one-third of the novel, after the two become adults. It is Shere Ali who motors the plot forwards and whose actions sustain its tension. In this section of the chapter, we will analyse the two readings that the novel produces, each following a different trajectory, to establish whether Linforth or Shere Ali is deemed the main protagonist.

In many respects, *The Broken Road* fits neatly into Allen J. Greenberger's 'Era of Confidence, 1880–1910', which, he suggests, is 'dominated by writers who presented the image of a confident and secure empire' (5). Indeed, the novel offers a narrative point of view, which functions as an objective voice in the paradigm of a Cartesian subject that is both autonomous and self-knowing. In an early chapter, the dying political agent, Luffe, anticipates the plot of the novel in surprising detail in a crucial mise en abyme as he talks to Major (later Colonel) Dewes:

> 'You take these boys, you give them Oxford, a season in London … You show them Paris. … You give them, for a short while, a life of colour, of swift crowding hours of pleasure, and then you send them back – to settle down in their native States, and obey the orders of the Resident. Do you think they will be content? … There's a youth now in the South, the heir of an Indian throne … In England he is treated as an *equal*; here … he is an *inferior* … The best you can hope is that he will be merely unhappy. You pray that he won't take to drink and make his friends among the jockeys and the trainers. He has lost the taste for the native life, and nevertheless he has got to live it. Besides – besides – I haven't told you the worst of it.' … 'There is the white woman,' continued Luffe. … 'Very likely she only thinks of him as a picturesque figure … she does not take him seriously … but he may take her seriously, and often does. What then? When he is told to go back to his State and settle down, what then? Will he be content with a wife of his own people? He will eat out his heart with bitterness and jealousy. And, mind you, I am speaking of the best – the best of the Princes and the best of the English women. What of the others – the English women who take his pearls and the Princes who come back and boast of their success? Do you think that is good for British rule in India?' (25)

The mise en abyme articulated through the mouth of the dying Luffe, whose impending demise bestows his voice of prediction with a bardic quality and pure objectivity, mirrors the trajectory that the narrative offers for Shere

Ali, including his schooling, the white woman, and the pearls. Luffe's dying statement thus becomes a prediction, a statement that defines and situates, as well as limits, Shere Ali's life. The disinterested nature of his judgement also makes Luffe into what David Lloyd terms a 'Subject without properties' (65) or an abstract subject, who conforms to 'the condition of universality' (65), thus articulating a common sense. By using Luffe as the preferred narrative point of view, the novel enlists the reader into reading it in this revelatory way, thus concealing the operation of an imperialist ideology that insists that Shere Ali can only ever be an inferior human being, merely because he is not white.

Furthermore, the novel reiterates this disinterested or objective point of view through the figure of Ralston, the 'unobservant' Commissioner of the Punjab that Shere Ali meets as soon as he arrives in India. The Commissioner is described as having a drawn face and hollow eyes 'tired with the strain of the hot weather' (70), suggestive of being yet another Englishman who was sacrificing himself for the natives, taking on the white man's burden. Thus, the reader's simultaneous (to Shere Ali) encounter with Ralston leads us to see him as being in accord with a common or public sense, 'giving [Shere Ali] sage advice with the accent of authority' (71). The reader also glosses over and overlooks Ralston's advice to Shere Ali that it was hoped that he would 'marry and settle down as soon as possible' (72) – a suggestion that he would have perceived as being too presumptuous on his part, had it been offered to Linforth or any other Anglo-Indian.

The narrative reveals its white perspective, not only by locating Luffe as having an objective, omniscient narrative point of view, but also through showing its preference for Linforth over Shere Ali in two distinct steps. First, it locates Shere Ali within the discourse of difference – unfathomable in many ways to the intended reader, who is situated in Europe or has a European sensibility. Notwithstanding his education at Eton and Oxford, Shere Ali is located within an impenetrable code, with his language and Chiltistani way of being functioning as an unbreakable cipher. For instance, upon his return to India, Shere Ali immediately recognizes as a compatriot the holy man with the blanket on his head – an individual who fools even the Hindus. Chiltistani semiotics is completely Other, unfathomable not only to the British, but also to other Indians. Other baffling signs are repeated within the text. The delivery of sacks of melon and grain from Shere Ali to the Mullah is interpreted by the Chiltistani as a signifier of rebellion and reclaiming of Islam: 'melons were the infidels which would be cut to pieces, even as a knife cuts a melon. The grain was the army of the faithful' (150). Again, when Linforth sees the transformed Shere Ali, they both repeatedly watch a water carrier with an earthen jug on his head as he negotiates a flight of steps to see if he will slip, as to do so would be an omen and signal of something unknown to the Anglo-Indian administration, with whom the reader is in alignment (189). Rendering Shere Ali as untrustworthy and seeking revenge (although the 'objective' narrative point of view never examines in any great depth what the forces of imperialism does to him in the first place to make him desire revenge) aligns the reader with the dominant ideology and, in alignment with the codes of imperialism, allows us to easily interpret him within the context of Homi Bhabha's notion of mimicry and Macaulay's 'Minute' on education.

The notion of mimicry is closely aligned with the aims of imperialism, in that the mimic man was always considered to be hierarchically inferior to the original, of which he was a copy. In 'Of Mimicry and Man', Bhabha traces the intellectual genealogy of the concept of mimicry via Charles Grant, who, in his reform of mission education in India during 1792, suggested that religious reform should be merely partial and not complete, since a complete reform might incite Indians to demand liberty. Bhabha locates Lord Macaulay's 1835 'Minute on Education' in alignment with Grant's partial reform. Macaulay conceived of a type of English education in India that would produce 'a class of interpreters between us and the millions whom we govern – a class of persons Indian in blood and colour, but English in tastes, in opinions, in morals and in intellect' (quoted in Bhabha 87).

Bhabha suggests that this religious and educational reform produces the mimic subject, who is a partial presence, '*almost the same but not quite*' (89), which, far from reassuring colonizing powers, instead functions as a threat precisely because it is a partial presence. Because of its partial nature, this subject also contains traces of the indigenous subject that cannot be erased, making them less transparent and therefore menacing – 'mimicry rearticulates presence in terms of its "otherness", that which it disavows' (91). For Bhabha, the ambivalence of mimicry – simultaneously soothing and menacing – is an effect of the indeterminacy or ambivalence at the heart of religious or educational reform. The ambivalent position that Shere Ali occupies – '*almost the same but not quite*'; 'the difference between being English and being anglicized' – ultimately makes him a menacing character to the reader, as much as to the Anglo-Indian power brokers. It is the initial incomprehension of the notion of mimicry that leads Linforth to exclaim of him: 'But he's loyal … There's no one in India more loyal' (166); completely oblivious to the power relations implicit in the notion of loyalty within Anglo-India.

Further, underpinning the references to racial hierarchies implicit in the concept of mimicry in *The Broken Road* lies another term – degeneration – which may usefully be unpacked to further our reading of the novel. This concept functioned in the nineteenth century as a counter-discourse to Darwin's theory of evolution, with its implications of continuous progress. Within the framework of social Darwinism, the concept of degeneration, with its classed and gendered undertones, mapped a range of unwanted behaviours and characteristics; prostitutes, the urban poor, criminals, the insane, and even feminists were all perceived as degenerate. As important as the classed and gendered boundaries that controlled degeneracy domestically were the racial boundaries that sought to control the threat of racial contamination in other parts of the Empire.

The discourse of degeneracy is also closely bound up with racial boundaries, in that, in scientific racism, the physique that was considered most evolved and ideal was that of the white race – an insight already implied in the Linnaean model that hierarchized human forms or what Anne McClintock refers to as the dominant metaphor of degeneracy: the Family of Man (50). While at the beginning of the nineteenth century, environmental and geographical influences were perceived as causing the degeneration of humans from their primordial form to create the five different racial types; by the middle of the century, certain races themselves were perceived as degenerate types. In particular, the Negro race was singled out by Georges Cuvier to be 'the most degraded human race, whose form approaches that of the beast and whose intelligence is nowhere great enough to arrive at regular government' (quoted in Stepan 98). Though degeneration was perceived as part of racial heritage, it was also considered a *process*, in that it indicated the deterioration within the limits of the racial type (see Stepan 98). This process was initiated when the races were removed from their proper geographical place, leading to degeneration. Thus, degeneration was associated with both bodies and actual geographic spaces. This concept became part of the discursive framework of colonialism. European colonists moving to the strange landscapes of Asia and Africa, with their intense heat and alien flora and fauna, often seemed to have high mortality rates, caused especially through the contraction of diseases such as malaria or yellow fever. This led to a medical judgement that whites degenerated in tropical spaces.

Finally, it must be pointed out that the anxiety of the prospect of degeneration through class-mixing that Europe faced domestically – the fear of crowds, slums, the urban poor, prostitutes carrying venereal disease, and so on – was mirrored by the anxiety of degeneration through race-mixing in the colonies, and the fear that intercourse between the races could lead to social ostracism or the deterioration and enfeebling of the white race. The theory of degeneracy, which mediated a comprehension of race relations, lasted from the middle of the nineteenth century through to the middle of the twentieth century. Laws against miscegenation, which were rampant throughout the colonies, stemmed from this theory. Domestically, degeneration had to be avoided through the maintenance of rigid class systems. Thus, the theory of degeneration was classed, gendered, and racialized.

The concept of degeneration is important to the discussion of this text, in that beyond the notion of mimicry – the lens through which Shere Ali can perhaps most revealingly be read – his character is marked by what Edward Chamberlain and Sander Gilman have called 'the institutionalization of fear' (xiv); in this case, the fear of degeneration. This explains Luffe's warning at the beginning of the novel against young Indian men being educated at Eton and Oxford: 'In England he is treated as an *equal*; here, in spite of his ceremonies, he is an *inferior*'. While Luffe attempts to frame his opinion by suggesting that an education in England would make the young Indian prince a stranger in his own land, he does not even begin to address the issue of *why* the educated Indian 'is an *inferior*, and will and must be so' (25). Obviously, the semiosis of Luffe's statement reveals the political advantage of maintaining racial hierarchy – 'must be so' – and reminds us that ideas about hierarchies are cultural and social constructions, rather than something natural, serving to benefit only white men like Luffe or Dick Linforth. Furthermore, Luffe's suggestion that Shere Ali should not be educated in Britain is proffered as the only way to protect the race boundary; the alternative option – that the British should not subscribe to racial hierarchies at all – is not considered even casually; indeed, racial hierarchies are deemed as a given. To echo Luffe, the political framework of imperialism *will* and *must* subscribe to racial hierarchies to justify and maintain itself.

So how do the interdependent concepts of mimicry and degeneration work in this text? Summoning Dick Linforth to mediate with Shere Ali, the political agent, Ralston, suggests that 'England overlaid [Shere Ali] with a pretty varnish ... That's all it ever does. And the varnish peels off easily when the man comes back to an Indian sun' (173). And in so doing, he dismisses Shere Ali's agony, grief, and overwhelming sense of loss about returning to Chiltistan after having spent ten of his formative years in England. Moreover, Ralston attributes Shere Ali's return to Islam to the rejection that he receives from the white woman, whom 'he knows he can never marry – because of his race. And so he's ready to run amuck' (174). Although Ralston never questions why Violet Oliver *cannot* marry Shere Ali, as if an interracial sexual relationship is physically impossible and the sexual boundary uncrossable, the issue of racial difference or hierarchy is central to the construction of Shere Ali. The narrative repeatedly underscores that, notwithstanding the sophisticated veneer that he acquired in England, it is his racial difference that remains dominant. For instance, while his appearance is very English – his colour no darker than a sunburnt Englishman and light enough to prompt Violet Oliver to exclaim 'You could hardly tell that he was not English' (58) – his superior skill on the polo field at Eton, his high-pitched intonation, and his full lower lip are carefully presented as the subtle markers of his racial difference. When he returns to India to find that he is no longer accepted as a social equal by the English with whom he had previously mixed, he crosses the class boundary to socialize with rough Englishmen – gamblers, boxers, jockeys – and the civilized veneer that he had acquired during his years in England begins to crack and peel off. Shere Ali's deterioration is specifically described in the scene in which he asks Dewes for help and is refused: 'All the fire went from his eyes, all the agitation from his face. ... It was as if a European suddenly changed before your eyes into an Oriental' (111). Thus, the narrative positions him as a cultural chameleon, whose always already degenerate body reverts back to its original form upon his return to India. Indeed, his degenerate condition is evident everywhere, from his preference for the company of socially inferior Europeans, to the way that he ignores his old friend Dick Linforth, to his treatment of Violet Oliver. When Violet Oliver rejects his offer of marriage, he does not take the rejection well, as, it is implied, an Englishman would, but rather becomes a threatening character participating in a failed attempt to kidnap her. Finally, his character becomes treacherous, organizing a rebellion against the British, thus proving the assessment that all Chiltis had 'gentle voices' and 'cut-throat ways' (24). In the desire to locate him as a degenerate figure, the narrative does not seem to call into question the social conditions that shape Shere Ali – his profound loneliness upon his return to Chiltistan, his sense that he is adrift between two worlds, rejected emotionally and intellectually by one and socially by the other, and his disappointment over Violet Oliver's rejection – all of which are caused by, or have their meanings imputed to, racial difference and hierarchy.

One further question needs to be asked at this point. What is the connection between the concepts of mimicry and degeneration? Bhabha's 'Of Mimicry and Man' seems to echo tropes of degeneration in the pithy phrases 'almost the same, *but not quite*' (86) and '[a]*lmost the same but not white*' (89) or again in 'the repetition of *partial presence*' (88). If the highest and most evolved physical form is that of the white male colonizer, like the Linforths, Luffe, or Ralston, then Shere Ali's attempt to mimic or approximate them, and his subsequent failure, especially signalled by the reference to his thick lower lip, reveals that he is 'almost the same, *but not quite*'. Attempts to create Shere Ali as the idealized or utopic Englishman reveals that he is only a '*partial*' representation of the image that subsequently crumbles and begins to fall apart upon his return to India. If Bhabha's analysis of the subversive figure focuses on the effect of the mimic on the original, the concept of degeneration, with its obsessive construction of racial gradations, reveals the effect of the original or the highest form on the copy. One could argue, even, that the terms mimicry and degeneration are mutually dependent. One cannot understand the true meaning of degeneration – of how places and races can make all the difference – without comprehension of the mimic, who is almost the same, but not white; similarly, the mimic, despite his menacing overtones, has no meaning, except within a framework of hierarchies.

Through the evocation of the notions of mimicry and Macaulay's 'Minute', the narrative purports to be a transcript of the reality that pre-exists its fabrication. It thus coerces the intended reader to subordinate other possible meanings to the transcendent meaning of Shere Ali as menacing, lacking loyalty, lacking the ability to be English, and lacking the ability to rise above his unfortunate racial origin and religious affiliations. The narrative encourages the reader to avoid reading it from Shere Ali's perspective in favour of a privileged and Anglo-Indian meaning. In its attempt to foreclose Shere Ali's perspective, it conceals all traces of presenting only one particular social reality – the Anglo-Indian. The reader must quite deliberately read against the narrative to gain a glimmer of any alternative meaning.

As its second strategy of advancing the social reality of Anglo-India, the narrative posits Linforth as the ideal hero. Indeed, the narrative underscores the romantic figure that he cuts with his genealogy, his great-uncle having disappeared (through choice) in India, and his father writing a last letter to his wife, as he awaits his death in the darkness of Chiltistan and the Road. (The narrative merely touches upon Sybil Linforth's loss of a husband and, eventually, her son to duty in Anglo-India, and associates white femininity with an overvaluation, a 'reverence'.) The perspective of the experienced India hands, which the narrative valorizes, recognizes the potential in Linforth. Sir John Casson, the late Lieutenant-General of the United Provinces in India, narrates:

> I was dining eighteen months ago at the Sappers' mess in Chatham. [Linforth's] face came out of the crowd and took my eyes and my imagination too … There seems to be no particular reason why it should happen at the moment. Afterwards you realize that there was very good reason. A great career, perhaps, perhaps only some one signal act, an act typical of a whole unknown life, leaps to light and justifies the claim the young face made upon your sympathy. (52)

Just as Luffe foretells Shere Ali's future and presents the narrative in a mise en abyme, Sir John Casson foresees the DSO that Linforth will receive for his heroic deeds in defeating the uprising that Shere Ali sparks. Linforth leads 100 Ghurkha soldiers to scale 1,400 feet of rock and liberate 'the position which, for eighteen days had resisted every attack, and held the British force immobile' (241). Finally, it is Linforth who is charged with pursuing the fleeing Shere Ali across the central Asian trade routes and capturing his closest school friend. The narrative urges the reader to interpret the final encounter with Shere Ali as a tragedy that affects both men in profound ways. Linforth is represented as a modern hero, brooding and affected by the politics and realities of imperialism, which demands the eschewing of the emotional ties of a friendship forged in childhood. The text thus makes him its tragic figure, rather than Shere Ali.

The alternative narrative that locates Shere Ali as its protagonist and goes against the dominant Anglo-Indian view can be traced even in Luffe's mise en abyme and later in Ralston's speech to Linforth. Luffe predicts that even 'the best of the princes' would become warped by the discriminatory treatment meted out to him by the Anglo-Indians. Ralston provides a corrective view to Linforth's unsophisticated understanding that valorizes imperialism in India unquestioningly:

> Shere Ali is the best of the Princes. But he has been badly treated, and so he must suffer … He's one of the best of them. Therefore he doesn't take bad treatment with a servile gratitude. Therefore he must suffer still more. But the fault in the beginning was not his. (219)

Ralston's statement that natives are badly treated in their own country becomes a recognition that is reiterated by the alternative narrative. For instance, in the chapter 'The Soldier and the Jew', Shere Ali, seated beside two English youths with similar accents from Eton and Oxford, overhears their anger at the treatment of English women at the hands of Indians: 'After all, if you are going to be the governing race, it is not a good thing to let your women be insulted'. When Shere Ali intervenes in their conversation, they silence him with an 'I don't think that I was speaking to you' (145) – a response that they would not have given him, had they been in England. Shere Ali realizes that he has been put in his place and feels the shame of having committed a social gaucherie.

While Shere Ali's privileged status of being a prince and his education at Eton and Oxford makes social inequities based on racial difference more visible, the alternative narrative appears to emphasize that his representation is a metonym for all Indians. In the chapter entitled 'Shere Ali's Pilgrimage', he is blocked from entering the Bibighar in Cawnpore, where many Anglo-Indian women and children had been killed at the onset of the Mutiny/Uprising, as this space was considered sacred to their memory and not to be sullied by the presence of natives. In contrast, however, when he enters the great mosque in Delhi, the Jamma Masjid, he finds a number of Anglo-Indians having a picnic within its grounds, eating their lunch and taking photographs. He realizes that Anglo-Indians 'were so careful of themselves, so careless of others' (171).

The alternative narrative also focuses on Shere Ali's relationship with Linforth and points out to its unequal nature in the emotion associated with friendships. When the two young men go walking in the Dauphiné Alps, it is Shere Ali who is determined to maintain the relationship at all costs. He exclaims: 'Nothing must come between us … Nothing to hinder what we shall do together'. Linforth's spare response to this outburst is: 'That's all right' (45). Again, when Violet Oliver tells Linforth that Shere Ali asked her to marry him, he states: 'He asked *you*! He must have been mad to think such a thing was possible' (182). Linforth's response suggests that he has no sympathy for his close friend's disappointment at his marriage proposal being turned down. Instead, as much as he is Shere Ali's rival for Violet Oliver's affections, his reply indicates his awareness and acceptance of racial inequality in India.

Finally, the alternative narrative also deploys an allegorical tale to underscore Shere Ali's lack of status. This allegory of the old woman that Hatch met in Mecca functions to indicate the similarity between her life and the life of Shere Ali. The old woman, without any rights or agency, was kidnapped during the 1857 Mutiny/Uprising in Cawnpore and passed on from one man to another, until she ended up a widow in Mecca, wishing to remain there until she died, as 'she had long since grown accustomed to her life' (120). While this narrative is supposed to underscore Shere Ali's intent to abuse Violet Oliver in a similar fashion, it also functions to expose his own status among the Anglo-Indians. Indeed, like the old woman in Mecca, Shere Ali had no say in the matter as to where he was to be educated. His treatment at the hands of the Anglo-Indians upon his return once again suggests his lack of agency or right to make decisions about most aspects of his life.

The narrative suggests that native men are feminized in their powerlessness, as Indian princes dress in silk jackets and wear jewellery like women (94); Shere Ali is summoned to return to Chiltistan from London by the Anglo-Indian Government, because of its various machinations and the political intrigue that it is caught up in (59); and he is urged to marry a Chiltistani woman. In the end (mirroring the fate of the woman in Mecca) he is exiled to Burma, his life and his rights being of no consequence to the Anglo-Indian Government. Indeed, this link between women and Indian men that emphasizes their similarities is further indicated in the framework of degeneration within which Violet Oliver's characterization can be read. Violet Oliver is implicated within the framework of this concept, not least because, being a woman, she lacks the perfect form of the white, masculine, colonial figure, but also because her breeding and behaviour – her lack of high morals or values, her shallowness, her acceptance of jewellery from Shere Ali, her flirtations with Shere Ali, as well as Dick Linforth, and her subsequent marriage to 'the offspring of some provincial tradesman' – make her a suspect figure. If Shere Ali's degeneration is evident in a comparison with Dick Linforth, Violet Oliver's lack of breeding is evident when she is compared with Phyllis Casson or Sybil Linforth, whose femininity and perfection are underscored through their prolonged absence from, and peripheral location within, the majority of the narrative. Thus, degeneration is performed in this text through the figures of Shere Ali, Violet Oliver, and various rough, working-class white men; it is evident, in other words, through race, gender, and class.

While Macaulay's 'Minute' perceives a practicality in the partial education that engenders the mimic, and Bhabha locates an indigenous agency in the menacing aspect of the mimic, neither of them explore the emotional outcomes – the anger and despair – of the mimic who is completely aware of the unequal status and treatment that imperialism bestows. Notwithstanding the promise of equality within liberal democratic discourse, which functions at the basis of Macaulay's 'Minute', of a production of a Westernized, specif-ically Anglicized, identity; in actual practice, it functions as a failure. Shere Ali's despair is one caused by a wounded identity – an identity deprived of its fullness of being that Eton and Oxford promised. In India, he is reduced to his race, which functions as a fetish. It signifies his reduced hierarchy and explains his untrustworthiness and, finally, his disloyalty to his upbringing. The text's repeated statement of his people and Islam's reclaiming of him thus dislocates this wound, this hierarchization, from its history – that the wound could have only been caused within the racially discriminating policies of imperialism. The despair that Shere Ali experiences when he leaves his adopted country and loses his closest friend and the woman that he loves – all because he is neither English nor white, as both Luffe and Ralston recognize – can only be treated within the parameters of an imperialistic Anglo-Indian framework as a lack of loyalty and gratitude.

Ultimately, Mason's *The Broken Road* is a novel about reading, as much as it is about imperialism in India. Indeed, if the act of reading forms our world and us as readers, it is both the reading for the plot, as well as the counter-narrative, that exposes the machinery and failures of imperialism. Its reinscription of, while critiquing, the dynamics of imperialism reveals this novel to be ahead of its time, in that contemporary comprehensions of otherness shape the representation of Shere Ali. In our analysis thus far, we have applied key terms in postcolonial studies, such as 'mimicry' and 'degeneration', to an Anglo-Indian novel to reveal the racial hierarchies that are contingent for the very development of the narrative and the reader's comprehension of it. The representation of Dick Linforth and Shere Ali as being similar in every way except racial origin forecloses other possibilities in the narrative development of their lives. Dick's choices either to support imperial rule or assert an individuated identity are mirrored in Shere Ali's choices of being subservient to the Empire or asserting an indigenous identity. The Great Game is thus played out, not just with Russia, but as a metaphor for the game that the Imperium plays with individual's lives. In the next section, we will analyse Rudyard Kipling's *Kim*, which is also set within the context of the Great Game and the demands that it plays on the individual within an Enlightenment framework. We suggest that Kim, though often interpreted as reinscribing imperial values, instead exposes the harsh demands of Empire and offers an alternative form of Enlightenment in its ambiguous conclusion.

Kim

The degeneration that adheres to Shere Ali is initiated as much by his diasporic condition living in England as it is by racial hierarchies within imperialism. Whilst Shere Ali is not, strictly speaking, a figure of diaspora, his migrant condition underpins and explains his degeneracy and is important precisely because it is a part of the pathological discourse that is associated with immigrants – forming criminal gangs or losing their moral centre or sinking into depression. As Nancy Stepan indicates: 'The meanings attached to "racial degeneracy" and the technologies they encapsulated became constituent elements, therefore, of the doctrine of social decay that emerged by the late nineteenth century' (98). Stepan proceeds to point out that, within race science, there was an idea that racial types belonged to their proper places, and degeneration occurred when the raced individual was out of place (99). It is interesting to note that the burden of degeneration and decay is borne by Shere Ali, but not Linforth. The narrative links his hierarchically superior position to his preservation from degeneracy. Instead, he becomes a romantic figure, lonely and exiled in the North West Frontier Province. But how would this discourse of degeneracy, diaspora, and decay affect the Irish, who were deemed inferior in Britain because of their colonized condition? In the second half of this chapter, we will examine Kipling's *Kim*, which examines these different signifiers in complex ways.

Rudyard Kipling's most famous work is the story of a young boy who lives a life of vagrancy in India, because both of his Irish parents are dead. Accepted as a 'friend of the world' by all the Indians that he meets on the Grand Trunk Road, Kim latches on to a Tibetan monk, who is in pursuit of the great river, while Kim is searching for his father's regiment. Kim grows very fond of the Lama and becomes his disciple. Simultaneously, he discovers his father's regiment and is sent to a school to learn to become white and acquire Western forms of knowledge. Thus, Kim is an ambivalent figure, both black and white. At the end of the novel, Kim is being trained to become a spy in the Great Game, even as he is learning the Buddhist ways of living and being.

In a crucial scene within Kipling's novel, Kim makes contact with his father's regiment, the Mavericks. When they open his upper garment and check his skin tones within, he transforms in front of their eyes from a young native thief to white, from a disavowal to an avowal, thus proving the provisionality of racial signs, as Kim's body and identity become a site of contest and revision. He now becomes the responsibility of the regiment and Anglo-India, for he is the son of a sahib – drunk, destitute, and vagrant, though his father, Kimball O'Hara, may have been. The regimental priests declare 'once a Sahib is always a Sahib' (88) and decide that Kim needs to be sent to a school and that the regiment will take care of him financially and make him 'as good a man as can be' (90). Thus, racial comprehension and racial characteristics (thieving Indian boy), though based on the body, appear to be arbitrary, predicated not on the racialized figure, but on the eye and interpretation of the beholder. We realize that, in Anglo-India, whiteness can be learnt or, rather, reawakened at school, so Kim can become properly masculinized and white. Kim, having forebears who themselves were colonized rejects of another geographical zone – Ireland – gets recycled as white and therefore useful to the Empire in ways that a vagrant in a bazaar cannot.

The attempts of Father Victor and Reverend Bennett to resignify Kim as white through education once again reminds the postcolonial reader of the text containing the oft-quoted lines of Lord Macaulay's 'Minute on Indian Education':

> We must at present do our best to form a class who may be interpreters between us and the millions whom we govern; a class of persons, Indian in blood and colour, but English in taste, in opinions, in morals, and in intellect. (237)

Reverend Bennett and Father Victor replicate Macaulay's intent for Kim; however, Kim functions as a reverse image, a mirror image, wherein he is Irish in blood and colour, but Indian in taste, opinions, morals, and intellect. In this next section, we wish to re-examine the politics and poetics of the mimicry that is implicit in Kim's reshaping and re-signification, Macaulay's 'Minute', and Bhabha's 'Of Mimicry and Man' that has helped shape postcolonial thought on identity, because we think that an examination of these various works permit readers to see the occluded text in Kim.

Lord Macaulay's 'Minute on Indian Education' was written while he was a member of the Supreme Council of India. Previously, Macaulay served as a Secretary for the Board of Control for the East India Company. As a member of the Supreme Council, Macaulay is best known for drafting the Indian Penal Code, which is still the basis for the current Indian Penal Code; advocating the freedom of the Indian press; arguing for the legal equality of Europeans and Indians; and, most importantly, for establishing a national system of education in India. The 'Minute on Indian Education' was written as an opposing viewpoint to the 'Orientalists' in Anglo-India, who proposed that higher education institutions in India should promote Sanskrit and Arabic alongside English. Macaulay was an Anglicist and favoured education in India to be conducted in English. The sum of money under debate was one lakh (100,000 rupees), and the debate was over how best to use the small amount, so that it could be utilized most effectively.

Macaulay advanced his argument in three points. First, that English was the language of modernity and of the rational sciences (in contrast to Sanskrit and Arabic, which belonged and looked to the past). So, for him, an investment into the promotion of indigenous languages was a waste of money. It is within this context of looking to the future that Macaulay suggests 'that a single shelf of a good European library was worth the whole native literature of India and Arabia' – a fact he claimed that even the Orientalists could not deny (230–31). Second, Macaulay naturalized the circulation and deployment of power by suggesting that the literature and languages of Western Europe had been enriched by the study of Ancient Greek and the Romans, rather than merely focusing on 'the old dialects of our own island' (232). He asks:

> [H]ad they printed nothing and taught nothing at the universities but Chronicles in Anglo-Saxon and Romances in Norman-French, would England have been where she is now? What the Greek and Latin were to the contemporaries of More and Ascham, our tongue is to the people of India. (232)

This argument of Macaulay's is underpinned by the idea that there was a continuum between Ancient Greece and Western Europe, which, for Martin Bernal, was a fiction constructed in the age of imperialism. In the eighteenth-century reconstruction of Greece as the cradle of civilization, Germany and Britain, in particular, saw themselves as having descended from the Greeks and their intellectual heirs, the Romans. Macaulay suggested that Russia's study of Western European languages as being central to their intellectual revival was an analogy for what English could do for the Indians: 'I cannot doubt that they will do for the Hindoo what they have done for the Tsar' (233). Macaulay's final reason for the promotion of English, rather than Sanskrit and Arabic in India, was that students who had been educated in the latter languages at public expense could not gain employment, even after graduation. He based this knowledge on petitions he had received from these students and felt that it was proof that Indians themselves wished to learn English. For him, maintaining Sanskrit and Arabic in universities in Benares and Delhi would be 'more than enough', thus freeing up funds to promote English at the Hindoo College in Calcutta and English language schools in the Presidency of Fort William (Calcutta) and Agra. However, being cognizant of the limitations of funds and the huge population of India, Macaulay felt that all the British could do was to form a class of interpreters, who would disseminate the knowledge that they had acquired to the great mass of the population. Ultimately, Macaulay's 'Minute' proved effective, as Lord William Bentinck – the Governor-General of Bengal, who also had authority over the Madras and Bombay Presidencies – adopted most of the policy changes that he recommended.

Notwithstanding the various pejorative remarks that Macaulay makes about Indian knowledge systems, his 'Minute' seems practical, given the limited resources at stake and set within its own logic. However, Macaulay's amalgam of accounting and ideology, his business acumen, and his colonial prejudice had been signalled on 10 July 1833, two years prior to the writing of this 'Minute', when he delivered a speech on the 'Government of India', defending the East India Company to the House of Commons:

> It is scarcely possible to calculate the benefits which we might derive from the diffusion of European civilisation among the vast population of the East. It would be, on the most selfish view of the case, far better for us that the people of India were well governed and independent of us, than ill governed and subject to us; that they were ruled by their own kings, but wearing our broadcloth, and working with our cutlery, than they were performing their salams to English collectors and English magistrates, but were too ignorant to value, or too poor to buy, English manufactures. To trade with civilised men is infinitely more profitable than to govern savages. (717)

How does this speech, delivered two years prior to the 'Minute' on Indian education, re-situate its ideological content? What profit is there to be made in the discourse of the white man's burden? If the two pieces by Macaulay are juxtaposed, one can interpret the reshaping of (an Anglicized) identity implicit in the 'Minute' to be one that is embedded in profit margins, for to study English would be surely to desire English broadcloth and cutlery. British hegemony is thus not only constantly reinscribed by the repeated citing of English, but it is good for business as well. Macaulay's intentions for Indians that veered between the discourse of business returns and the supremacy of an English education is also implicit in those of Rev Bennett and Father Victor for Kim. Indeed, notwithstanding that, at 300 rupees per year, St Xavier's School was the most expensive option for Kim's education and paid for by the Lama, the focus of Kim's education is his ability to spy for the government in the intrigues of the Great Game.

Further, the training in whiteness that he is subjected to is always a partial representation of Britishness. The education that he receives does not focus on Greek, Latin, science, philosophy, or history, the subjects to which young boys in British boarding schools would have been exposed. Instead, he is trained in mapping terrains and memorizing details, so he can learn to be more observant. In one of the few scenes in which the narrator makes an appearance, Kim is represented painting the map and contours of Bikaneer. Using rosary beads instead of survey chains, along with his survey paint box of 'six colour-cakes and three brushes' (170), he paints the city of Jeysalmir (Jaisalmer) in Rajasthan. He also uses his compass to gain his bearings and writes up a report with details on how many soldiers of the British Army the desert could support, the number of breaches in the city wall of Jeysalmir, and 'the temper and disposition of the king' (170). The narrator, who makes himself momentarily present, informs the reader that: 'The report in its unmistakable St. Xavier's running script, and the brown, yellow, and lake-daubed map, was on hand a few years ago (a careless clerk filed it with the rough notes of E.23's second Seistan survey)' (170), suggesting that, years later, the map drawn by the teenage Kim was still in circulation, still being used.

Within postcolonial discourse, mapping and surveying are considered to have imperialistic overtones, in that the art of mapping is embedded in power relations, often reflecting the cultural meanings as constituted by the hegemonic group. Chandra Mukherjee suggests: 'The meanings of land as property [in the New World] to be consumed and used as Europeans was written into the language of maps' (31). Indeed, the East India Company created the post of Surveyor-General of Bengal as early as 1767 (Carens 613). In her analysis of the Rani of Sirmur in *A Critique of Postcolonial Reason*, Spivak comments on another Anglo-Indian, Robert Ross, who maps the hill country in northern India, and remarks: 'What is at stake is a "worlding," the reinscription of a cartography that must (re)present itself as impeccable' (228). Spivak suggests that the mapping by colonial forces re-narrativizes history, so that in the new rendition of (cognitive) mapping, the native is rewritten as other. Within the context of *Kim*, Kim's mapping and surveying of the princely states of Rajasthan is undertaken in order to assess the chances of British victory and dominance in these regions, thus, if utilized, effectively rewriting the native as other in their own space.

If earlier in our reading of Shere Ali in *The Broken Road* we touched upon Bhabha's essay, Kim's mimicry and performance of both whiteness, as well as blackness, begs for the juxtaposition of Bhabha's 'Of Mimicry and Man' with Kipling's novel. In his essay, Bhabha suggests that the reproduction of the native as a copy does not locate him as passive. In fact, it is precisely the native's difference manifest in his excess (in comparison with the original) and slippage that not only provides for the ambivalence in the text, but also locates the native within an agency. The ambivalence that is visible in the text underscores power's inadequacies, its failure to control meaning, and thus disruption to its authority. Colonialism and colonial discourse reveal the ambivalence within Enlightenment discourse, upon which Charles Grant's 'Christianity' and Macaulay's 'Minute' are predicated. For Bhabha, Macaulay and Grant's texts construct the colonized as metonymies of presence, in that they are only partial representations of the original. Thus, he insists that the mimic 'is always produced at the site of interdiction. It is a form of colonial discourse that is uttered *interdicta*: a discourse at the crossroads of what is known and permissible and that which though known must be kept concealed' (89).

While Bhabha's notion of the mimic is predicated on racial differences between white and black, Kim disrupts the fixity of this racial difference, not only because he can perform both, but also because, as Irish, he is simultaneously categorized as both black and white. In a crucial scene that reveals the close bonds of affection between Mahbub Ali and Kim, the former presents him with

> a gold-embroidered Peshawur turban-cap, rising to a cone, and a big turban-cloth ending in a broad fringe of gold. There was a Delhi embroidered waistcoat to slip over a milky white shirt, fastening to the right, ample and flowing; green pyjamas with twisted silk waist-string; and that nothing might be lacking, Russia-leather slippers, smelling divinely, with arrogantly curled tips. (170–71)

This Pathan outfit that Kim wears is juxtaposed with that of his St. Xavier's school uniform and his outfit as the lama's *chela* – all of which equally confer on him an authentic identity. Kim's excess of identifications imbues authenticity with the notion of ambivalence. His shifting significations suggest the ways in which racial/ethnic identities are enacted, appropriated, and imitated, thus calling into question not only the hierarchy between originals and copies, but also between racial identities.

The ambiguity in the text largely coheres around Kim's body, so that not only is it multi-ethnic, but it also contains all the uncertain significations of the Irish body: is it black or white? Kim's parents are Irish, Kimball O' Hara and Annie Shott. Although the number of Irish soldiers (in the Indian Army) declined after the Mutiny, joining the army was one of the few job opportunities available to the colonized Irish. Noel Ignatiev suggests that Irish immigrants in nineteenth-century America were referred to as 'niggers turned inside out'. Alternatively, African-Americans were referred to as 'smoked Irish' (41). In Britain, the Irish were referred to as 'the white negroes.' Most importantly, in John Beddoe's influential 1862 work on the races of Britain, he produced an 'Index of Negrescence', in which the prominent Irish jaw was perceived as being similar to that of Negroes. Kipling's deliberate representation of Kim as being of Irish origin is meaningful, in that in the two decades prior to the publication of the novel Anglo-Irish relations were prominent in British politics and newspapers. In 1882, Thomas Henry Burke, who had been appointed Chief Secretary of Ireland, was murdered, along with Lord Frederick Cavendish – the nephew of Prime Minister Gladstone – by Irish Republicans in Phoenix Park. These murders were set within the larger debate over Irish Home Rule, which Bill was defeated in the House of Commons in 1886. In 1896, the second Irish Home Rule Bill was also vetoed (Gray 53). To represent Kim as Irish was not only to enhance the ambiguity that was inherent in his racialization, but also to interrogate any comprehension of a homogenized whiteness. By deliberately underscoring Kim's liminal status in this text, Kipling problematizes and heterogenizes white presence in India.

Further, Kipling also cites Kim's poor white status to add to the stack of ambiguities in the text. Kim is 'a poor white of the very poorest' (1). In popular representations of the Raj, Anglo-Indians are perceived as belonging largely to 'the middle-class civil servants [who had] appropriated an aristocratic style of ruling and living' (Arnold 105). Yet, as David Arnold, among others, has pointed out, nearly half of the 150,000 or more Europeans living in India at the end of the nineteenth century belonged to a group called poor whites. This group was composed of soldiers (like Kimball O'Hara), sailors, semi-skilled workers, and intermediaries in government departments that liaised between Europeans and Indian subordinates, such as, for instance, the police, the railway, in jails, or as domestic servants, nurses, midwives, clerks, and teachers (Arnold 104–05). A proportion amongst these poor whites was composed of vagrants, convicts, prostitutes, and lunatics. While the novel *Kim* is often read almost as a fairy-tale – a vagrant child or foundling who discovers he belongs to the upper echelons of society – the reality in India was more depressingly mundane. Arnold suggests that although the poor whites morphed in social status with the Eurasians, the former 'jealously guarded their separate racial identity' (106). As well, the white vagrants lived their lives like poor vagrant Indians. In *Kim*, no Indian character is particularly surprised to discover Kim's racial background; it is only the Anglo-Indians who perceived poor vagrant whites as discrediting 'the entire British race' in India (Arnold 114). *Kim* must also be contextualized within the Vagrancy Act of 1869, which was amended in 1871 and again in 1874. This Act, aimed at destitute Europeans, was based on British Poor Law legislation and functioned to dispose of vagrants in India by sending them to poorhouses or prison. Vagrant European women, though, were shipped back to Britain as soon and as discreetly as possible, because it was feared that they might work as prostitutes in India.

Not only is the attitude to vagrancy central to our reading of Kim, but also to white orphans. Earlier, we suggested that Kim faced a range of three options for his further education. Orphanages and schools for children of European origin had been established since the 1780s, and the skills taught to children were to assist them in gaining employment in the military or railways. Girls were trained to become 'low-grade teachers, midwives and nurses' (Arnold 112). Girls were also not trained beyond Standard IV, because any further training 'might have a tendency to make them dissatisfied with the station in life for which they were destined' (quoted in Arnold 112).

Kim's value lies in his ability to pass for a native. His agency in the school can be negotiated only by his changeability; ironically, precisely that which his education attempts to erase from his character in trying to resignify him as white. This changeability signifies a freedom, class, and racial ability that are at the locus of his agency. Kim's metamorphosis – sometimes a native, sahib, student, or spy, sometimes Muslim, Hindu, Buddhist, or Catholic, sometimes vagabond or part of the ruling class – dislocates him, not only from bodily and racial significations, but also from the very fixity of the signified: his body and identity become a free play of signifiers. If comprehensions of racial hierarchies are written on the body as black/white, then Kim's figure can only underscore the dissonances amongst these comprehensions. Kim learns at school to become British white, though this process is undermined by his being a poor Irish white; further, his racial performances are simultaneously coded by the variations of Indianness, as well. Kim's representation goes beyond a heterogenizing of whiteness. His figure resists all categorizations, in that he is not quite native, as he is white; he is not quite white, as he is Irish; he is not quite Irish, in that he revels in his life as a native; he is not quite an orphan, in that he thinks of the lama and Mahbub Ali as father figures, and they reciprocate accordingly; he is not quite a spy, as he is also a lama in training; he is not quite a vagrant, as he has a sense of belonging; and he is not quite a poor white, as he exceeds the fate written for him at the orphanages by being both a successful junior lama and spy. Kim is produced/produces himself at the intersection of these various categorizations and significations.

If within post-structuralist thought, the subject is discursively produced, in that it is the occupation of set structural spaces that initiates a subject's speech, then Kipling's representation of Kim defies such an organization of the subject. It is precisely such a way of being – discursively produced, while exceeding that discourse – that brings Bhabha's mimic man to mind. For Bhabha, the menacing aspect of the mimic becomes visible when the original intention goes awry and meaning falls apart. We suggest that Kim's simultaneous occupation of so many different positions undermines the necessity to occupy only one discursive position at any given time. Kim is aware of such a fashioning of his identity when he asks: 'I am Kim. I am Kim. And what is Kim?' (282). Indeed what is produced at the site of interdiction in the text is Kim's radical nature, which underscores a multiplicity of being without prioritising any one of it in a space charged with hierarchy and clear racial delineations.

As if to underscore the ambiguity and celebrate the multiplicity of being that it produces, the novel signals it again in the conclusion. Postcolonial critics as wide-ranging as Edward Said and Gail Low have read *Kim* as a text of imperialism, as a result of which, Kim's enunciations of his multiple positionings are foreclosed in their readings. For instance, Said suggests that Kipling's representation of Indians is underpinned by the notion that 'the inferiority of non-white races, the necessity that they be ruled by a superior race, and their absolute unchanging essence' (182). For Gail Low, Kim is a white colonizer, who is able to contain and equate different national identities. At the conclusion of *Kim*, he is faced with two futures: to continue as a spy in the Great Game or find the River of the Arrow, which would give both himself and Teshoo Lama enlightenment. The novel concludes ambiguously. Mahbub Ali and Teshoo lama debate over whom Kim will follow. Mahbub Ali urges the Lama to persuade Kim to return to the Great Game. Teshoo Lama instead suggests: 'Why not follow the Way thyself, and so accompany the boy?' (285). In the closing lines of the novel, Kim does not state his preference; it is the lama who confidently states: 'Certain is our deliverance' (289). Thus ends *Kim*, leaving the reader uncertain of the path that he will choose. But if the idea of mimicry underpins this novel, then we can imagine that Kim will choose both.

Conclusion

Thus far, we have focused on the character of Kim in Kipling's novel and Shere Ali in Mason's, particularly in relation to mimicry and degeneration. However, while both *Kim* and *The Broken Road* on one level undoubtedly reinscribe the scientific racism of late nineteenth-century imperialism, they simultaneously appear to question the very racial hierarchies that they valorize.

In *The Broken Road*, Mason both reinscribes and questions racial hierarchies by making Shere Ali and Dick Linforth mirror images of each other and showing that the opportunities afforded to both men have been identical in almost every respect. The two men are born within a few months of one another, share privileged backgrounds, and, when the decision is made for Shere Ali to be educated in England, appear to share the same opportunities. They meet on Shere Ali's first day at Eton, and, from then on, they are inseparable. They have India in common, and soon they share the same aspirations for the progress of the Road. They fall in love with the same woman, Violet Oliver, both propose marriage to her, and both have their suits rejected. And while their lives appear to take different courses once both men are in India, there are indications that their actions are, in fact, equally circumscribed by the politics of the Road. Even after Shere Ali's campaign on the borders of Chiltistan has been put down; their paths continue to run parallel. The novel ends with Shere Ali in exile in Burma and Linforth in England on furlough. By carefully highlighting the similar opportunities that the two men enjoyed, Mason also draws attention to the one difference that caused their paths to diverge: Shere Ali's race. If Shere Ali is fashioned as a mimic man in Britain through its cultural capital, could we not say the same of Linforth – that, in India, he is Shere Ali's mimic man, reduced to visiting England only occasionally and destined to live in a masculine world in the isolated mountains of Chiltistan, reshaped by its lack of cultural capital? If mimicry and degeneration are produced at the intersection of the differences among races, geographical spaces, and the knowledges that these impart, then wouldn't the same effects shape Linforth's life in Chiltistan as well?

Kim's ambivalent positioning as both black and white, lama in training and spy in training, Indian and Irish, vagrant and having a sense of belonging, all point to a post-racial future when social hierarchies cannot be articulated through racial demarcations. Kim also exposes the way that whiteness is underpinned by class demarcations – in sum, that whiteness is also a bourgeois formation, which cannot countenance white poverty and vagrancy. Through Kim's ambivalent positioning, we can fathom the composition of whiteness: being educated, having a family, having a home, and having a sense of social superiority. (Indeed, by these particular characteristics of whiteness, Shere Ali in *The Broken Road* is white.) Kim also reveals the difference between race and class formations. By juxtaposing the two protagonists, Kim and Shere Ali, both of whom function as mimics, we see the fluidity of class formations, in that Kim, notwithstanding his Irishness, can eventually evolve into becoming acceptably white. For Shere Ali, racial formations and racial hierarchies dictate his destiny. Notwithstanding that he is, in every way, better off than Kim, it is the latter that becomes acceptable.

And why must this lesson be taught against the backdrop of the Great Game? The Great Game's demand of a monastic masculinity – its eschewing of the private, alienation of women, rejection of love amongst friends and within masculinity, suppression of domesticity, exposition of the naked political manoeuvrings of imperial powers, exposure of the posturing between European powers, underscoring of racial hierarchies, and insistence that social hierarchies are predicated on racial hierarchies – lays bare the scaffolding of power upon which the niceties of Anglo-India – love, marriage, the civilizing mission, decency, and Enlightenment values – were based.

Finally, while the compound signifier imperialism-diaspora underscores duty as the scaffolding upon which it attains its meaning, what it also accidentally reveals is the consequence: degeneration. If the sojourn in foreign spaces can cause bodies, habits, mentalities, and sensibilities to devolve, can both imperialism and diaspora be degenerate conditions?

CHAPTER 3

The Missionary's Position:
Love and Passion in Anglo-India

In this chapter, we will examine Anglo-Indian fiction featuring missionaries, as they, along with working-class whites and non-commissioned soldiers in India, belied the image of the 'bourgeois aristocracy' that largely underpinned Anglo-Indian fiction, as well as popular representations of the Raj in the British imagination. Considered to be members of the lower-middle class, the missionaries problematized the boundaries around whiteness, through living in close proximity to native lines and their daily interactions and intimacy with native lives. In a hierarchical system frequently likened to the Indian caste system, with the 'heaven born' members of the Indian Civil Service (ICS) at the top, missionaries, like the domiciled whites, Eurasian community, and British Other Ranks 'all considered to be on a par with the lower castes, were either ignored or patronized by the rest of the Anglo-Indian community' (Collingham 155). Their socially ambivalent position was further compounded by their strong sympathy for the native population, as if such an emotion provided a barrier to their ability to think within the white imperial frame that enabled their very presence in India.

While not being white enough for the Anglo-Indian community on the one hand; on the other hand, Indians saw missionaries as forcing alien, white systems of faith on them. Indeed, Christianity's association with the West and modernity that filtered through the missionaries in India seemed to suggest that other forms of religious beliefs were archaic and outmoded. Christian missionaries in India functioned at the nexus of modernity, colonial politics, and whiteness, provoking discomfort amongst the local population. In this chapter, we unpick the ambivalent nature of missionary fiction, not only within the context of race, but also within the form of the narrative structures of the Anglo-Indian novel itself. Indeed, the Anglo-Indian novel is generally perceived as belonging to the genre of romance, as they contained within them a marriage plot, with the male and female protagonists falling in love against the exoticism of India. Evoking genealogy from the Anglo-Indian romance written by women and the Mills and Boon/Harlequin romances, Hsu-Ming Teo suggests that: 'The colonial order was necessary for the production and sustenance of romantic fantasies' (2). Further to the exotic locale, for Teo, India as a background provided the 'fulfilling fantasy of meritocratic upward mobility, whereby middle-class initiative and talent were rewarded with rapid entry into the elite ranks of society – both the British upper classes as well as Indian royalty' (2). Indrani Sen defines these romances as the 'station romance', which was 'preoccupied with the scripting of the social life of the station' (73). Sen interprets this focus on the social life of the station as being 'rooted in a need to make the writing of fiction in the post-1857 context as an act of self-definition, an articulation of self-identity, as well as a prescription of this society's code of conduct' (73).

But where does the novel about missionaries fit within this romance genre? Far from being peripheral to the politics of Empire, the missionary movement in Britain was central to it, in that the growing power of the East India Company is closely linked to the influence of evangelical Anglicans, as represented in the figure of Charles Grant, who was chairman of the British East India Company, as well as a member of the Clapham sect. His religious beliefs shaped his political and commercial beliefs and influenced the governance of India. As G. Kitson Clarke points out in his analysis of Victorian England, 'in no other century, except the seventeenth and perhaps the twelfth, did the claims of religion occupy so large a part of the nation's life, or did men speaking in the name of religion contrive to exercise so much power' (quoted in Thorne 143). The economic power of Christian Britain was so great by the end of the nineteenth century, that British churches had over 10,000 missionary operatives in total, with a budget of £2m, which was equivalent to what the British Government of that era spent on civil service salaries (Thorne 155). Thus, while popular representations of missionaries depict them as unimportant or peripheral to the Empire, their genealogy in India suggests that, to the contrary, they were influential in shaping the morality and intellect of a god-fearing public in both Britain and Anglo-India. Susan Thorne points out that the British public's first encounters with the colonial other were through the stories brought back by missionary societies. She suggests that: 'In the course of their fund-raising efforts, missionary societies disseminated information about colonised peoples and encouraged if not required reflection on the Empire's *raison d'etre*, the legitimacy of British rule' (146–47). The missionary's role in the story of Empire manifested itself in narrative forms, which could not sustain a linear model of storytelling about religion. Religious narratives had to be mixed up with a sense of racial otherness. If the genre of the social realist novel of the nineteenth century, which focused on material reality and class differences and functioned as a mirror of social reality, was the closest contemporary to Anglo-Indian fiction, the latter, heavily influenced by this model, also simultaneously rewrote it by focusing almost solely on imperial identity and concerns. Thus, the grittiness of the social realist novel manifested itself as the dirt and poverty of India, but without the overt self-reflection and political and social critique that were central to the canonical writers of the Victorian period. Within this context, the missionary novel was further anomalous, as its focus tended to be on soul-making and conversion, rather than on any overt preoccupations with the unchristian nature of imperialism.

This chapter, then, will focus on the thematics of missionaries and conversion and their place within the genre of Anglo-Indian fiction, which commonly focuses on romance, adventure, and heroism. It will consider how the missionary novel fits within this schema, when the only passion that could be represented was for Christ and the only adventure a wrestling for the soul. We will begin our discussion by contextualizing the missionary novel within missionary history, before going on to analyse two interesting novels, which reshape our understanding of Anglo-Indian fiction – Margaret Wilson's *Daughters of India* and Alice Perrin's *Idolatry*. Wilson's American nationality gave her sufficient objective distance to critique the British Empire in *Daughters of India*. Perrin, on the other hand, critiqued the missionary zeal to stamp out idolatry. Both intersect different genres of the realist novel, mingling religious zeal and the desire to convert with that of love and marriage. Finally, we will consider the relationship between imperialism and missionaries in India and the various ways in which a diasporic sensibility is manifested in missionary activity.

Missionaries in India

Prior to the nineteenth century, while some Catholic and German Protestant missionaries followed in the footsteps of Father Thomas Stevens – the first British missionary in India, who arrived in Goa in 1519 – the East India Company, concerned that its commercial enterprises might be damaged by evangelical activity, discouraged or even blocked the entry of missionaries into India, fearful that the Indian population would resent such activity and cause trouble for the Company's commercial ventures. Indeed, the mutiny at Vellore in southern India in 1806 – the first revolt of Indian sepoys against the Company – was blamed on the proselytising activities in the area and interference with religious customs, such as shaving styles for Muslims and the prohibition of caste marks for Hindus. However, following the renewal of the East India Company's Charter in 1813, the ban on missionaries was removed. As Betty Joseph explains:

> The ritual of renewing the charter at regular intervals, since its original granting in 1600 by Queen Elizabeth I, always served as an occasion for various constituencies among the British public to have a say in deciding who was to benefit from Indian trade. (156)

Bowing to pressure – notably from the Clapham Evangelicals, who argued that

'British domination was robbed of all justification if no efforts were made to reform native morals' (Viswanathan 36) – the Charter of 1813 opened India up to proselytising by British missionary societies, as well as to free trade. Evangelicals were now able to spread the Christian message to the idolatrous, heathen Indians, building on the legendary work of the Reverend William Carey and the Baptist Missionary Society in Serampore – a Danish settlement north of Calcutta, which, at the time, offered a haven for missionaries in the face of the East Indian Company's strong opposition to Christian missions in India. According to Anna Johnston, William Carey's 'arrival in 1793 as the founder of the Baptist Missionary Society's mission in India represents the start of a significant influx of British Protestant missionaries' (65), which soon saw the Church Missionary Society, the London Missionary Society, and the Wesleyan Missionary Society join the Baptist Missionary Society in its efforts to translate the Gospels and establish schools. By the 1820s, the practice of Orientalism that had been favoured by Company officials prior to the 1813 Charter was superseded by a policy of Anglicism – reaffirmed by the India Act of 1833 and evident in Thomas Babington Macaulay's infamous 'Minute on Education', dated 2 February 1835 – and missionary activity became part of a larger movement designed to improve or Westernise the people of India. However, in the face of strong resistance to Christian evangelizing from the Indian population, including sepoys, as well as continued resistance from some British quarters, the missionaries had to learn to adapt their practices to suit the local situation. As Nancy Paxton notes, traces of their struggle to define colonial policies and practices in India in the period between 1830 and 1857 'find expression in both British and Anglo-Indian novels' (22), many of which see misguided missionary zeal as one of the underlying causes of the Mutiny.

Following the Mutiny, educational and medical missions became a pivotal feature of missionary work and the principal vehicles for conversion. Schools were established in villages near the missions and became gender-segregated in the face of what was seen as local prejudice, with the male missionary supervising the boys, while 'Native Female Instruction' would be left to the care of his wife. Christian texts, of course, notably the Gospels, were used as teaching tools across both the male and female curricula. However, the disappointing experiences of these early village schools, which largely only attracted the children of the already marginalized lower castes, led to the development of 'zenana visitation', which saw British women visiting small groups of Hindu women in their own compounds. Zenana work was recognized as an integral part of the evangelical mission in India, and, after the 1860s, the employment of single women missionaries was seen as the most efficient way of achieving the Christianization of Indian households, so much so that by the end of the nineteenth century, there was a predominance of female, rather than male, missionaries in India. At the same time, as Johnston explains,

the cooling of evangelical fervour and an increasing trend within the British community (both at home and abroad) away from purely religious ministrations towards a more secular aid-based philanthropy meant that the influence of missionaries in India towards the end of the century had waned. (71)[1]

As the number of missionaries in India increased during the nineteenth century, alongside the belief that spiritual progress was one of the benefits of British rule, so the volume of missionary literature pouring out of India grew exponentially. These works, 'written about India by missionaries, or containing the lives of missionaries who have died in the country' (Mullens 41), joined the travel narratives, journals, letters, and histories being written by the East India Company officials and their dependents. They were used to promote missionary activities to their readers, both in the colonies and at home, and took the form of 'autobiographies; biographies of individual missionaries, missionary wives, or Indian converts; local, regional, and colonial histories; and non-fictional (although often fanciful) accounts of Indian life and customs, education, women's place in society, to name only the most popular genres' (Johnston 81). From the 1860s onwards, books about the plight of Indian women, particularly zenana literature, became increasingly popular. A good example is the Reverend Edward Storrow's *The Eastern Lily Gathered* (1852), which Antoinette Burton suggests 'typifies the male missionary view, emphasizing the superior position of women in Christianity and the degrading customs of early childhood marriage and widowhood imposed by both Hinduism and Islam' (72), and which Johnston discusses in detail within *Missionary Writing and Empire, 1800–1860* (85–96).

Alongside this body of missionary literature, there are also numerous Anglo-Indian fictions which focus on missionary activity or feature missionaries prominently. The earliest of these fictions is probably *The Missionary: An Indian Tale* by Sydney Owenson [Lady Morgan], published in 1811. This romantic novel, which was admired by the poet Percy Bysshe Shelley amongst others, describes the celibate love story of Hilarion, a Portuguese Franciscan missionary, and a Hindu *devidasi* or temple dancer, Luxima. Owenson's romantic idealization of Hinduism would not generally survive in the fiction that followed the Christian evangelicalism that began to flow more freely across the subcontinent and influence colonial policy in the 1830s and 1840s. In *The Hosts of the Lord* (1900), Flora Annie Steel, in common with many of the late nineteenth- and early twentieth-century Anglo-Indian writers who wrote missionary novels, portrays the lack of success that missionaries had in converting Hindus to Christianity and presents a clear opposition between Christianity and Hinduism, with the former being linked to Englishness and whiteness. Alice Perrin deals with the subject of missionary life in India in several of her stories and novels, including *Idolatry* and *The Vow of Silence* (1920) – 'a clever psychological study of Harold

---

1 For a concise chronology of missionary activity in India, see John F. Riddick's *The History of British India: A Chronology*. In particular, see Chapter 9, 'Religion and the Missions', pp. 147–56.

Williams, a gawky youth who comes out to India as a missionary' (Singh 148). Like many Anglo-Indian writers, Perrin is not enamoured of missionaries and, as Singh notes, citing Mrs Cartmell, the wife of the missionary in *The Vow of Silence* as an example: 'She admires their selfless labours, but ridicules the narrowness of view which missionary life tends to engender' (148). In *The Outcaste* (1912), Mrs F.E. Penny – herself the wife of a prominent Christian missionary, Frank Penny (author of *The Church In Madras* [1904]) – presents the conversion of Ananda to Christianity. What makes the book both unusual and interesting is the way in which Penny describes the persecution that Ananda patiently suffers following his conversion, while also recognizing the terrible pain that his actions cause his wife, Dorama, and the misery that it is causing his parents. As the young Miss Wenaston sagely comments, echoing the views of many Anglo-Indians writers towards missionary activity in India:

> I am of the opinion that he might have had more consideration for his father's feelings. Why should existing relations that seem so satisfactory be disturbed? There is a time for all things. It is too soon to ask educated India to accept Christianity; the way is studded with such colossal difficulties. (157)

Indeed, for an Indian to become a Christian was also to be like the diasporic other. Penny deals with the terrible consequences of conversion in *The Swami's Curse* (1922), where the high-caste Hindu, Savalu, knowing that, as a Christian, he will only be allowed one wife, but unwilling to renounce either of his two wives, solves his dilemma by killing his first wife, Thiara. Conversion is also presented in a negative light in Perrin's novel, *The Waters of Destruction* (1905), when the evangelical missionary, Mr Tod, pressures Stephen Dare into marrying the Hindu widow, Sunia, in the hope that he will then be able to convert her to Christianity. Moreover, as Paxton explains:

> Mr Tod is defined as a threat to public order because, in his efforts to convert Hindus to Christianity, he lives too close to them and transgresses the supposedly natural racial boundaries that should, in Perrin's view, separate the colonizer from colonized. (203–04)

As these examples demonstrate, both Perrin and Penny are sensitive to the harm that missionary activity can cause, and, indeed, most Anglo-Indian novels and stories written about missionary life not by missionaries themselves tend to be ironical or satirical in tone, as Singh observes (151).

In *'Curry and Rice,' on Forty Plates; Or The Ingredients of Social Life at 'Our Station' in India*, first published in 1859, Captain George Francklin Atkinson satirizes British officials and residents in the fictional Anglo-Indian station of Kabob, affectionately referred to as 'Our Station'. The people and places mentioned are probably caricatures of those Atkinson encountered during his military career as a captain in the Bengal Engineers. Atkinson, a keen artist, drew all forty plates in the book, each of which is accompanied by a short chapter, in which he mocks the people and institutions of Kabob with

Figure 10. 'Our Missionary', in George Francklin Atkinson, *'Curry and Rice,'* *on Forty Plates; Or The Ingredients of Social Life at 'Our Station' in India.* London: Day, 1859. Reproduced from the collection of the Australian National Library.

his acute observations. Among the station figures that he makes fun of is the missionary, the Reverend Emanuel Fruitz – a German.

The plate (see Figure 10) depicts the missionary discussing a point of scripture with two Indians, while passers-by and street urchins pause to listen to the doctrinal debate. The chapter on 'Our German Missionary' (41–44) succinctly captures the many trials and tribulations of missionary life on a small station. The missionary family live in a bungalow on the edge of the bazaar, apart from their fellow Europeans and surrounded by the few native converts to their faith. While Fruitz works untiringly, but with little success, his wife looks after the school that he has established in the bazaar.

In a somewhat different vein, Henry Bruce's *The Song of Surrender: An Indian Novel* (1915) and *The Temple Girl* (1919) both satirize the Ritualist Mission in India, while Rudyard Kipling's story 'Lispeth' is a stinging attack on missionary hypocrisy. The eponymous protagonist of this story is a young Indian hill girl, who has been brought up as a Christian and is now a servant to the Chaplain's wife at the Kotgarh Missionary Station. While out walking, she finds an injured Englishman, whom she nurses back to health and falls in love with, convinced that he will marry her when he recovers. The Englishman is amused by her devotion and plays along with her, even though he is already engaged to an English girl at home. When it is time for him to leave, the Chaplain's wife, 'being a good Christian and disliking anything in the shape of fuss or scandal' (10), advises him to tell Lispeth that he will be coming back to marry her. Finally, after three months have passed, the Chaplain's wife tells Lispeth that the man never had any intention of marrying her. When she understands that she has been lied to by both the Englishman and the Chaplain's wife, she reverts to her own people, which causes the Chaplain's wife to remark: 'There is no law whereby you can account for the vagaries of the heathen, ... and I believe that Lispeth was always at heart an infidel', which, in turn, prompts the narrator to venture the opinion that '[s]eeing that she had been taken into the Church of England at the mature age of five weeks, this statement does not do credit to the Chaplain's wife' (11).

Other missionary novels include the American Margaret Wilson's *Daughters of India* and *Trousers of Taffeta: A Tale of a Polygamous City*, Mary Scharlieb's *Yet a More Excellent Way* (1929), and Honoré Morrow's *The Splendour of God* (1929). This last novel focuses on the service of the missionary Adoniram Judson – the first missionary of the American Baptist Foreign Mission Society, who landed in Burma in 1813 – and his wife, who could not work in India, due to the East India Company's opposition to missionary activity there. The body of missionary literature was greatly swelled by the numerous children's stories and narratives containing missionary themes, which were produced by writers such as Mary Martha Sherwood, who accompanied her officer husband to India in 1804 and produced a staggering total of over 400 titles based on her experiences in India.

While many missionary novels are penned by devout Christians, few depict successful conversions. More commonly, both in missionary novels and in references to missionaries and missionary activities in Anglo-Indian fiction more generally, missionaries are portrayed as unscrupulous in the methods that they employed to convert Indians or, when they are presented as genuinely devout and optimistic about conversion, their attempts (like those of their historical counterparts) meet with little success. When conversions do occur, they are invariably either problematic or bred from convenience, rather than conviction. In William W. Hunter's *The Old Missionary* (1895), the protagonist accepts that he has not made any real converts, although he does hold out hope for the children of those he has baptized. In most missionary novels, the missionaries do not display even this level of optimism. Frequently in Anglo-Indian novels, the Church, like the Club, is used as a symbol of Britishness, thus the efforts of missionaries to welcome Indians on an equal footing is resented. The extent to which this view pervades Anglo-Indian fiction is evident in a passing reference to missionaries early on in E.M. Forster's *A Passage to India* (1924), where, joining the general response to Adela Quested's expression of desire to meet Indians, a lady who had been a nurse in a native state prior to marriage comments: 'I am all for chaplains, but all against missionaries' (48). She sees chaplains as ministering to the white residents, while it is the missionaries who desire to take Christianity to the Indians and, as a consequence, bring Indians into contact with white

Christians. Maud Diver, however, does not concur with the deprecation of missionaries that is common in Anglo-Indian fiction. In *Ships of Youth* (1931), she presents a particularly positive picture of a medical missionary in Grace Yolande. Margaret Wilson, too, is largely positive in her depiction of missionaries in her Indian fictions.

To sum up, Anglo-Indian missionary fictions cohere around three main issues. First, and in keeping with the larger body of Anglo-Indian fiction, missionary fiction constructs the native as superstitious, dirty, and idolatrous. Within this context, issues pertaining to the ill-treatment of native women by their men, the problems of caste, and poverty are all discussed, though not within the politics of imperial governance (as in other Anglo-Indian fictions), but as something local and as the exploitation of the masses of uneducated and poor Indians by their upper-caste, middle-class counterparts. Second, missionary fiction explores the tension between the passion for Christ and worldly passion. Missionary protagonists, both male and female, are often faced with a choice between a secular life, which includes marriage, and a life devoted to Christ. In these novels, married life is treated as a binary opposite to true devotion to Christ and a sense of a religious calling. Finally, underpinning missionary fiction, there is a sense of bewilderment and a condemnation of the natives, which is caused by the lack of successful conversions. The sacrifices, hard work, and living amongst the heathen poor do not appear to be rewarded in these novels. The failure of the missionary enterprise is blamed on the native's ingratitude. Thus, the missionaries become Christ-like figures, their lives sacrificed at the altar of faith before a host of undeserving natives.

Daughters of India

The American writer Margaret Wilson, who won a Pulitzer Prize for her 1923 novel *The Able McLaughlin's*, published a series of eight 'Tales of a Polygamous City' and two novels, *Daughters of India* and *Trousers of Taffeta*, all of which drew on her experiences as a missionary in India in the service of the United Presbyterian Church of North America between 1904 and 1910. The eight 'Tales of a Polygamous City' and two Indian novels share much in common. The vivid descriptions of the Indian landscape, villages, mission hospitals, and Indian households, as well as the convincing translations of Punjabi speech patterns which marked the stories, are honed in the novels. Indeed, names and scenes from the earlier stories are recycled in the novels, particularly in *Trousers of Taffeta*, which, like the stories, focuses on polygamous marriage and the pressures exerted on (and the apparent desire of) women to perpetuate the male line. The story of Fatma, for example – the unloved second wife in 'Speaking of Careers' – and Gulam – the barren first wife who looks after her husband and Fatma's five children after Fatma dies following her fourth pregnancy, the birth of twin sons, and years of neglect by her husband – is repeated in *Trousers of Taffeta* in the story of Bilkis – the second wife of Raja Mohammed Salim Khan – and Rashid – his barren first wife, who cares for him and the children after Bilkis dies.

Though, at times, Wilson's missionary novels may appear moralistic and somewhat didactic to the modern reader, they nevertheless occupy an important place in the genre of Anglo-Indian fiction. In part, at least, this is because they were penned by an American missionary woman, who, as Everett Wilkie observes, 'infused a Christian and feminist fervor rare in the first third of the twentieth century' (163) into her Indian novels – a fervour which most obviously manifests itself in her novel *Daughters of India* with the three independent, Christian, female characters: Davida Baillie, an American, and Taj and Miss Bhose, two Indians. Moreover, as an American and a missionary, Wilson was not a member of the Anglo-Indian 'club', and this outsider status is reflected in the fresh perspective that she offers of the Anglo-Indian experience. *Trousers of Taffeta* is arguably the more accomplished of Wilson's two Indian novels, both in terms of plot and character, with a clear focus on polygamous marriage and the position of women in a patriarchal Indian society. Yet *Daughters of India*, which borrows its title from a non-fiction work of the same name, published in 1908 by Mary Jane Campbell – a missionary with the United Presbyterian Church in India (Wilkie 163) – is of more interest to the postcolonial reader, because it is looser and baggier in its structure and offers a broader perspective on the sociology of India in the early twentieth century than can found in most Anglo-Indian missionary novels of this period.

Daughters of India focuses on the relationship between the two main American characters – Davida Baillie, a missionary teacher (and thinly veiled portrait of Wilson), and John Ramsey, her superior in the mission in Aiyanianwala – their work with the Christian and Moslem communities from the Flowery Basti, and the breaking-up of a kidnapping ring in the nearby village of Pir Khanwala, which provides the novel with a plot, although ultimately it is little more than a coat hanger on which to hang the critique of imperialism that is at the heart of this missionary text. The protagonists of this novel are both Americans and members of American Christian missions. Wilson's critical positioning in this novel is strategic, as Davida's and John's whiteness bestows upon them acceptance from the Anglo-Indian community; yet the fact that they hail from a country that had been colonized by the British gives them an objectivity which permits a fresh critique of Empire. The rather thin and episodic plot, which Wilkie sees as both its greatest flaw and chief strength, 'for it allows the reader to concentrate on Wilson's masterfully compressed vignettes' (163), also opens up the novel to the possibility of multiple readings. In other words, *Daughters of India* sustains the reader's interest, precisely because of the way that Margaret Wilson straddles multiple genres – the missionary novel, the romantic novel, the feminist novel, and the colonial adventure novel. In what follows, we will begin to unpack some of the possible ways the novel might be read within and across the frameworks of these genres.

First, of course, *Daughters of India* is a missionary novel, which highlights self-abnegation, the choice of living a life of poverty, and the attempt to alleviate the suffering of the other. The missionary trait of abnegation is roundly condemned by Flora Annie Steel and Grace Gardiner in their domestic manual for memsahibs, *The Complete Indian Housekeeper and Cook*. In their chapter on 'Hints to Missionaries and Others Living in Camp and Jungles', the authors specifically emphasize the need to eat well: 'practical, experimental knowledge of missionaries leads to the belief that missionaries, as a rule, think [food] of no consequence – if not worldly or derogatory to their spiritual calling – to give a thought to anything so commonplace' (154). And with regard to housing, they are equally stern in their advice:

> In India a soldier in barracks is allowed in his dormitory 1800 cubic feet. European hospitals allow 2400 cubic feet to each patient. Missionaries' lives are equally valuable, and they should not have less. It may be a laudable desire to imitate the natives by living in mud huts, but native constitutions and ours are not alike. (158–59)

The references to St. Francis and the parable of the Good Samaritan in *Daughters of India* are crucial if it is to be read as a missionary novel. Davida's preoccupation with St. Francis, who preached renunciation and poverty, is linked to the long-dead Ferguson, to whom she was romantically attached; but it is also, ironically, at odds with both the pomp and ceremony of the Raj, as well as its imperial agenda. More interesting, though, and central to any reading of the novel as a missionary text, is the introduction of the parable of the Good Samaritan early in the novel. This story, which appears only in the Gospel of Luke, is one of the most important of the many parables that appear in the Gospels. In response to a legal scholar who asks who is his neighbour, Jesus tells him the story of a Jewish traveller who is robbed, beaten, and left for dead at the side of the road. First a priest and then a Levite pass by and ignore the man. Then a Samaritan comes upon the man, and, despite the mutual antipathy between Jews and Samaritans, he stops to help, tending the man's wounds and taking him to an inn to recover, promising the innkeeper that he will cover all of the man's expenses. In the context of the novel, the parable can be read as a strong condemnation of the Raj, which both discriminated against Indians and promoted interracial (British–Indian) and interreligious (Hindu–Muslim) tensions, in order to further its colonial aims. Moreover, the parable highlights the contrasting actions and beliefs of the British Raj, whose rule was based on an absolute belief in racial superiority, and the missionaries, who, in actions that recall those of the man from Samaria, frequently tested that belief. This is evident, for example, in the response of the English police Sahib, when he discovers that the 'dying sister' – an earlier victim of the kidnapping ring that he is now investigating – is living in Davida's house: "'Do you mean to say" – [the Police Sahib] looked disgustingly at Ramsey – "that you've got a common bazaar woman – trash – living here with you – in this house – full of – disease?"' (124). The missionaries, in stark contrast to the only official representative of the Raj to appear in the novel, see the dying sister only as a victim who needs their help, which, like the Samaritan, they offer unreservedly.

While this is, of course, first and foremost, a missionary novel, the multiple layers of the work are revealed when we read beyond the missionary frame and consider it as a feminist novel, with a female protagonist who gives up the comfort of her home and country to work for the uplifting of the downtrodden Indian woman; as a romantic novel, with its tragic undertones, which simultaneously emphasizes the comfort and companionship of a heterosexual pairing; and as a colonial adventure novel, complete with kidnappings, plucky escapes, and immense wealth, albeit in the form of Christian understanding. We do not wish to suggest, of course, that the various readings of the novel can be neatly partitioned off, but rather that by allowing that Wilson maintains all four genres simultaneously, we can see better how she moves the plot forward and how as she does so she immerses the reader in the quotidian of the poverty-stricken community of Aiyanianwala in the northern Indian state of Punjab.

In interesting ways, Margaret Wilson's novel echoes the work of her compatriot, Katherine Mayo, whose *Mother India*, which purports to reveal the truth about Indian hygiene and traditional practices, such as child marriage (which was the subject of a vigorous public debate in 1925), created considerable controversy when it was published in 1927, a year before the publication of *Daughters of India*. Gandhi, for example, writing in *Young India* – the weekly journal that he edited from Ahmedabad during 1919 to 1931 – famously described the book as 'the report of a drain inspector sent out with the one purpose of opening and examining the drains of the country to be reported upon, or to give a graphic description of the stench exuded by the opened drains' (539).

In 1925, Mayo decided to write a book about India, because most Americans, as she claimed, knew nothing about it. Nuanced by an awareness of globalization and an increasingly small world, Mayo felt an urgency to observe 'common things in daily human life' (20). For Mayo, the gravest social problem that India faced was the insidious combination of child-marriage, misogyny, and a powerful Hindu patriarchy.[2] Thus, the focus on Indian women and the material conditions of their lives in Mayo's text becomes a shorthand reference for the barbarism and backwardness of Indians. The first wave of Western feminism did not necessarily critique imperialism; rather, its reinscription of colonized women as objects of inquiry and pity becomes an imperialistic move. As Chandra Talpade Mohanty asks in her well-cited article 'Under Western Eyes':

2 In 'Three Women's Texts and a Critique of Imperialism', Spivak points out that within the context of colonialism, the status of women becomes not only a marker of the progressive nature of a culture, but also a form of assessment of the colonized country.

What happens when this assumption of 'women as an oppressed group' is situated in the context of Western feminist writing about third world women? It is here that I locate the colonialist move. By focussing on the representations of women in the third world … it seems evident that Western feminists alone become the true 'subjects' of this counter-history. Third world women, on the other hand, never rise above their generality and their 'object' status. (351)

How, then, are we to read Davida's sense of her mission to uplift the poor masses, especially the women in India, within this framework? How should we read this novel within the context of American women themselves, who were only granted suffrage and equal rights in 1920? What does Wilson's novel add to the relationship between Western feminism and colonialist discourse?

By now, it is commonplace to gesture at the collusion or imbrication between the history of imperialism and imperialist presuppositions of missionary work, on the one hand, and the complicity between the church and state in the history of British colonialism on the other. Our aim in this discussion of Wilson's novel, however, is not so much to emphasize the way in which it takes part in the discourse of colonialism; that discourse is evident everywhere in the narrative – in its depiction of, and adverse reaction to, the poverty, dirt, baffling behaviour of the natives, their general untrustworthiness, pettiness, and cowardice, and the general muddle of India – and needs little teasing out. Instead, we wish to focus on Wilson's representation of love and sexuality and what it reveals of the relationship between the races.

Specifically, the novel explores the split between passion and asexual love by providing the American missionary, Davida Baillie, with an Indian counterpart in Taj – a young schoolteacher and beautiful widow who suddenly disappears from the town. The story initially begins to unfold around Taj's disappearance, which is then followed by the disappearance, first, of Ramsey and, later, of Davida. By the end of the narrative, the text makes clear the distinction between attitudes to love in the Western world and love in India, largely through the figures of Davida and Taj and the reasons behind their disappearances: while Davida disappears in order to take care of a pregnant woman, Taj elopes. In juxtaposing Davida as American, white, and in love with a memory and faithful to the past and Taj as Indian, brown, and in love with herself and the present, the text imputes racial differences to the differing attitudes to love and sexuality. This contrast is particularly underscored in the narrative when Taj returns to the mission after her marriage and visits Davida, who asks what she will do if her husband comes for her earlier than she expects:

Taj smiled then. Or the memory of many little kisses hovered smiling on her red lips. She turned her face away …

'A woman's place,' she said, 'is in her home. In that case I would go home with him.'

She went serenely away to Miss Bhose's, leaving Davida stricken again of an old passion – sick unto death, she felt. Life, of a sudden, wasn't good enough. It wasn't worth while. 'A woman's place,' said Taj, unutterably glad of her conviction, 'is in her home.' 'But I am homeless,' said Davida. 'I have no place in the world. How cozily love wrapped her round! But I am naked, uncovered. I can't let her, that naughty little native sweeper, stir me up all through and through, again. What do I care if she marries? They marry every day. They love easily. Anybody will do for them.' (161–62)

The narrative concedes that passion is, universally, bodily – written on the lips or the naked body. However, it also immediately and sharply delineates the difference between Taj and Davida in racialized terms, which also become classed terms (Taj is a schoolteacher and not a sweeper). Difference is written on the abject working-class and racialized body, rather than on the bourgeois white body.

In Denis de Rougement's classic text *Love in the Western World*, the world is divided into two halves in its attitude to love, passion, and desire. For Rougement, the East (by which he means Asia) subscribes to a complete fusion with God. Human love is 'mere pleasure and physical enjoyment', but simultaneously devoid of passion (71). The Easterner, governed by Eros, does not form attachments to fellow creatures, but is absorbed into divine perfection. In contrast, with the onset of Christianity, the West subscribed to agape and the belief in communion (but with no union of essence) and a love of one's neighbour. Far from the complete eschewing of passion, according to Rougement, '[t]he cultivation of passionate love began in Europe as a reaction to Christianity (and in particular to its doctrine of marriage) by people whose spirit, whether naturally or by inheritance, was still pagan' (74). Passion, for Rougement, is always marked by suffering, and he offers, as an example, the narrative of Tristan and Isolde, in which both characters repeatedly seek out barriers to satisfaction. Postmodern views of passion are marked by Rougement's geographical divisions, in that, within contemporary society, passion has become an outmoded emotion and has been replaced by the concept of desire. Mediated through the framework of Freud and Lacan, sexuality in modernity, too, is always doomed to disappointment and dissatisfaction, as it is bound to a sense of originary loss.

Daughters of India fits into the framework suggested by Rougement, in that love and passion, sexuality and spirituality are all explained through the differences between East and West. In this way, attitudes to love not only locate any character in the novel within the framework of religion, but also appear to racialize them (notwithstanding the presence of a number of characters who are converts to Christianity). To echo Rougement, Taj's marriage can only ever be 'mere pleasure and physical enjoyment' (71), because, in Davida's words, Indians 'love easily. Anybody will do for them' (162).

Another way in which the relationship between love and sexuality can be read in this novel becomes evident if we consider it for a moment in relation to Charlotte Brontë's iconic feminist novel, *Jane Eyre* (1847). Like Wilson's novel, Brontë's novel, too, contains elements of the enmeshing of several different genres: feminist, colonial, the search for identity, and the romantic novel. The difference between the two novels, however, becomes evident if we compare similar scenes from each work. In *Jane Eyre*, St. John Rivers – Jane's long-lost clergyman cousin – explains to her why he cannot marry the rich and beautiful Rosamond Oliver: 'Rosamond a sufferer, a labourer, a female apostle? Rosamond a missionary's wife? No!' (329). Jane asks him if, in that case, he will then relinquish his desire to become a missionary. His response is swift and unequivocal:

> Relinquish! What! My vocation? My great work? My foundation laid on earth for a mansion in heaven? My hopes of being numbered in the band who have merged all ambition in the glorious one of bettering their race – of carrying knowledge into the realms of ignorance – of substituting peace for war – freedom for bondage – religion for superstition – the hope of heaven for the fear of hell? Must I relinquish that? (239)

Rivers instead proposes to his cousin Jane, because, as he says, she is 'formed for labour, not for love' (354). Not surprisingly, Jane turns him down, because she yearns for romantic and sexual love with Mr Rochester. The conclusion of the novel is only too well-known: Rivers's missionary work in India foreshortens his life, as India often foreshortened European lives, while Jane thrives in England after her marriage to Mr Rochester. *Jane Eyre* posits missionary work – the love of Christ – and romantic love as mutually exclusive categories; Jane and St. John have to choose one or the other.

Wilson, on the other hand, though a series of elisions and displacements that make her narrative strategy rather more complex than it at first appears, presents romantic love and the love for God not as mutually exclusive, but as simultaneously possible. In a revealing moment early in the novel, Davida Baillie's colleague, John Ramsey, refers to her dead lover, Ferguson:

> 'I was thinking what Ferguson said one day, about this. Do you remember that morning when he –' John Ramsey had his limitations. But he had known beauty when he had seen it in her man, Davida said to herself. And he knew how to use the memory of it. Never too often, never without delicate loveliness, just at the right moment, in the right tone, he mentioned her lover. (20)

We see that, despite Ferguson's death, Davida's passion is sustained precisely because he is dead; his death ensuring a circumvention of any form of closure to their love relationship. Notwithstanding his physical absence, the Christ-like Ferguson continues to be an important presence in Davida's life, structuring her priorities and mediating her goals. In terms of gender and missionary agency, her passion for Ferguson also reflects the need for a missionary woman to be guided by a patriarchal authorizing figure. Wilson further manages to include the structure of heterosexuality alongside the self-abnegating love of God by triangulating the relationship between Davida and Ferguson to include another patriarchal authorizing figure, John Ramsey.

Davida Baillie and John Ramsey are close friends and colleagues, who are thrown into companionable isolation by a series of absences. Not only has Ramsey's wife, Emma, returned to the United States with their children while her husband continues his work in India, the mission's 'First Lady' – the now elderly Miss Monroe, who functions as a quasi-chaperone – is also, at the time, back in the United States. As the narrator reminds us in a prescient moment, both Emma Ramsey and Miss Monroe are crucial to the story, and '[t]heir absence is the setting of its stage' (53). And while the text insists on the circumspect nature of Davida and Ramsey's relationship, it also locates them as heterosexual partners, in that they support each other spiritually and by confiding in each other. Among other indications of their (chaste) pairing are Davida's concern that Ramsey eats nutritiously; Davida's agitation when Ramsey is missing; Ramsey's extreme agitation when Davida is presumed kidnapped; and Davida's support for Ramsey when he has to appear in court. And throughout, the text constantly reiterates that any misunderstanding of their relationship reveals an Indian mindset that cannot acknowledge opposite-sex friendships. In the passage quoted above, Ramsey appears to 'woo' Davida through evoking the image of Ferguson, thus keeping the latter alive as the mediator of their relationship. Though the mediator is dead, the mediation is not. Therefore, a desire according to an Other is inaugurated in the text. If Ramsey 'woos' Davida through the figure of Ferguson, her response to him is more an impulse towards Ferguson. The structure of triangulated desire thus transforms Ferguson into a figure that is Christ-like, yet erotically charged, in the novel. Yet it is precisely the unconsummated love between Davida and Ferguson that also structures the relationship between Davida and Ramsey. They, unlike Jane Eyre and St. John Rivers, enjoy the chaste love of God as well as passion and loss, while also participating in the comforts, if not the sexual desire, of heterosexuality.

Comparing *Daughters of India* with *Jane Eyre* also allows us to unpack a little further the nuanced differences between the white British missionary and the white American one. Such delineation is necessary, because the colonial British missionary is enmeshed in the history of British colonialism in a way that an American missionary is not and never can be. Indeed, the novel makes few textual allusions to the Indian Independence struggle, beyond a passing reference to the Amritsar massacre and another to Gandhi, then newly returned to India from South Africa. And while any direct engagement with colonial politics is largely outside the orbit of this text, Davida does signal her dislike of British colonialism through her attitude towards representatives of British imperialism, such as 'His Majesty's Superintendent of Police'. In a self-critical moment, she also admonishes herself for seeing the world in terms of the racial hierarchies established by a colonial power, whose history she disassociates herself from: 'I am as bad as the Police Sahib, as bad as the silliest arrogant Englishman who ever vaunted the superiority of his white skin' (146).

Within the context of whiteness studies, there is often an uncritical understanding and acceptance of the term whiteness. Frequently, little attention is paid to geographical, historical, gendered, and sexual particularities, and all white bodies are perceived to signify identically. Such homogenization is, in part, the unwitting result of works like Noel Ignatiev's *How the Irish Became White* or Richard Dyer's *White* and a postmodern comprehension of the term, which is located within the politics of contemporary multiculturalism. But whiteness, too, has a history and its own geographic, gendered, and classed specificities. Reminding ourselves of these specificities is salutary, because it permits us to see the differences between St. John Rivers and Davida (or John Ramsey). Jane thinks that St. John Rivers

> was of the material from which nature hews her heroes – Christian and Pagan – her lawgivers, her statesmen, her conquerors; a steadfast bulwark for great interests to rest upon; but, at the fireside, too often a cold cumbrous column, gloomy and out of place. (346)

The emphasis in Brontë's text is on the imperial rule of India, even among missionaries, without taking into consideration the heterogeneity of the British population that lived in colonial India, with their varying differences. Imperialism and whiteness become monolithic.

Being part of the dominant culture, missionary groups in colonized spaces have asserted a moral and spiritual authority that is in continuum with the political and imperial authority asserted over the subject population. Yet, as Gauri Viswanathan has pointed out in *Outside the Fold*, such a reading of missionary activity as imperialism enacted on another arena needs to be nuanced by the underpinnings of British/Indian history. It needs to be contextualized within the secularization of colonial rule (matched by the simultaneous development of a tolerant civil society within Britain itself). If Britain's aim in India was to transform Indians into deracinated versions of the British, then it was its secular face that needed to be emphasized. To this extent, missionary activity to Christianize Indians was looked upon with disapproval by the official machinery of British India after the Sepoy Mutiny of 1857. Conversion is, as Viswanathan puts it in *Outside the Fold*, 'arguably one of the most unsettling political events in the life of a society' (xi), because it threatens the cohesion of a community, alters the demographic equation, and causes numerical imbalances within society.

The point we want to make through our comparison is that, by juxtaposing *Jane Eyre* with *Daughters of India*, attention can be paid to the violence of religious conversions. What St. John cannot say in *Jane Eyre*, because that text is a part of imperialistic discourse, Margaret Wilson can write in *Daughters of India*. The kidnappings, the hostility from the British civil authorities, the lack of religious fervour among the converted, and the general lack of success of the missionary work in India that forms the second half of Wilson's novel can only be expressed in a work that does not emerge from the same history of imperialism. Wilson's text emphasizes desire to educate and convert the disenfranchised. This desire contrasts greatly with that of Brontë's St. John

Rivers and the type of missionary imperialism that he appears to advocate in *Jane Eyre*:

> 'Yes,' said he, 'there is my glory and joy. I am the servant of an infallible master. I am not going out under human guidance, subject to the defective laws and erring control of my feeble fellow-worms: my king, my lawgiver, my captain, is the All-perfect. It seems strange to me that all around me do not burn to enlist under the same banner, – to join in the same enterprise.' (353)

Davida's more modest desire is expressed diffidently and simply: 'how nice it would be if it did come, the glorious kingdom' (176). By asserting American difference, Margaret Wilson can not only explore the insecurities of being a proselytising and religious white in an administration that insisted on the secular, but can also, through Davida, offer a different relationship across race than the obviously imperialist discourse that Brontë provides through the figure of St. John Rivers.

To summarize our arguments thus far, Wilson's use of an American protagonist permits her to make a critique of imperialism – a position which she obviously felt could only be made by someone not participating in that system. This radical critique by Wilson is, however, tempered to a large extent by her depiction of white femininity along traditional lines, through her representation of Davida doing women's work and furthering the civilizing mission, which is the white (wo)man's burden. Indeed, Wilson's critique cannot appear any more radical, because of her conflation of the missionary novel with that of the woman's romance, with its demands of stereotypes of white women, as well as poor Indians. Thus, in Wilson's hands, India becomes an exotic arena that enabled selfless service in white missionaries.

Idolatry

In a letter to Syed Ross Masood written in mid-January 1911, E.M. Forster writes:

> I am reading Lyall's hand book about the English in India – the sort of thing I required [for preparation for travels in India]. Also I have failed to read another of Alice Parin's [sic] novels called *Idolatry*. The other I tried was good, but this is about missionaries & wicked Hindus and most tiresome.' (120)

Bhupal Singh does not share Forster's negative opinion, suggesting instead that 'Alice Perrin draws an excellent picture of a missionary household in *Idolatry*' (148), while the reviewer for the *Times Literary Supplement* praises the novel for its vivid presentation of 'the humiliations, the trials to faith and hope, the small and yet painful anxieties which beset every missionary who goes to work in the Indian field' (53).

Alice Perrin – who was an exact contemporary of Kipling (she was two years older than him), Flora Annie Steel, Maud Diver, B.M. Crocker, and F.E. Penny – was born into an established Anglo-Indian family, her grandfather being both director and chairman of the East India Company. Educated in England, she returned to India after marrying Charles Perrin, who worked for the Indian Public Works Department.

When Anne Crivener's father dies in Perrin's *Idolatry*, her mother, the daughter of a missionary, hands the baby Anne over to her wealthy paternal grandmother and remarries. When the novel opens, the grandmother has recently died, after carelessly squandering her family fortune, thus leaving her granddaughter, Anne, in an unhappy financial position. Anne discovers that her mother is the wife of a missionary, John Williams, and that, fortuitously, she is living in Sika – the very place in India where the wealthy and eligible Captain Dion Devasse is about to be posted. Seizing her opportunity, she resolves to visit her mother and marry Devasse. An engagement follows, according to plan, but a complication arises when Anne finds herself increasingly drawn to the handsome, devout missionary, Oliver Wray, her step-father's junior colleague. Wray, meanwhile, is more intent on saving Ramanund – the son of the local Rajah – from the grips of idolatry, than getting involved with Anne or, indeed, any other woman who might distract him from his evangelical duty. Although he and Anne do eventually fall in love, she realizes that it is impossible for her to marry him or distract him from his calling, and, breaking off her engagement to Devasse, she returns to England as 'a sadder and better person' ('An Anglo-Indian Story' BR134). There, inspired by Wray's example, she rents a tiny flat in London and devotes her time to investigating cases for a charitable association. When Devasse comes back on leave, she is finally ready to marry him for love, rather than for his fortune.

At first glance, the novel seems to be not only apolitical, but also not particularly interrogative of anything, because of its protagonist, who, although she needs to marry for money in order to sustain an upper-class lifestyle in England, is generally likeable and well-mannered. Furthermore, though in the guise of a missionary novel, it highlights the lack of success in converting natives to Christianity. By the end of the novel, the focus is back on London, rather than India, and it closes with Anne's impending marriage to Dion Devasse, a non-missionary. How can a novel that occupies a liminal space of two different genres be categorized? What is invested in invoking multiple forms of the novel? What is the status of marriage and how does desire function in a novel that straddles two different genres? Where are the politics in this novel? We would like to suggest that, just as Anne is offered her choice of two different men, so are readers offered two different genres – the romance and the missionary novel – and multiple readings of the term 'idolatry'. It is within the multiple possibilities and readings that the novel offers, that a political critique of life in Anglo-India starts emerging in the text.

Initially, in order to keep both forms of the novel open, Perrin clearly delineates between the secular and religious worlds. Her novel focuses on sharp contrasts: first, between London and Sika; second, between the civil lines, where the Anglo-Indian population clusters, and the ambiguous geographical zone that the missionaries occupy near the native bazaar. Further contrasts are made through the juxtaposition of the domestic, interior spaces of the civilian Anglo-Indians and that of the missionaries. The secular household that is central to our reading is that of the Stapelys, which is contrasted with the missionary household of Anne's stepfather, Mr Williams. The very different positions occupied by Mr Stapely and Mr Williams, within the complex Anglo-Indian hierarchy, are reflected in every aspect of their households.

The Stapelys, who represent the civilian population, live in a large bungalow located in the civil lines and surrounded by other Anglo-Indian families, where they are attended to by a host of servants and lead lives typical of Anglo-Indians on the upper rungs of the social ladder. They have twin fifteen-year-old sons at 'a leading public school' (43) in England and a younger son, whose departure to England should be imminent. Mrs Stapely, who has been living in India since the age of fifteen, has transmuted from an English girl to an Anglo-Indian memsahib. Her two obsessions in life – the reader soon discovers – are her son Babba and carefully administering her kitchen towels, which she collects every evening and hides in a box, as her Indian domestics had been known to use them to make dresses for their children. Mr Stapely is forced to delay sending their youngest son Babba to England at his wife's insistence, against his better judgement, and, indeed, that of medical opinion of the time. Sir Joseph Fayrer (the same Dr Fayrer who was the Residency Surgeon at Lucknow during the Mutiny), writing from decades of experience in the Bengal Medical Service, suggests, in *European Child-Life in Bengal* (1873), that, by the age of seven, an Anglo-Indian child

> must be sent to England, or it will deteriorate physically and morally – physically, because it will grow up slight, weedy, and delicate, over-precocious it may be, and with a general constitutional feebleness ... morally, because he learns from his surroundings much that is undesirable, and has a tendency to become deceitful and vain, indisposed to study, and, to a great extent, unfitted to do so, – in short, with a general tendency to deterioration, which is much to be deprecated, and can only be avoided by removal to the more bracing and healthy (moral and physical) atmosphere of Europe (quoted in Buettner 29).

The narrative depicts Babba as a child spoilt by deferential and indulgent servants and a mother who is reluctant to allow him to be 'orphaned' just yet, but who, as Maud Diver puts it in her non-fiction work *The Englishwoman in India*, is painfully aware of 'the rival claims of India and England; of husband and child. Sooner or later the lurking shadow of separation takes definite shape; asserts itself as a harsh reality; a grim presence, whispering the inevitable question: "Which shall it be?" (37). In this way, the narrative appears to represent everyday domestic life in an Anglo-Indian civil station for the 'middle-class aristocracy', which formed a large part of the civilian population of Anglo-India.

If Mr Stapely is numbered amongst the overtly 'upper-class' of Britons in India, Mr Williams, as a Protestant missionary, is, at best, located amongst the lower-middle class of Anglo-Indian society (see Buettner 7). In contrast to the Stapely bungalow, the Mission House is problematically located outside the civil lines, beyond the market, and close to the native lines. While the Stapely home is filled with comfortable furniture and quality ornaments, the missionary's home, with few servants and filled with the knick-knacks that the Williams women have made in order to raise money for the mission, lacks the trappings of a comfortable Anglo-Indian home and identifies them as poor whites. No alcohol is served in the house, and, instead of Westernized meals, such as those served in the Stapely household, the Williams family survives on 'the staple Indian dish of dal and rice' (143).

As David Arnold has shown, the families of missionaries (and other similar groups of 'poor whites') rarely feature in studies of domestic life in British India,[3] and this absence is reflected, too, in Anglo-Indian fiction. The missionary's close relationship – both geographically and in other ways – with the native population results in their status in the Anglo-Indian community being as ambiguous as the food that they eat. Yet the narrative also simultaneously undercuts such stereotypical representations of white wealth, by implying that civilian life in Anglo-India is a façade of bourgeois aristocracy in Britain. For instance, the Stapely household is shaped and reshaped, not only by Anglo-Indian mores, but also by financial constraints. Judge Stapely cannot send Babba to England, even though his departure is long overdue, as he cannot afford it. Again, Mrs Stapely is proud of her thrift at the parties that she hosts, cooking most of the food herself or serving leftovers. Her mother has to manage within her small pension and chooses to live in the hills in India, as her standard of living would be higher there than in Britain (90). Thus, the narrative both reiterates the semblance of white wealth, while interrogating it and exposing the hidden narrative of Anglo-Indian poverty. To this extent, the missionary narrative's emphasis on thriftiness facilitates the discourse of thrift that runs through Anglo-India, as well as London, when Anne returns there and has to live within her meagre means.

The strategy of contrast is also evoked in the representation of the two main male characters, Dion Devasse and Oliver Wray, who function as reverse images of each other. If Dion moves from poverty to wealth through the course of the novel, Wray has an opposite trajectory, rejecting his comfortable life and inheritance for a life of denial in India. Again, while Dion is passionately in love with Anne and is willing to give up his career in the army to return with

---

3 See David Arnold, 'European Orphans and Vagrants in India in the Nineteenth Century' and 'White Colonization and Labour in Nineteenth-Century India'.

her to England, Oliver, though in love with her, is entirely unwilling to consider giving up his missionary work, much as St. John Rivers refuses to give up his vocation for Rosamond Oliver. Thus, the representation of the imperial ideal functions as the Christian mission's binary opposite.

The narrative emphasizes Anne's choices between the two men through a further series of narrative strategies. It first differentiates sharply between Anne and her mother and then conflates them, in order for the reader to perceive them as repetitions of each other. Initially, the text represents the two as polar opposites: whereas Anne is from a wealthy background, young, healthy, and pretty, Mrs Williams belongs to a poor missionary family and is now faded in appearance and frail. However, the text's description of one is soon applicable to the other as well. For instance, Mrs Williams is described in an Austenish vein early in the text as 'a little insignificant "nobody," the daughter of a missionary, having neither connections nor money, nothing in the world to her advantage save a singularly pretty face' (9) – a description that, following the death of her grandmother, describes Anne, too, who suddenly finds herself the daughter of a missionary, with few connections and less money, but still in possession of a pretty face. At another juncture, reading through her mother's letter to her grandmother, Anne imagines her mother's life as 'a narrow, monotonous life of duty and self denial – the one romance of her young heart buried deep out of sight' (25); and later, Anne's mother, Mary, exclaims: 'I pray God that if ever you love a man as I loved your father you may never know the bitter grief of losing him, the hopeless longing, the despair –' (87), which acts as a portent for Anne's future, which is realized at the end of the novel, when she finally settles for marriage to Dion, echoing Jane's decision to marry Rochester in Brontë's novel. Thus, in this interplay of condensation and displacement, the narrative suggests that Anne's future has been lived by her mother, Mary Williams, in a reverse of sorts in the past.

We want to suggest that these processes of displacement and condensation are central to the mixing-up of narrative forms here, in that through displacement or the transferring of intense emotions and the fate of Mary Williams to her daughter Anne, it can still posit itself as a romance, rather than as a missionary novel. Through the process of condensation – a narrative movement that can represent composite images drawn from a group of people, places, and objects – and specifically through the composite figure of Mary and Anne, different generations, classes, and locations (London and Sika) emerge. This composite female figure signals to the reader the future emotional life of Anne. Thus, the reader who simultaneously interprets and is confounded from interpretation sustains their interest in the narrative form and its progression. Indeed, one can point to the deliberate attempt of the narrative to heighten and sustain the reader's interest by its predicting and then thwarting of endings, until, in the final paragraph, it is revealed that Anne is going to marry Dion after all, notwithstanding her hopeless love for Oliver Wray: 'She paused, and in the significant silence that followed, as he looked into the future with confidence and hope, Dion did not fail to acknowledge, humbly, ungrudgingly, how deep was his own debt, also, to Oliver Wray.' (396)

Thus, the novel seems to suggest two forms of love and desire: immature and impossible love and one contracted in maturity. Three characters experience love twice: Anne for Oliver and then Dion, Anne's mother for Major Crivener and then Mr. Williams, and, finally, Mr. Williams for his first wife and then for Anne's mother. Unlike other station romances, this novel suggests that love can only be successful within the context of compatibility, rather than physical desire, within the context of shared class and values.

Furthermore, beyond the strategies used in the narrative to sustain the reader's interest, Perrin critiques missionary life, not only through Anne's choice of husband, but also by foregrounding and critiquing the notion of idolatry. If the novel takes its title from the act of idol worship that the Hindus indulge in, it soon seems to suggest that there are three idolatrous relationships in the novel: the Hindus worship of their gods, Anne's desire for Oliver, and even Oliver's passion for Christ. If idolatry can mean both the worship of idols and immoderate attachment to another person, both Anne and Oliver love idolatrously. While Anne is able to overcome idolatry, neither the Hindus nor Oliver can love, except through idolatry. Oliver, though he loves Anne, prefers to give her up, so he can follow his love for Christ. In fact, the narrative suggestion that he gives her up because he thinks she loves Dion proves to be a ruse. At the end of the novel, he decides to live like a Hindu holy man and spread the word of Christ. In the conflation of Oliver Wray and the Hindu lies the critique that Perrin makes of missionary activity – that a secular life is far less idolatrous. There is a sense in *The Flower of Forgiveness* (1894), repeated in Wilson's *Daughters of India* and present in Steel's story 'For the Faith', that adopting Indian dress, like passing in Mutiny fiction, is a potentially dangerous activity and that it is always better for Christians to maintain their own white, visibly European identity, rather than attempt to assimilate to India. Even when the aim is conversion, the end does not justify the means.

Finally, Perrin's argument against missionaries treads familiar grounds in the culture wars that persisted in Britain concerning the validity of missionary activity overseas and their compassion towards racial others in the face of a lack of compassion accorded to the domestic poor in Britain, who endured similarly wretched lives. In *Bleak House* (1852–1853), Charles Dickens highlights the 'telescopic philanthropy' of Mrs Jellyby and Mrs Padiggle, while in *Middlemarch* (1871–1872), George Eliot criticizes Mr Bulstrode as one 'whose charity increases directly as the square of the distance' (quoted in Thorne 154). As Thorne explains: 'For evangelicalism's influential critics within the English intelligentsia, foreign missionaries and especially their home supporters embodied all that was self-righteous and hypocritical, effeminate and ineffectual, cloyingly sentimental and culturally illiterate, about the evangelical bourgeoisie' (154). Perrin's clear representation of what missionary life did to its women – Mrs Williams's death from an unnamed illness, which readers recognize as exhaustion, and Anne's step-sister fated to share her mother's end after years of working tirelessly for a patriarchal missionary society, which would not recognize the contributions of women, preferring to support the men, who were, however, mostly unsuccessful in India – suggests that, like Dickens and Eliot, she believed in working charitably to uplift the uneducated and suffering masses of poor British (as she has Anne do in the conclusion of the novel), rather than attempt to convert Hindus to Christianity. Moreover, she shows that there is no desire for conversion in the broader Anglo-Indian community that subscribes to racial hierarchies, since conversions threatened to transform the heathen into fellow Christians, nominally the same as the Anglo-Indian, but, of course, not quite.

In this chapter, we have focused on the missionary figure in Anglo-Indian fiction, which was an important one in the assessment of imperial lives in India. We have suggested that Wilson's *Daughters of India* functions contrapuntally to Brontë's *Jane Eyre* to reveal conversion to be both a violence and violation of indigenous identities and, through its protagonists, who are deemed to be outside British colonialism, it offers a scathing critique of missionary practice. On the other hand, *Idolatry*, written from a secular perspective that finds any form of evangelical activity to be slightly improper, plays upon and opens up the meaning of idolatrous behaviour, so that the missionaries who found it to be an anathema were themselves espousing a form of idolatry. Thus, both novels seem radical in their interrogation of colonialism and evangelism. Yet, we, as readers, must hesitate to overstate this point, as both novels, notwithstanding their attempt to interrogate power relations, must surely also be reiterating them, as both writers lived in India, and Perrin was clearly a part of the Anglo-Indian community. As such, they repeated the same structures of power and knowledge that they found problematic. Yet both novels have their subversive moments. The missionaries, despite their whiteness and because of their practice of Christianity and Christian principles, became uncannily transformed, creating ambivalence in the circulations of imperial power. As Anglo-Indians – even, if in Wilson's case, on the periphery – they problematize imperial identities and transform the discursive conditions of dominance through their very presence and religious convictions and offer resistance to the very genre of Anglo-Indian fiction.

Finally, and somewhat contradictorily, though imperialism (the imposition of a foreign power) and Christian missionary activity (the spreading of the Christian values of equality, kindness, and faith) are often perceived as functioning as binary opposites, they are actually in a dialectical relationship with each other. In India, each needed the other to validate its own existence and give meaning to its activities. The power implicit in imperial government was camouflaged as a means of bringing India into modernity by leaving behind superstitious ways of life and teaching democratic ways of being. In turn, missionary activity in India needed the support and presence of imperialism and its implied Christian white superiority to effectively spread the word of a true religion in an idolatrous space. Furthermore, both needed the heathen Other to validate their own identities.

Both imperialism and missionary activity were aspects of the diasporic lives of the Anglo-Indians. Khachig Tololyan suggests that the tendency of diaspora scholarship to avert its gaze from the deployment of power has resulted in a perception that diaspora is anti-state and anti-nationalism. In so doing, what the diasporic gaze glosses over is the movement of power, with its drive for location and re-territorialization. In both of the texts that we have analysed in this chapter, the missionary church reveals its impulse, unsuccessful though it may be, towards institutionalization. Missionary activity and the Christian church in India were always political: in craving converts, it craved expansion. Like its imperial relative, it wanted to be bigger and more powerful. By trying to convert natives, to make them into weak imitations of themselves, the Christian missionaries in India attempted to naturalize their own diasporic lives.

CHAPTER 4

The Laws of Desire:
Intimacy and Agency in Anglo-India

In this chapter, we will examine the status, politics, and semiotics of Anglo-Indian interracial marriage, because, encapsulated within it are competing discourses, which infuse this topic with ambivalence – as simultaneously inevitable and forbidden, as sexually desirable, but politically and socially unacceptable – revealing the complex relationship between power and sexual desire that is represented as binaries and, finally, interracial desire as the very condition of narration itself. Both in the United States, with its problem of slavery, and in the British Empire, with its colonies, along with the prominent role that Britain played during the slave trade, miscegenation was the sexual taboo of the nineteenth century; the intimate relationship between a black and a white signified the Victorian version of the love that dare not speak its name. This simultaneous fear and intimacy with the (racialized) Other was the impetus to the development of racial science, as well as one of the cornerstones for the development of the natural sciences of the nineteenth century. If comprehensions of the dominant self and body in the nineteenth century were predicated on an immediately visible physical otherness that demanded the strict demarcation between black and white bodies, then there was an urgency to confront and root out any form of race-mixing. Indeed, even in the twenty-first century, our attitudes to race are the legacies of the racial science that first originated in the nineteenth century, whether we fill out our racial identity in equal opportunity forms or are categorized in precise ways because of our racial appearance. Structured and constructed in the nineteenth century, our racial histories are central to our interpellation in the twenty-first century as well.

In this chapter, we specifically wish to explore love, intimacy, and desire in Anglo-India. Notwithstanding the taboo of sexual intimacy between colonizer and colonized – in fact, the taboos become part of official discourse throughout the British colonies, as seen, for example, in the Burma Circular of 1867 and the Crewe Circular of 1909 – the large bi-racial population everywhere in the colonies suggests the constant violation of that taboo. The Empire's attempt to repress Anglo-Indian sexuality – either in the form of social taboos against interracial unions or in the disproportionate outnumbering of white women by white men in India, leading to the construction of British men as being sexually decent, moral, upright, and interested only in their duties[1] – is simultaneously matched by an alternate discourse of the Empire functioning as sexual opportunity, as seen in the work of Ronald Hyam. In this line of reasoning, the Empire was an antidote to a repressed Britain consumed by the Purity Campaign launched in the last three decades of the nineteenth century, which was obsessed with raising the age of consent and disapproving of masturbation, schoolboy sex, and homosexuality. Hyam's interpretation evokes the Empire as a site of unbridled, unregulated sexuality – just compensation for the ennui of being far away from the comforts of home and delights of a civilized Europe, in order to govern, tame, and civilize it.

Additionally, since the publication of Edward Said's *Orientalism*, it has become a commonplace notion in postcolonial thought that rape becomes the gendering metaphor for imperialism, with the colonized functioning as the supine, raped, feminized body. Within colonialism, the female body is essential to represent power and politics; in fact, imperial politics and power relations are played out upon her body. In colonial discourses, the comprehensions of race and sexuality are so tightly braided together that one cannot be considered without the other, functioning as compound nouns, 'a racialized sexuality [or] a sexualized notion of race' (Stoler 34), thus suggesting that the insistence on racial purity is also simultaneously revealed as sexual desire for the Other. Ken Ballhatchet's statistic that, in 1901, the Eurasian population numbered 89,000 is more than ample testament of this desire for the Other (6).

This chapter will begin with the premise that, far from a repression of sexuality, there was, in fact, an intimacy between Britain and India, which became, in turn, both visible and invisible. Examining the trajectory of Anglo-Indian desire, we see a narrative development – one that moves from the possibility of interracial sexual relations in the eighteenth century, where racial identities had not yet rigidified to a repression and denial of desire and hardening of the boundaries of racial identities in the long nineteenth century. Here, racialized anatomies functioned as destinies. In the next section of the chapter, we want to explore this narrative development, through the

---

1 See, for instance, E.M. Collingham's *Imperial Bodies*, in which she describes: 'the body of the sahib divided into a symbolic ceremonial body and an active, self-disciplined bureaucratic body' (p. 117); also see Indrani Sen's *Woman and Empire*, where she suggests that the valorization of the boyish woman in Empire fiction 'is in some sense a reaction to the fear of female sexuality in the colony' (p. 78).

iconography and fiction produced in these periods. We will start by drawing upon the shifting attitudes to race-mixing in the history of Anglo-India, before we examine two very different novels, Victoria Cross's *Life of My Heart* (1905) and Maud Diver's *Lilamani: A Study in Possibilities* (1911).

Tracing the history of Anglo-Indian desire in the late eighteenth century, we find evidence of considerable tolerance of cross-cultural relationships between European men and Indian women. Perhaps the best-known example is that of Colonel James Achilles Kirkpatrick (1764–1805), Resident at Hyderabad, and his Mughal wife, Khair un-Nissa, whose love affair, which transcended religious and political boundaries, as well as cultural ones, is the subject of William Dalrymple's *White Mughals: Love and Betrayal in Eighteenth-Century India* (2002). Another example is that of William Palmer (1740–1816), a high-ranking official and personal friend of Governor-General Warren Hastings, who, in 1786, commissioned Francesco Renaldi to paint a portrait of himself and his family.

Renaldi's painting, *The Palmer Family* (1786) (see Figure 11), shows Palmer seated in the centre, surrounded by his household of two Muslim wives, three children, and three female servants:

> On the left side sits Bibi Faiz Bakhsh, a Muslim lady of aristocratic background with whom Palmer lived from 1781 until his death in 1816. ... She holds in her lap a sleeping baby, a boy named Hastings, and on either side of her stands a toddler, a son William, and a daughter Mary. ... On the right side of the painting sits Palmer's second bibi. ... This younger bibi is childless in the painting, and leans against Palmer's leg. He holds her hand, but his face is turned away from her and toward Bibi Faiz Bakhsh and her children. Two maidservants stand in opposite corners, echoing the doubling of wives and underscoring the balance between the two sides of the paintings. (Tobin 112–14)

As Betty Joseph explains in *Reading the East India Company, 1720–1840*, 'the painting creates a multiplicity of positions that depict the two women not as passive possessions of the white man but as his emotional and sexual companions in the private domain' (98). In Renaldi's idyllic rendering of the Palmer household, there is a sense of reciprocal affection between the Englishman Palmer and his Indian bibis, which is borne out by the fact that Palmer lived with Faiz Bakhsh for more than thirty-five years and bequeathed her his house in his will (Tobin 113). Significantly, the painting depicts an Englishman who moved beyond the acceptable custom of taking an Indian mistress in the absence of Englishwomen to challenge colonial identity, through his evident contentment with, and in, his Indian household, where he lived with not one, but two wives, who his fellow countrymen would have seen as both morally and intellectually inferior to British women. Yet, at the same time, the painting is set up to present Palmer as a man to be envied by his fellow Europeans: a man with two exotic wives.

The racial integration and social acculturation displayed by men like

Figure 11. *The Palmer Family*, by Francesco Renaldi. Oil on canvas, 1786. Reproduced with permission of The British Library Board (Foster 597).

Kirkpatrick and Palmer, reflected in their adoption of Indian dress and ways of living, was continued by such prominent figures as Sir David Ochterlony (1758–1825), who was appointed Resident of Delhi in 1803, and Sir William Fraser (1784–1835). Ochterlony, who liked to be addressed by his Mughal title, Nasir-ud-Daula (Defender of the State), had thirteen Indian wives and is depicted in one painting by a Delhi artist in full Indian dress, smoking a hookah, and watching a nautch in his mansion (see Figure 12).

In this miniature painting, a white-haired Ochterlony reclines on the floor amidst pillows and bolsters, smoking his hubble-bubble pipe and evidently enjoying the entertainment being performed in front of him. A female servant is bringing refreshments on a tray, while a male servant stands behind him with a fly whisk, poised and ready to strike. Ochterlony looks entirely comfortable in this setting, displaying a level of assimilation into Indian life, which, while not uncommon, was nevertheless frowned upon, as the four family portraits including three officers in full uniform looking down at him censoriously attest.

If Ochterlony set the tone, Fraser, who, in 1805, was sent from Calcutta to be Ochterlony's assistant, bettered the example of his superior: 'part severe Highland warrior, part Brahminized philosopher, part Conradian madman', 'he pruned his moustaches in the Rajput manner and fathered "as many children

Figure 12. *Sir David Ochterlony in Indian Dress and Smoking a Hookah and Watching a Nautch in his House in Delhi*, by an anonymous artist working in the Delhi style. Watercolour, circa 1820. Reproduced with permission of The British Library Board (Add.Or.2).

as the King of Persia" from his harem of Indian wives'.[2] Such behaviour was not unusual at the time, and there were many other continental Europeans and Britons who lived cosmopolitan lives on the edge of Empire in the late eighteenth century. The Frenchmen Claude Martin (1735–1800), Antoine Polier (c. 1741–1795), and Benoît de Boigne (1751–1830), in Maya Jasanoff's words, all 'spanned Indian, European, and British cultures both professionally and personally' (90). The Irish soldier of fortune George Thomas (1756–1802) married Zeb-un-Nisa, the Begum Samru of Sardhana, who was the widow of another European mercenary, Walter Reinhard (1723–1778), while the East India Company servant and scholar Neil Edmonstone (1756–1841) had a family of four children with his Indian 'wife' in the 1790s. However, tolerance of such lifestyles would largely evaporate by the end of the first decade of the nineteenth century.

As Christian evangelicalism began to direct colonial policy in the 1830s and 1840s, racist and puritanical attitudes made cross-cultural intimacy increasingly rare, and, following the Mutiny of 1857–1858, any such tendencies were carefully censured, by invoking a 'racial memory of the 1857 uprisings as the barbaric attack of Indian savages on innocent English women and children'

2 William Dalrymple, *City of Djinns*, p. 99.

(Sharpe 85). The Mutiny, then, brought to an end the tolerance of cross-cultural intimacies, which, in any case, had been treated with growing unease in the preceding decades, as increased links with Europe altered the complexion of Anglo-Indian society, and the cantonments and civil lines increasingly became places of refuge where European women could be isolated and the white race protected from the threat of racial contamination. Indeed, Cynthia Enloe suggests that Robert Baden-Powell, who began his military career in Lucknow and spent over ten years in India, founded the Boy Scouts in 1908 in part because he believed that intermarriage of the races was endangering the maintenance of Britain's imperial power (49–50).

One of the earliest British novels of India, Phebe Gibbes's epistolary novel of sensibility, *Hartly House, Calcutta*, published anonymously in 1789, includes an important early literary representation of the possibility of a cross-cultural relationship between an English woman and an Indian man. In the introduction to his recent scholarly edition of the novel, Michael J. Franklin notes that contemporary reviewers praised the novel for its accurate representation of colonial life in Bengal (xxi), adding that:

> It certainly provides what is in many ways an accurate sociological picture of colonialist life in the Bengal of the 1780s, which usefully complements the travel writing of Jemima Kindersley, the *Original Letters* of Eliza Fay, the *Memoirs* of William Hickey, and William Hodges's *Travels in India*. (xxxvii)

But what is especially notable about this novel in the context of our discussion of love, intimacy, and desire between Anglo-Indians and Indians is that Gibbes – whose heroine, Sophia Goldborne, is sexually attracted to her Hindu Brahman tutor (and later to the Muslim Nawab of Bengal) – appears to accept the possibility of desire and intimacy between a European woman and Indian man. Even in the eighteenth century, when the interracial marriages of men like Kirkpatrick and Palmer were officially tolerated if not officially sanctioned, this would have been met with disfavour and may only be permissible here because of the young heroine's stated belief, as evident in her letters to Araballa – her correspondent in England – that Brahmans are celibate, thus, as Franklin notes, avoiding 'the spectre of miscegenation' (xxviii).

The spectre of miscegenation was not avoided, however, in the numerous Anglo-Indian novels that do deal with mixed marriage and the problems arising from cross-racial intimacy. As the lives of men like Kirkpatrick and Palmer demonstrate, it was not uncommon for Englishmen to marry Indian women in the eighteenth century, and even in first quarter of the nineteenth century there was little prejudice against such marriages, either in Anglo-Indian society of the time or the fiction of the period.

However, by the second quarter of the nineteenth century, these marriages were no longer looked on with the same degree of tolerance. Yet while Captain Forester's marriage to a Muslim woman, recounted in one of the stories in *The Baboo and Other Tales* (1834), may not be approved of by his countrymen, it is not seen as unusual. And, indeed, even at the end of the century, it is clear from stories such as 'Yoked with an Unbeliever', in which the planter Phil Garron marries a hill-girl who makes a better man of him, that Rudyard Kipling did not regard them as particularly singular. Nevertheless, as Benita Parry explains, by the mid-nineteenth century, and even more so by the late Victorian period, intermarriage with Indians (or even Eurasians) had begun to be seen as a symptom of degeneration (32), so much so that Bhupal Singh was moved to observe in *A Survey of Anglo-Indian Fiction* that the 'device of killing or putting aside the Indian girl is followed by almost every Anglo-Indian novelist' (167). In Maud Diver's story 'Sunia: A Himalayan Idyll', the eponymous Indian woman Sunia gives her life to save her British lover, intercepting a snake bite that would otherwise have struck Phil Brodie, who is left to contemplate the narrow escape he has had from an 'an act of sentimental folly, which would probably have ruined his career' (27) and isolated him from the company of men and women of his own race. At the outset of Flora Annie Steel's *On the Face of the Waters*, discussed in detail in Chapter 2, Jim Douglas is living in Lucknow with his Indian mistress, Zora, and working as the Nawab's horse trainer. His assumed name, James Greyman, highlights his ability to live between two cultures and links him to such historical figures as Benoit de Boigne and James Skinner, who moved freely between the two worlds. However, in order to 'purify' her hero, Steel informs her reader, early in the novel, that Jim sees Zora's impending death as offering him freedom from 'a life which had grown distasteful to him' (32) and of the relief that he felt when his half-caste son, the product of his degeneration, died at birth:

> How many years was it since he had seen Zora weeping over a still little morsel of humanity, his child and hers, that lay in her tinselled veil? She had wept, mostly because she was afraid he might be angry because his son had never drawn breath, and he had comforted her. He had never told her of the relief it was to him, of the vague repulsion which the thought of a child had always brought with it. (35)

Similarly, in G. Dick's *Fitch and His Fortunes: An Anglo-Indian Novel* (1898), the zemindarin Savitri Bai commits suicide, thus saving Fitch from an unholy marriage; in Victoria Cross's *Self and Other* (1901), the obstacle to Francis Heath's future in the Indian Civil Service is removed when his Indian 'guest', Narayanah Chandmad, is carried off by the plague; and in Donald Sinderby's *The Jewel of Malabar* (1927), the English officer Sir John Bennville, who is determined to marry Kamayala, a Nayar widow, is saved from the folly of his passion when she suddenly (and rather unconvincingly in an otherwise convincing novel) converts to Christianity and enters a convent. In this novel, as Bhupal Singh observes, the reasons why an Englishman should not marry an Indian woman are clearly set out and are typical of the reasons that inform many novels of mixed marriage:

> [T]hat an Englishman cannot marry a black woman, that it is simply not done, that he would have to live in 'this God-forsaken country' for the rest

of his life, that Indian girls are dangerous and put something in one's drink, that his children would be 'half-chats,' that he has a decent English line to keep up, and that an officer of the Musketeers married to a native is an unheard-of horror. (Singh 168)

Novels of mixed marriage fall into two distinct categories: those that deal with the marriage of an English man to an Indian woman; and those that deal with the marriage of an English woman to an Indian man. During the first 200 years of the 'Kampani Bahadur', or East India Company rule, there were very few English women in India. Even as white women began arriving in India in increasing numbers during the nineteenth century, instances of mixed marriage between an English woman and an Indian man were rare, as the women were quickly placed into a colonial purdah, which kept them apart from Indian men. The twentieth century, however, brought with it new opportunities for the races to mix. Indians, mostly men (but some women, too, including Cornelia Sorabji), began to travel to Britain for education or pleasure. Some married British wives, whom they took back with them when they returned to the subcontinent. Sir E.J. Trevelyan, writing in the *Journal of Comparative Legislation* in 1917, noted that: 'During recent years Indians have come to England in increasing numbers, and have in many cases married English wives', adding that:

> In the majority of cases such alliances must lead to unhappiness. The views of the East and the West differ considerably as to the meaning of the marriage relationship, and as to the position of women in Society. Differences of religion, of habits of life, and of education prevent the complete union which is necessary for happiness in the married state. (223)

Such marriages also attracted the attention of Anglo-Indian writers, who, by and large, condemned them. Mrs Penny takes up the subject in a number of her more than thirty novels set in India, including *A Mixed Marriage* (1903), *A Question of Colour* (1926), and *A Question of Love* (1928). In all of these novels, she expresses (albeit somewhat patronizing) sympathy for her central Indian characters – all cultured men, who have lived in England and want something more than Indian women, bound by tradition, can offer them. But, significantly, even though she brings the Indian man and English woman together, she also brings about their separation and never allows a marriage to take place. The pattern set by Penny and followed by many other Anglo-Indian novelists who wrote about mixed marriage between a brown man and white woman is neatly summarized by Bhupal Singh:

> An Indian, cultured, enlightened, more or less Europeanized and belonging to a rich, if not a princely family, gets to know a beautiful, intelligent English girl, either in England or India. They fall in love with each other, thereby exciting the jealousy or anger of some Anglo-Indian lover or guardian of the girl. Some sensational incident is then introduced – devil-worship or a local riot involving the girl in danger. Finally the English girl is married to her

Anglo-Indian admirer and the Indian is left alone to realize that his desire
to marry an English girl was wicked and impossible – 'a desire of the moth
for the star'. (172)

Other novelists, however, do allow such marriages between East and West to
take place. In *Voices in the Night* (1900) – where the London-educated Brahmin
Chris Dravenant (Krish Devanund) marries an English girl – and again in
The Law of the Threshold (1924), Flora Annie Steel, like Penny, explores some
of the difficulties brought about by the Westernization of young Indians.
More commonly, though, novels which feature marriages between an English
woman and an Indian man do so in order to record the plight of the poor
English woman and the tragedy of mixed marriage and, in doing so, reveal – as
E.M. Forster's *A Passage to India* so painfully highlights – that racial prejudice
was perhaps even deeper and more pronounced in the early twentieth century
than it had been in the nineteenth century.

In Victoria Cross's *Life of my Heart*, published in 1905, it is the white woman
who initiates the relationship, the white woman who is given agency to go
beyond the constraints of colonial hierarchy to cross racial boundaries in a
gesture which reinforces the colonizer/colonized binary, while simultaneously
reversing the male/female one. On a related topic, Prem Chowdhry notes:

> This transgression challenges the whole system of racist and masculinist
> domination and subverts the concept of racial superiority. An alliance or
> contact between the native male and European female went against the
> notions of male and superior white racial domination. It recreated fears of
> loss of race, class and status. (207)

Conversely, in Maud Diver's 1911 work, *Lilamani: A Study in Possibilities* – the
first of a quartet of novels dealing with mixed marriage and its aftermath
– the relationship is between an English man and an Indian woman. Both of
these novels, written in the early years of the Edwardian period, mark a shift
from earlier Anglo-Indian fiction written in the wake of the Mutiny, which
emphasized the vulnerability of Anglo-Indian women caused as a result of
their sexual desirability and had the threat of rape as a central motif. In
juxtaposing these two novels – one which has a white female protagonist who
falls in love with a Muslim man and the other which has an upper-middle class
British male protagonist who falls in love with a high-caste Indian woman
– we hope to track the dense configuration of terms like power, whiteness,
blackness, and desire, in order to examine how gender and sexuality were
shaped and mediated by the demands and mores of the Empire.

Life of My Heart

In *Writing Under the Raj*, Nancy Paxton describes Cross's 1905 novel *Life of My
Heart* as 'one of the most ideologically radical novels of this decade' (215),
because of its intersection of the trope of the New Woman with that of

imperialism, both of which process their relationship to power in diametrically opposed ways. While imperialism is a form of global, white, patriarchal dominance, the politics espoused by the New Woman – the forerunner of the first wave of feminism – is aimed at destabilizing patriarchy by insisting on the agency of women. The synopsis of the novel is as follows: the protagonist of *Life of My Heart*, Frances Wilson, aged twenty at the start of the novel, has just returned to Jungpur in India after a classical education in England to be with her father, a retired general in the Indian Army. Being a young, white woman optimizes her chances of getting married, due to the gender imbalance in Anglo-India, yet Frances does not find the selection of available British men in Jungpur appealing. Instead, she is attracted to Hamakhan, a Muslim *chetai-wallah* or mat weaver from Peshawar, who claims to be fifteen years of age, but whom Frances believes to be seventeen or eighteen years old, as, like all natives of his class and region, he could not properly know his exact age. Here Cross breaks the pattern of this type of interracial desire, which dictates that the Indian man should be of good birth or cultured or, ideally, both, 'before they could entice any Englishwoman' (Mukherjee 142). As they fall in love with each other, Hamakhan moves into her home as a domestic servant. When General Wilson discovers their relationship, they elope, effectively severing Frances's ties to her family and Anglo-India. The second half of the novel tracks their life together living within Hamakhan's means, the birth of their child, and the various other tribulations that they face. It concludes, melodramatically, with their death.

If the first half of the novel is set in Anglo-India, the second half is set in working-class Muslim colonial India. The location of Frances as a sexual being – albeit a failed one, making improper choices – is the radical breakthrough of this work, especially within the context of the gradual desexualizing of Anglo-Indian men and women since the Mutiny of 1857. Indeed, there were clear codes of acceptable behaviour for the imperial couple. In juxtaposing these disparate spaces of Anglo-India and working-class native India, the text explores not only the relationship between the native and ruling elite and the taboo subject of white women's sexuality along with interracial sexuality, but also the status of white women in these relationships. Far from being an overvalued being, her whiteness is a status that is bestowed upon her through her relationship to her father or her heterosexual relationships within Anglo-India.

In this section, we will examine the figure of the New Woman, enmeshed in this intersection of imperialism, racial difference, and sexuality. We will consider the way the text resolves the opposition between formed attachments, which are considered to be part of the private realm and at the core of one's very identity, and the public nature of social practices that govern and mediate those attachments. In other words, we want to look at the way in which Anglo-Indians govern the love between the protagonists. We will also consider how it transforms private intimacies into discursive public acts. Finally, we will address what constitutes the Althusserian 'hey you!' that interpellates them as subjects of the British Empire and what that has to do with the desire and intimacy represented in this work.

New Woman, the Station Romance and *Life of My Heart*

Within Anglo-American feminist history, the figure of the New Woman is closely linked to the United Kingdom's Married Women's Property Act of 1882, which legislated that married women could retain control and keep all personal and real property that was acquired before and during marriage, thus striking a blow upon Victorian patriarchy. The figure of the New Woman was celebrated in the closing years of the nineteenth century, particularly in the 1880s and 1890s, becoming metonymically linked with the very notion of modernity at the turn of the century.[3] Angelique Richardson points out that over 100 novels and even more short stories were written by, or contained the figure of, the New Woman in the last years that proceeded the twentieth century (5). Additionally, Ann Ardis argues that the New Woman replaced the figure of the Angel in the House, which became popular in the mid-nineteenth century (quoted in Richardson 7). Thus, the figure of the New Woman is associated with modernism, with the challenge to traditional comprehensions of femininity, and with disruption and subversion. The New Woman interrogated marriage and heterosexuality, supported socialism, and was perceived as being simultaneously asexual and mannish, as well as hypersexual and emphasizing the importance of physical passion. Ultimately, the figure of the New Woman constituted a heterogeneous group, espousing new attitudes to femininity, marriage, and sexuality, while also simultaneously endorsing the attitudes of the eugenicists, for whom the maternal figure was central to the production of healthy citizens (and, consequently, for the very maintenance of the Empire).

How does the figure of the metropolitan New Woman, with her emphasis on education and her anti-marriage stance, translate in the colonies, with its own peculiar fashioning of, and requirements for, the feminine? Indrani Sen points out that, in the aftermath of the 1857 Mutiny, there was the dominance of the station romance in the literary productions of Anglo-India, which, although following a romance format, also focused on the social life of the station. Sen suggests that

> this preoccupation with encoding the life of the community was rooted in a need to make the writing of fiction in the post-1857 context an act of self-definition, an articulation of self-identity, as well as a prescription of this society's code of conduct. (73)

She further adds that the narrative trajectory of the heroine, deployed by the station romances, moves from 'ignorance to knowledge and from moral

---

3 See the introductory chapter of Angelique Richardson's *Love and Eugenics in the Late Nineteenth Century: Rational Reproduction and the New Woman.*

disorder to order' (74). Sen concludes that the focus on romance leading to marriage was part of the shaping and contouring of Anglo-Indian women to become imperial citizens – 'the making of a memsahib' (74). Indeed, station romances functioned as a training manual for feminine imperial identity, with their predominantly Anglo-Indian women readers. Further, the emphasis on marriage functioned in two ways: first, as the central trope that subjectivated Anglo-Indian feminine identity (just as war against the rebellious natives became central to the formation of Anglo-Indian masculinity); and, second, as a metaphor for the social order and stability that Anglo-India represented in India.

If marriage was a necessary narrative feature in Anglo-Indian fiction while validating the Anglo-Indian presence in India, then one can see it as being at odds with the very ethos of the New Woman, with its emphasis on independence. *Life of My Heart* negotiates between the contrasting ethos, by both repudiating, as well as redefining, marriage, through its representation of the protagonist, Frances Wilson. Furthermore, Cross's adaptation of the station romance structure underscores desire, intimacy, and sexuality to be central to our reading of the novel. Through her use of the New Woman as protagonist, Cross seems to suggest that the costs of imperial identity are the passions of the body – a very excision of it. This depassionating of the body is suggested in the opening pages of the novel, which maps out Frances's everyday life: the routine of waking up and saying goodbye to her father General Wilson, who, though retired, goes to work on weekdays between eleven o'clock in the morning and four o'clock in the afternoon; in his absence, reading, listening to music, entertaining a stream of callers, including her older sister, and taking lessons in Hindustani and Persian from her tutors; eating a seven-course lunch with wine everyday (19–22); on her father's return from work at four o'clock, leading him to the dining room, where he would have his peg of whisky and sandwiches; getting ready for their daily evening drive, during which they would meet and greet other Anglo-Indians. On occasions, they might go to the Gardens of Jungpur to listen to the military band. Indeed, the everyday life of Frances was meant to provide her with opportunities to meet young marriageable men – a fate for which a station romance heroine was destined. However, Frances's experience of life as the heroine of a station romance is an empty signifier:

> Of the men and women she met there, the latter seemed to know nothing, and never to have known anything, and the former seemed to have known something much against their will and to be trying hard to forget it. (24)

Thus, the narrative's metonymic link between the station romance resulting in marriage and an imperial identity is perceived by Frances as being predicated on an absence: 'to know nothing'; 'never to have known anything'.

Therefore, in representing Frances as a New Woman, the figure of identification for its predominantly female Anglo-Indian reader, the novel offers an alternative reading position – that of interrogating the dominant ideology's production of an imperial identity. This alternative and interrogative mode is further reinscribed in the novel's inclusion of Frances's sister, May, within the narrative. May, unimportant to the development of the plot or to Frances's life, is, nevertheless, central for providing the reader with the empty horror of the station romance heroine. May, married to General Harding, had 'a loveless marriage, in strict accordance with orthodoxy and propriety' (104) and accepts Frances's desire and love for Hamakhan: 'Can I honestly dissuade her from this natural joy and happiness, and urge her to follow the correct and orthodox cause? What has it brought me?' (104). In her recent critique of monogamy and marriage, Laura Kipnis describes them to be 'a system of exchange: an economy of intimacy governed … by scarcity, threat and internalized prohibitions; secured ideologically … by incessant assurances that there are no viable alternatives' (11) – a description that is particularly apposite to May's sense of her marriage to General Harding. Indeed, at the end of the novel, May responds to the news of her sister's death by asking: 'Was her sister's fate worse than her own? … Was the plain where her sister was buried more desolate than the stretch of empty, cheerless, unimpassioned life before herself?' (386–87). Thus, in comparing Frances's death with her life as a post-station romance wife, May turns notions of intimacy, the private, and the Anglo-Indian home on their head, by focusing on the unwritten narrative, the everyday life in marriage, rather than the idealization of it.

Intimacy and Desire in *Life of My Heart*

If the space of intimacy and desire is generally considered to be located in the domestic, the social mores of Anglo-India complicate these terms. Indeed, what is deemed private is mediated by the public, the politics of race, and comprehensions of power relations under the aegis of imperialism. In *Life of My Heart*, Anglo-India learns its internal life publicly, theatrically, through guide books on behaviour, with the civilizing process learnt through a constant fix on racial difference and the authority that imperial rule confers upon whiteness. The split between the Victorian notion of the public and the private evaporates and even entertainment – normally belonging to the personal and domestic – is mediated through the lens of imperialism. Frances discovers the empty theatricality of her life during her daily drives to the park, while playing whist, and at dances. Within the context of always being on display, always having to bear a sense of white propriety, Frances's equation of passion with secrecy and a focus on the body is a natural consequence of the excision of the body and the private in Anglo-India.

An examination of the boundaries between the public and private is fruitful for an understanding of intimacy and desire in the text. It is a commonplace to state that nineteenth-century notions of the spatial division of the public and private have functioned in the social as well, in that these binary oppositions also function to divide male and female, work and family, colonizer and colonized, and hetero- and homosexual (Berlant 3). In these paradigmatic divisions, the public, male, colonizer, work, and the hetero-sexual have traditionally been associated with the rational and instrumental, whilst the latter terms are associated with emotions. In 'Intimacy: A Special Issue', Lauren Berlant points out that there is a close relationship between comprehensions of intimacy (generally located in the space of the private) and the development of the public sphere. Berlant uses Jürgen Habermas's notion of critical public discourse, which argues that it is within 'the intimate spheres of domesticity' that one learns to experience internal lives publicly. She states that:

> The development of critical publicness depended on the expansion of class-mixed semiformal institutions like the salon and the café, circulating print media, and industrial capitalism; the notion of the democratic public sphere thus made collective intimacy a public and social ideal, one of fundamental political interest. Without it the public's role as critic could not be established. (3)

For Habermas, this development of a critical publicness was important to the representation of the public's interests against that of the state. Berlant explains that comprehensions of intimacy and the internal life within liberal society are paradoxically learnt through public discourses that have an audience, such as novels and newspapers. Thus, nineteenth-century notions of public and private are problematized within terms such as collective intimacy and critical publicness.

How, then, can we use these terms to inform our reading of *Life of My Heart*? If the narrative can be seen as perpetuating dominant ideology – a how-to manual for Anglo-Indian women – how does it function to produce a public and collective intimacy? In *Imperial Bodies*, E.M. Collingham analyses the peculiar relationship that Anglo-Indians have with their bodies, by focusing on food, clothes, and social rituals. Collingham suggests that tinned foodstuffs from Britain were valorized, as eating Indian food threatened to deplete the whiteness of Anglo-Indians; evening dress was considered essential at dinner, even when dining alone and even if the fabric of the clothes were inappropriate for India's hot climate; and, most importantly, the social rituals around visiting each other were deemed central to the daily reinscription of Britishness and whiteness practiced by the Anglo-Indians. However, as Collingham adds,

> What made the Anglo-Indians appear more British than their compatriots in the metropole was their embodiment of an idea of Britishness which belonged to the nineteenth century. This left the Anglo-Indians with a body which was as socially outdated and archaic as it was politically out of touch. (164–65)

While the social rituals that Collingham enumerates as being public in their display reinscribe Anglo-Indianness, how can we discuss collective intimacy in this novel? *Life of My Heart* makes a clear distinction between intimacy and desire, in that while the former is very closely aligned with a public mode of identification, the latter, desire, as represented through Frances and Hamakhan, appears to destabilize whiteness and its close braiding with power – the very thing that Anglo-Indian life was supposed to stabilize. While Anglo-Indian marriages belong to the side of intimacy and seem to be publicly engendered, bodily desire can only be expressed through Frances and Hamakhan's relationship. Indeed, Frances and her sister May's relationships with their partners function as a study in contrasts. May is not only bored by the theatrical nature of her marriage to a husband who espouses proper Anglo-Indian values, but also has to listen 'to his honest snores' (390) at night; the term 'honest' signifying idealized Anglo-Indianness, while detracting from his physical attractiveness. (In fact, the only attractive male in the novel is the exoticized Hamakhan.) In contrast, the narrative places Frances and Hamakhan at the locus of bodily desire, in an absence of Anglo-Indian propriety, completely secluded. Additionally, another point of contrast between May and Frances is that, while the former's life is quite public and part of a collective intimacy, Frances's life becomes increasingly more private and secret in the novel. Frances and Hamakhan's desire can be enacted only in enclosed places, without becoming a part of public discourse or the collective intimacy of the Anglo-Indians. This textual incarceration of Frances is spatially manifested in the way she moves into the native city and is sequestered in the innermost room of the hut that she shares with Hamakhan, far away from Anglo-Indian spaces. If whiteness were perpetuated through the consumption of British food, evening dress, and social mores, as Collingham would have it, then Frances's life with Hamakhan is one that is completely dislocated from whiteness, as she wears Muslim clothes, eats native food, and socializes with hardly anyone by the end of the novel. In the last instance, the paradigmatic cluster – public, male, work, colonizer – all closely align to form a public intimacy, whereas the other cluster – female, family, and colonized – function at the level of desire, revealing a paradox that bodily desire can be expressed only through cross-racial relationships, because notions of intimacy and desire are racially and spatially bound in the text.

What we have argued thus far is that, through the figure of the New Woman, the novel offers the radical possibility of interracial relationships – one that joins a white woman with a non-white man within the context of racial imperial rules. In order to enable this radicalization, Cross's narrative separates intimacy from desire, rendering the former as public, legal, permissible only within racial boundaries, and stable. Desire, on the other hand, can only be deployed on condition of secrecy, illegality, and interracial relations. We now want to examine whether the novel can sustain this radicalization and to consider how it caters to the genre of the romance and the predominantly Anglo-Indian readership, who would, for the most part, subscribe to imperial rule in India, as it validated their presence. We wish to examine, in particular, the status of ambivalence in a text where the Indian male protagonist is perceived as Greek, where the New Woman – notwithstanding her Muslim clothes – remains authoritatively British, and where the child – the product of the miscegenation – disappears from the text.

Ambivalences or the Conclusion in *Life of My Heart*

Notwithstanding the radical turn of the novel, Cross's text is nevertheless laced with ambivalences. While, on the one hand, the novel espouses cross-racial love as the only solution for the excision of the body and desire in Anglo-India, it simultaneously moves to Europeanize the cross-racial nature of that desire. For instance, Hamakhan is frequently likened to a statue: 'It was as if one of those figures whose beauty lives in the pages of Plato and Aristophanes had stepped out of them before her' (52); 'If a bronze statue from the Vatican had been taken from its pedestal and set there upon the chick with the Indian light upon it, it could not have looked any different' (53); and

> It is strange how the ancient Greek type is renewed in the Pashawuri Pathans. With few exceptions, their faces are strictly classical ... [She wondered] if the Greeks in India could have anything to do with settling their particular beauty in this race. (143–44)

Similarly, seeing Hamakhan, Frances remembers that, as a child, 'she had read with fervour over and over again Herodian's description of Heliogabalus as he danced before the sun-god with all the eyes of the soldiers fixed on his beauty' (239), and she likens Hamakhan's form to that of Heliogabalus. This Europeanizing of Hamakhan is also coupled with his grooming, being taught to read and write, as well as learning table manners from Frances.

The Europeanizing of Hamakhan functions in two ways in the text. First, in likening him to an ancient Greek form, Hamakhan is rendered archaic and unthreatening, as a figure who will not upset the status quo in Anglo-India. Rendered aesthetically pleasing, he can be assimilated into European forms in Britain, if not in Anglo-India. Such an implication is made when Frances decides that, when she inherits her property, she will return with Hamakhan to Britain. Second, it is not coincidental that the narrative metonymically links him to Greek forms. Within the eighteenth and nineteenth centuries, the Greek revival re-imagined the Greeks as ancestors of Western Europeans. In *The Victorians and Ancient Greece*, Richard Jenkyns suggests that late eighteenth-century German thinkers, such as Winckelmann, Goethe, Lessing, and Schlegel, rediscovered art forms like sculpture and architecture and reinterpreted Greece as a metaphor for the pure form of ancient European life (41). However, the repetitive references to Frances's preference for Greek forms, aesthetics, and philosophy functions problematically in the text, because, in a skewing of vision, when she sees her Indian, she sees a Greek instead. Finally, the radical nature of cross-racial love that the narrative seems to advocate is rendered less radical than at first glance.

The ambivalence in the text is further signalled in its conclusion. It is not an exaggeration to state that the conclusion of the novel is contrived, in that, with the birth of their child and subsequent move to Naimarabad, the narrative loses its focus and trajectory, as if the author does not know how to conclude. Indeed, one could go so far as to say that, if in the first half of the novel Anglo-India and its mores conspires to keep them apart, in the second half, it is the narrative form itself that conspires to prevent them from enjoying a happy life together and prevent the novel from having a happy ending. After Frances and Hamakhan elope, the narrative shifts from a focus on interracial desire in the first half of the novel to a focus on cultural differences in the second half. Here, differences are signalled in the narrative through an enumeration of Muslim attitudes to women, their jealousies and their treachery towards even their own friends when sexual desire is at stake, and the unreasonable demands of loyalty. Within this writing of racial and cultural differences, even the birth of Frances's child proves a momentary distraction in the text. Finally, the conclusion is contrived when Hamakhan is forced to prove his loyalty to his friend Gaida, by delivering, on his behalf, a sack containing the severed heads of three Hindus to a town called Lalpur. Gaida is prevented from doing this himself by a broken ankle and calls upon Hamakhan to make the gruesome delivery. When Frances discovers the heads in the sack, she exclaims, 'How could you take the blood of another man's crime on your head and hands? They belong to me!' (339). The narrative comes to an inevitable conclusion with both Frances and Hamakhan being apprehended with the sack of heads by the police, followed by Hamakhan killing both Frances and himself to escape the law.

But why can there be no happy ending to this story? Beyond the disapproval of Anglo-India towards their match, the narrative provides various and regular impediments to their happiness: a jealous Hamakhan; various attempts by Muslim men, who are in pursuit of Frances and would not hesitate to kill Hamakhan to possess her; and, finally, the episode with the sack of Hindu heads. Why is the predictable happy ending of a station romance not possible in an interracial romance such as this? What is invested in such an ending, especially for a radical novel that intersects the New Woman as heroine in an interracial relationship within imperialism? Ironically, the text seems to undo what its protagonist deems as problematic in Anglo-India – the erasure of desire and excision of the body.

How, then, can we interpret the repeated attempts at foreclosures in the novel? If the function of the station romance is to end in a marriage, then *Life of My Heart* seems to foreclose marriage itself, by having Frances elope with Hamakhan, but not marry him. And since they cannot retroactively marry, the narrative attempts to finish itself by drawing their relationship to a close in alternative ways. In this final section of our analysis of the conclusion, we would like to begin by posing three questions: if Frances signified the New Woman, as Nancy Paxton would have it, what happens to the notion of agency generally associated with this figure? If agency is enacted through Frances's relationship with Hamakhan, how is her increasingly incarcerated role in the second half of the novel explained? How can the fantastical and contrived conclusion of the novel, which has Hamakhan attempt to help his friend who has murdered three men, be interpreted? Nancy Paxton states:

> [I]n this odd turn from romance to a fantastic sort of allegory, Cross reasserts the hegemony of British standards of law and justice by describing how Hamakhan's failure to recognize the reach of colonial law causes the tragic death of both lovers. (223)

Thus, in Paxton's reading, agency can only be asserted in its opposition to colonial, Anglo-Indian law, and Hamakhan's inability to read the almighty reach of British law kills off Frances's agency.

However, to posit the notion of agency as something that exceeds the law is problematic, in that it assumes that agency is always deployed by the individual will of the subject and that the law functions as a barrier to individual will. In *The Psychic Life of Power*, Judith Butler suggests that there cannot be a conflation of the term individual with that of subject, because the latter term is a linguistic category – a site that individuals come to occupy, in order to articulate themselves and come into intelligibility. For Butler, the idea of the subject functions in both active and passive terms, in that the subject is constituted within, as well as subject to, power. Using Foucauldian suppositions, Butler points out that the power assumed by the subject (as in agency) is both an extension and reiteration of the very same power that enables the constitution of the subject. Therefore, any notion of agency as merely oppositional is limited and blinkered.

If we read the trajectory of Frances in *Life of My Heart* within the framework described by Butler, we see that her self-assertion and her sense of self as superior and powerful are enabled by her being Anglo-Indian. Her preference for intellectually superior company is not unlike that of her Anglo-Indian peers, who wish for socially acceptable company. Thus, her love for Hamakhan, far from being a democratizing move, is constituted through her belonging to Anglo-India. As such, her decision to be partnered to Hamakhan and elope with him comes from her imperious/imperial temperament. In fact, once taken out of the Anglo-Indian community and hidden behind 'purdah', her agency disappears. She gives Hamakhan control over her life. Indeed, the narrative structure reiterates and reinscribes the structure of authority, in that it makes a number of attempts to rein in her sense of agency, so that it is once more subject to Anglo-Indian mores and belief systems.

But does agency always only ever conform? Does it buckle down to the pressure of power? Butler adds that:

> Agency exceeds the power by which it is enabled. One might say that the purposes of power are not always the purposes of agency. To the extent that the latter diverge from the former, agency is the assumption of a purpose *unintended* by power, one that could not have been derived logically

or historically, that operates in a relation of contingency and reversal to the power that makes it possible, to which it nevertheless belongs. (15)

For Butler, therefore, power's ambivalence becomes visible through the concept of agency. In our text, with the death of the white woman and brown man who have transgressed racial and cultural boundaries, the ambivalences in the text reinstate the Anglo-Indian status quo, while simultaneously seeming to create a space for the construction of the critical and ethical reader as well. If the relationship between Frances and Hamakhan threatens the idea of imperial whiteness in Anglo-India, based on myths of racial hierarchies, it also invites a reading of both the hybridized nature of the imperial experience and the hybridized nature of reading. In his classic texts 'Of Mimicry and Man' and 'Signs Taken for Wonders', Homi Bhabha attributes agency to subversive forms. In 'Of Mimicry and Man', he develops the Lacanian concept of mimicry. Bhabha's mimic, a colonial subject, *'almost the same'* as the colonizer, *'but not quite'*, *'almost the same but not white'* (89), calls into question the unchallenged authority of dominant hegemony, as well as its ethics. In 'Signs Taken for Wonders', mimicry is displaced by the concept of hybridity that subverts the narratives of colonial power and dominant cultures, 'so that other "denied" knowledges enter upon the dominant discourse and estrange the basis of its authority' (114). Within the context of *Life of My Heart*, Frances's eroticized desire for Hamakhan 'reverses the effects of the colonialist disavowal' ('Signs Taken for Wonders' 114). In foregrounding this desire as its starting point, the first half of the novel can be read as a discursive treatment of denied knowledges. It lays bare the repressed text, which denies racial hierarchies and permits heterosexual desire between white and brown to be consummated, notwithstanding the background of imperial rule. In this respect, Frances's relationship with Hamakhan opens up to the reader an ethical relationship to the other – the possibility of seeing the other as equal and loving, of finding beauty in the other, not as an extension of the self, but always as other. The novel's hybridity thus functions as a counter-narrative – a critique of the Anglo-Indian canon and its exclusion of other narratives; it creates what Bhabha, in 'The Commitment to Theory', refers to as a 'Third Space of enunciation' (37), where colonial identity can be challenged, re-imagined, and rewritten, albeit briefly.

Lilamani

The long-term relationship that is not sustained between the white woman and brown man in Cross's *Life of My Heart* is sustained between the white man and brown woman in Maud Diver's *Lilamani*, thus raising interesting questions about the relationship between agency and white femininity, as if the latter signifier was a contradiction in terms – white and femininity cancelling each other out. In *Lilamani*, Maud Diver describes the meeting between an

English aristocrat, Nevil Sinclair, and a beautiful, high-caste and cultured Rajput, Lilamani, and the events that led up to, and immediately follow, their interracial marriage. What makes Diver's novel interesting to us, particularly in relation to *Life of My Heart*, is that the *mésalliance* she describes has a happy conclusion. In *Lilamani*, a marriage between East and West is seen not only to be possible – hence the subtitle 'A Study in Possibilities' – but, with its happy conclusion, acceptable, if not desirable. In this novel, Diver challenges Kipling's axiom from 'Beyond the Pale': 'A man should, whatever happens, keep to his own caste, race and breed. Let the White go to the White and the Black to the Black' (127), which is famously reinforced in what Nancy Paxton calls his 'endlessly repeated tag line' (194): 'Oh East is East and West is West, and never the twain shall meet' ('The Ballad of East and West'). Contrary to the widely held view that opposites repel each other, her male hero, Nevil Sinclair, believes that binary opposites can sustain each other:

> Mighty opposites were they – irreconcilables? By no means. Six weeks of closest intimacy, of spelling out letter by letter the unknown quantity he has taken to wife, inclined him to believe rather that East and West are not antagonistic, but complementary: heart and head, thought and action, woman and man. Between all these 'pairs of opposites' fusion is rare, difficult, yet eminently possible. Why not, then, between East and West? (171)[4]

Different, but complementary; yet it is worth noting the correspondences in these pairs of complementary opposites: heart, thought, and woman; head, action, and man. Despite the novel's apparent non-conformity, Nevil is nevertheless always cast as the dominant partner, with Lilamani as the submissive or dependent one. Thus, despite in many ways going against the grain of Anglo-Indian fiction, *Lilamani* maintains the colonizer-colonized relationship, depicting Britain as the dominant partner and India as the submissive one, even reinforcing it in the marriage that it portrays between England and India. If Lilamani is presented as an ideal woman, it is because only an *ideal* Indian woman could possibly be worthy of an English husband.

The consequences of this marriage of East and West are explored further in three later novels that complete a loosely connected Sinclair family quartet: *Far to Seek: A Romance of England and India* (1921), *The Singer Passes: An Indian Tapestry* (1934), and *The Dream Prevails: A Story of India* (1938). Together, the four Sinclair family novels offer the reader a portrait of Anglo-India that encompasses significant Indian characters and the Eurasian baronet, Sir Roy Sinclair, the son of Sir Nevil and Lilamani, as well as the more familiar civil and military representatives of the Raj, who are the usual subjects of Anglo-Indian fictions.

By focusing in *Lilamani* on the life of an Indian – specifically an Indian woman – in Europe and England, rather than on Anglo-Indian life in India,

4 See Paxton, p. 194.

Diver opens the way for an exploration of female agency and mixed marriage within the contexts of both the British Indian Empire and late Victorian Britain. With the advent of the New Woman and the attendant 'Woman Question' in late Victorian Britain (which she pointedly introduces in the novel), Diver appears to have consciously depicted Lilamani as an embodiment of 'all the feminine qualities that [were] under threat in England' (Ghose 64). It is precisely because the novel deviates in these several ways from the usual pattern of Anglo-Indian fiction (including those which deal with mixed marriage), precisely because the novel does not unquestioningly parrot nineteenth-century views on miscegenation or unconditionally reproduce nineteenth-century theories of degeneration, that *Lilamani* is of interest to the modern-day reader.

The novel does, of course, inevitably follow many of the conventions of romantic adventure fiction, and the stock characters of the genre can as readily be found in *Lilamani* as elsewhere in Anglo-Indian fiction. The racist views of Nevil Sinclair's sister, Lady Jane Roscoe, echo those voiced by English memsahibs in numerous Raj novels and stories, while Mrs Despard amply performs the less common role of the more liberal or enlightened memsahib. Similarly, Nevil's brother, George, who has served in India with his regiment, is typical of the boors found in both the Presidency towns and 'up country' stations. Of more interest, though, and what we will focus on in our reading of the novel, is Lilamani's relationship with Audrey Hammond and the trope of miscegenation that brings to the fore some complex issues concerning masculinity, femininity, and sexuality in the Empire context.

The interaction between Lilamani and her mentor, Audrey Hammond, under whose patronage she has travelled with her father to Europe, raises important questions about the relationship between British and Indian women. How does the women's movement of the late Victorian period inflect their relationship? How do racial hierarchies function in the construction of femininity within imperialism? How does the triangulated relationship between British men, British women, and Indian women function in the production of desire?

Overtly, the text devotes very little space to Lilamani's and Audrey's shared relationship. Audrey seems important to the plot only insofar as she gives Lilamani access to Europe and Nevil Sinclair access to Lilamani. Once she fulfils these requirements of the narrative, she is largely written out of the story, reappearing briefly only at the very end of the novel, where we see her once more at the Cap d'Antibes, waiting to return to India, and to 'take up regular work again' (313). Audrey is not the Victorian Angel in the house; instead, she is carefully positioned as the New Woman, influenced by the suffragette movement, aware of her abilities to do medical work (traditionally a male preserve), keen to complete 'an article on nerve crises for a semi-scientific magazine' (313), and free to travel.

During the course of the novel, she is variously described as a 'bachelor-girl' (36), someone who cultivated her 'brain and ego at the expense of the natural emotions' (36), and a woman who had 'boyish straightness and suppleness of limb' (8). In contrast, Lilamani is exoticized throughout the text as a 'pale lotus-bud' (14), a 'purdah lady' (29), and someone who combines a 'peculiarly eastern mingling of demure aloofness with a delicately direct appeal to the senses and the heart' (141). Her clothing is similarly exoticized and frequently described in detail; at the Cap d'Antibes Hotel, dressed in a sari, Lilamani is represented as an exotic bird, 'an iridescent vision of grey and gold, shot through with mother-o'-pearl tints that shimmered changefully when she moved' (30), whereas the dull plumage of the 'full evening dress' (32) worn by the European women at the hotel is represented as a norm that warrants no particular description. Notwithstanding this exoticization and the stereotypical racial remarks directed at Lilamani and her father, it is Audrey – unfeminine, unmarried, intellectual, and independent – who is presented as aberrant to the values of Anglo-India perpetuated in the text. Despite the fact that Lilamani is Indian, her femininity and, later, her worship of her husband make her more acceptable to Anglo-Indian, and perhaps even late Victorian, values than Audrey, who insists on her independence and pursues a traditionally male career.

Though perhaps of minor interest to the early twentieth century reader, it is instructive for the modern reader to consider Audrey's positioning in the text in relation to the changing roles of women within the context of British imperialism. While bourgeois women were frequently located as the Angel in the House in the mid-Victorian period, by the end of the century, women's roles had started to change. Alongside the suffragette movement, there was increasing demand for university education for everyone, including women, municipal suffrage, marriage law reform, and the abolition of the Contagious Diseases Acts. In particular, the struggle for the repeal of the Contagious Diseases Acts, successfully led by the feminist Josephine Butler, galvanized the women's movement within Britain, and, when the repeal movement turned its attention to India, eventually led to its direct involvement with the politics of Empire.

The language of imperialism is present in, and in many ways defines, Audrey's relationship with Lilamani: the parameters of cultural superiority, political trusteeship, and modern English behaviour are all carefully established. As Antoinette Burton points out in *Burdens of History*,

> [f]or feminists the British Empire was evidence of the superiority of British national culture and, most important, of the obligations that British women were obliged to discharge – for the benefit of colonial peoples and, ultimately, for the good of the imperial nation itself. (7)

British feminists saw Indian women as helpless victims, who lived lives of backwardness. The practice of sati became a metaphor for Indian women's lives and the zenana, where women and girls were secluded, was further proof of their imprisonment within Indian culture and patriarchy. According to Florence Nightingale, British feminists had to seriously think about their 'stewardship in India', while, for Josephine Butler, it was inevitable that British feminists had to next campaign for the reform of prostitution in India. Most importantly, Mary Carpenter insisted on the educational work that needed to be done in India by professional women teachers from Britain. Thus, the plight of Indian women became a rationale for explaining the British presence in India, and the alignment of British feminists with imperialism was a means of demonstrating their attachment to national-imperial culture and therefore that they were worthy of suffrage alongside British men. Indeed, British Feminism was able to articulate itself especially within the structure of the racial hierarchies enabled by colonialism.[5]

Audrey's relationship with Lilamani is distinctly inflected with the historical nuances of late Victorian British feminism, as well as the parent-child binary of Empire. She feels charged with the role of educating Lilamani, so that she can 'do greater things for her self-restricted sisters in a few years than I could do in a lifetime' (12), and, along with Sir Lakshman Singh, appears to exercise a parental role over Lilamani. In response to her ministrations, Lilamani acknowledges that Audrey, 'the woman she loved and respected only less than her own mother' (34), 'stood in place of Mataji' (322). Interestingly, Mataji's exclusion from the text and the way that Audrey replaces her as the maternal figure introduces a second moment of miscegenation into the text, ostensibly positing the 'family' grouping of Sir Lakshman Singh, Audrey, and Lilamani as an alternative nuclear family.

If Audrey, as a British feminist, or New Woman, can access some control over her own future, can she also access control over Lilamani's future? In other words, is the notion of agency only ever gendered or racialized in the text? It is obvious that the British feminist's work in India was predicated on the Indian woman's lack of rights. In *Mother India*, her enormously popular work on Indian women's rights, Katherine Mayo states: 'A girl child, in the Hindu scheme, is usually [considered] a heavy and unwelcome cash liability. Her birth elicits the formal condolence of family friends' (60). Mayo, an American, was hardly non-partisan in her approach to the topic. *Mother India* was written at the instigation of a British officer, J.H. Adams, whom she met in London and who worked for the Indian Political Intelligence Department, which functioned to counteract the growing Indian nationalist propaganda. Mayo's work suggests that, unless Indian women were given more rights, India would continue to remain both intellectually backward and poor. The issues of Indian nationalism and agency were thus explicitly tied to the condition of its women by Mayo.

Lilamani must be read within its cultural context. Within the framework of Indian women's rights, Lilamani has no agency. Indeed, first, her mother arranges a marriage for her with a man much older than herself, and then Audrey determines an alternative future in medicine for her. In his cornerstone article on the construction of the Victorian Indian woman's femininity and her rights, 'The Nationalist Resolution of the Woman's Question', Partha Chatterjee

5 See Mary Carpenter, *Six Months in India*.

points out that the difference between the colonizer and colonized in India, or Western and non-Western, materialized in a series of binary opposites – outer/inner, material/spiritual, world/home, male/female – which were all paradigmatically linked. The woman, representing the inner life, was given the task of maintaining greater spirituality and was also confined to the home. The Indian male, in contrast, was given access to public spaces, but also ones that were contaminated by Western mores, behaviours, and ideas. Maintaining pure Indianness was thus entrusted to the Indian woman, who, under colonialism, was relocated within a neo-patriarchy that was both Indian and British.

How is Lilamani located within such a configuration? Does she have any agency? For instance, she is undoubtedly submissive towards Nevil, openly proclaiming that 'the measure for an Eastern woman's submission is the measure of her love' (96) and that '[f]or the Indian woman religion is all; and marriage is a chief part of that religion' (116). She is posited as a 'pure Hindu woman in her capacity for sacrifice of self' (114). As she tells Nevil: 'In my country – husband of every true woman is even as her God' (143) – a sentiment that may recall Milton's *Paradise Lost*, but which is nevertheless meant to be read as outdated in the West.[6] The way that Lilamani is constantly exoticized and subordinated renders her mute, suicidal, ill, and almost anorexic, her physical fading miming the way that she is silenced by the text and within British imperial culture.

Lilamani's lack of agency is further emphasized by the fact that Nevil does not intend to expose himself to the stigma that would attach to him if he were to visit India as the husband of an Indian woman or as a man with an Indian father-in-law. The depth of his feeling about India and, more generally, the 'East' is evident during his brief sojourn in Egypt with Lilamani and Sir Lakshman Singh. He may love Lilamani, but he is not, at this stage, willing to embrace her country or her culture, except in so far as he can exploit it for his own profit, whether that be in terms of his wife's slavish devotion to him or, more literally, as a subject for his art. In this sense, he continues to tread the imperial path that has always marked Britain's relationship with India. Anything else would be interpreted as a form of regression or degeneration. It is Lilamani who must make all of the sacrifices, and she must make them in the name of progress.

Here, again, Diver departs from the stock-in-trade pattern of Anglo-Indian romance. As discussed earlier, in most examples of the genre, it is the Englishman – or occasionally the Englishwoman, as in *Life of My Heart* or E.W. Savi's *The Daughter-in-Law* (1915) – who marries an Indian that makes all the sacrifices, risking, through a single act of folly, his career and his (or her) standing in the community. In this novel, though, Diver insists that Lilamani, rather than Nevil Sinclair, is the one who makes the sacrifices, giving up her home, her religion, and her family, in order to marry an Englishman.

---

6 John Milton, *Paradise Lost* (1667), Book 4, line 297: 'He for God only, she for God in him'.

What is of particular interest to the modern reader of this novel, which is written from an Anglo-Indian viewpoint that predates postcolonial studies, is the issue of agency, which is so central to any consideration of race, gender, and nation. We can see that, notwithstanding the dislocation of Lilamani from any sense of power or ability to control her fate, within the frameworks of imperial British feminism, Indian patriarchy, and British patriarchy, the text does offer her a sense of agency, albeit one so faint that it can only be established, negatively as it were, through moments of refusal. The first of these moments is her refusal to marry her mother's choice of a husband, which, we are told, was supported (and thus made possible) by her father and led to her embracing the alternative of travel to Europe and training in medicine, as proposed by Audrey. The second moment of agency is, ironically, her refusal to accept Audrey's prescribed role for her, in order to marry the man of her choice. In so doing, she appears to move back towards the traditional role of wife initially offered to her by her mother, but with a difference. By exercising choice, by opting for a love-match, rather than an arranged marriage, Lilamani appears to be permitted a degree of agency. Yet if the Indian woman's confinement to interior spaces is read as lacking the freedom that her English counterpart enjoys, Lilamani's embrace and creation of 'the Inside' or zenana and the establishing of her shrine at Sir Nevil's ancestral home, Bramleigh Beeches, suggests that notions of agency should not be read in a literal way, but through the framework of the politics of difference. Rather than signalling a lack of agency, this is another moment when Lilamani's agency is predicated on a refusal – this time her rejection of the role of the English wife, which highlights the trope of miscegenation.

The trope of miscegenation or race-mixing is, of course, central to the mixed marriage that lies at the heart of this novel. It is important to unpack this trope within the text, because the reconfiguration of British and Indian masculinity and femininity all seem to converge around Lilamani's marriage to Nevil Sinclair. Further, miscegenation functions as a taboo in this text, as it does throughout most Anglo-Indian fiction. However, as Kenneth Ballhatchet points out in *Race, Sex, and Class Under the Raj*, historically, this had not always been the case. As outlined earlier, in the seventeenth century there were many interracial sexual liaisons, which were actively encouraged by the East India Company to facilitate British and Indian interactions and which, over time, led to an increase in the Eurasian community in India (96). Nevertheless, by the late nineteenth century, racial hierarchies strictly underpinned comprehensions of British and Indian interactions. In fact, the so-called Indian Mutiny of 1857 was instrumental in the solidifying of this taboo, as it shifted the meaning of British masculinity by reconfiguring it within a militaristic framework: adventurous, athletic, and with an emphasis on homo-social bonds between men. This reconfiguration, constructed on the terrain of colonialism, also meant that British masculinity appeared to be in a diacritical relationship to Indian masculinity. In other words, both British and Indian forms of masculinity seemed to be constructed in relation to each other, rather than in relation to their respective femininities. If British masculinity became more militaristic, then Indian masculinity, following the events of 1857, became more duplicitous and untrustworthy.

Racial hierarchies between white and brown men are articulated in the text through the figures of Nevil Sinclair and Sir Lakshman Singh. Though the latter is older than Nevil, he is frequently (though not quite always) presented as deferential to his white son-in-law. The text posits Sir Lakshman Singh as an acceptable Indian (just as it posits Lilamani as both dutiful and beautiful), in order to make the miscegenation palatable to its readers. Sir Lakshman Singh is positively portrayed as an enlightened Indian, primarily because he is so strong a supporter of Empire and recognizes the superiority of British culture. He is Diver's idea of a perfect Indian, precisely because he believes absolutely in British rule in India. Significantly, during a discussion of Indian nationalism, it is Sir Lakshman Singh who urges a strong hand to deal with anti-British agitation in India: 'In my belief ... no worse harm could befall to India than that Great Britain should cease to be paramount power. But only this – in order for being paramount she must be, in the best sense, a *power*' (83–84). Like Rudyard Kipling, Diver has no room for pro-nationalist voices in her fiction. For all its liberal views on interracial marriage, *Lilamani* frequently demonstrates what Benita Parry calls Diver's strident 'pride in the British as a master-race' (70).

The modern reader influenced by the cultural and theoretical discourses within postcolonial studies is struck by the fact that, notwithstanding the text's desire to keep racial differences foregrounded in the story and to maintain the British as superior within any context of race-mixing, *Lilamani* simultaneously seems to posit that both races are mutually interdependent. The text posits a more syncretic viewpoint. The textual strategy of undercutting that it appears to valorize and hold dear is present throughout and causes interesting ambivalences in the text. For instance, it attempts to circumvent the horror of miscegenation by positing Audrey as a possible wife for Nevil. However, Lilamani and Nevil's growing intimacies become utterly problematic for Audrey right at the beginning of the narrative. Interestingly, modern readers recognize the ambivalence in the novel, as they are never sure whether Audrey is jealous of Lilamani's conquest of Nevil or Nevil's conquest of Lilamani. The conflation of Audrey's desire for Lilamani to be remade in her image with that of her desire for Nevil, as well as that for Lilamani, gives the text an ambiguity that foregrounds the escape of rigid gender and sexual boundaries. Furthermore, the maintenance of rigid boundaries between Britain and India is once again scrambled when Nevil seems to eschew anything that has to do with India, with the exception of his wife. However, he is soon dependent on ideas about, and attitudes to, India in his very work. His reputation as a painter and his ideas for painting are predicated on Indian mythology, so much so that the *Ramayana* paintings and Lilamani's shrine room become prominent features of Bramleigh Beeches. This aspect of the novel, which can be read as an invasion of the metropolis by the colonies, points to a wider crisis of Empire, rather than a crisis pertaining to the Sinclair family alone. Soon, race-mixing in the novel is overtaken by a mixing of ideas that seem to get away from the social and cultural limitations that Diver attempts to place on her novel. If Sir Lakshman Singh is an acceptable Indian because he is almost white, then Nevil establishes his reputation as a painter because of his Indian ideas. And by accepting his wife's husband-worship and the Indianization of Bramleigh Beeches, Sir Nevil himself is relocated as an Indian husband and effectively feminized. Thus, despite the valorization of Anglo-Indian values and the superiority of whiteness in the authorial comments in the text, it is precisely the collapse of the boundaries within gender and race hierarchies that renders *Lilamani* fascinating to the modern reader.

Diver continues her exploration of the subject of mixed marriage in three further novels that make up her Sinclair family quartet. In *Far to Seek*, Sir Nevil and Lilamani's son, Roy, who appears to inherit the best of both cultures, visits India, where he falls in love with his Oxford-educated cousin, Arúna. But Diver refuses to endorse a further interracial marriage, and Roy is dissuaded from this course, which would have emphasized his Indianness over his Englishness. Then, after a further visit to India in *The Singer Passes*, in the last volume of the quartet, *The Dream Prevails*, the Eurasian Roy, who, as Greenberger observes, is 'the *successful* product of such a mixed marriage' (172), plays on her racial prejudices to persuade the English girl Chrystal Adair that marriage to her Pathan admirer, Sher Afzul Khan, is impossible, because of the gulf that separates the two races:

> You might be happy with Afzul just at first, if his world and yours would let you. But they won't. And it couldn't last. ... Could you face the prospect of growing old among those wild hills and alien people, cut off from your own world, your friends, your art – (379)

And later, Diver endorses Roy's advice, when Chrystal realizes that Roy 'had saved her ... from a marriage that might have spelt tragedy for her, as for Afzul no less' (490). It is significant that Maud Diver, who considered the subject of mixed marriage more thoroughly than any other Anglo-Indian novelist, finally rejected it. It is important to note, however, that in the first volume of her quartet of novels on the subject, the marriage that appears to be successful – and, indeed, is shown to be successful in later volumes – is between an English man and an Indian woman; the marriage she rejects as impossible in the final volume is between an English woman and an Indian man.

We have suggested that, incorporated within the history of miscegenation in Anglo-India, there are some interesting insights into the status of women, both white and non-white. Notwithstanding the discourses of the New Woman that permeated Britain in the latter part of the nineteenth century, the deployment of this figure in Anglo-Indian fiction highlights the tenuousness of the white women's agency. Victoria Cross's *Life of My Heart* reveals that Anglo-Indian women were like chameleons, whose whiteness seeped away from them in their heterosexual relations with black men – the conferring of racial superiority being possible only through white patriarchy.

Further, even when the privacy accorded to matters of sexuality is taken into account, what sexual relations in Anglo-India reveals is the public nature of the mediation of desire, heterosexuality, and sexual reproduction. Sexuality is part of public culture, and Frances and Hamakhan queer the very nature of desire in initiating an interracial sexual relationship. On the other hand, *Lilamani* reveals that only white masculinity can reproduce whiteness, even when coupled with a non-white woman. Moreover, this miscegenation gives Nevil the right to imagine an Empire, a vocation, and a topic for his painting. In short, what these two novels reveal is that public sexual desire and Empire are two sides of the same coin in Anglo-India.

There is one final question that we wish to posit concerning the impact of diaspora on the shaping of sexuality in Anglo-India: while the sexual activity of Anglo-Indians was overwhelmingly shaped and controlled by imperialism, to what extent was it also influenced by their diasporic sensibility? It is a commonplace to point out that the maintenance of a collective identity is dependent on the control of sexuality, particularly female sexuality. In Anglo-India, the strict maintenance of a collective identity was facilitated by both law and the discourse of racial science, as much as it was by peer pressure and unwritten institutional rules that influenced career advancement. Sexual injunctions that sought to restrict cross-racial relationships in Anglo-India did not, of course, seek to restrict relationships with their counterparts in Britain, with whom they increasingly shared little in common.

Thus, the maintenance of a collective identity was predicated on the myth of common origin and ties to a common nation, and it is this relationship to Britain that governed the sexuality of Anglo-Indians, rather than the demands of imperial rule. Indeed, one could argue that it was the anxiety to have their identity in continuum with those in Britain that allowed their private desires to be governed by public life. Intimacy and desire, as practiced in Anglo-India, was riddled with the anxieties of their displaced citizenship. In the words of Lauren Berlant, the 'political public sphere' was an 'intimate public sphere' (4). An unproblematic British citizenship could only be purchased by the negating of the individual self (usually developed and nurtured in the private sphere), as well as the legislation of sexual desire itself. This depletion of the self was matched by an erosion of the private sphere in Anglo-India. Indeed, to be a powerful Anglo-Indian meant *nothing* if it was not combined with this unprob-lematic connection to a British identity and citizenship. Anglo-Indians had to embody Britain.

Conversely, in Britain during this period, citizenship, the shaping of desire, and the reproduction of a bourgeois identity were hinged on other demands, which had more to do with maintaining class difference than racial difference, which was a pressing issue only elsewhere: in the colonies, in India. The genealogy of sexual desire in Anglo-India is a matter not of the individual and family, but of the nation and diaspora.

Imperialism as Diaspora

Diaspora has been an occluded term in the analysis of British imperialism. While British imperialism has fundamentally been read through the lens of power or race, its close relationship to a diasporic sensibility – along with the changes, migrancy, syncreticism, and transculturation that accompanied it – has consistently been ignored. The shifts brought about by diaspora not only affected the imperial subject nation, but also the imperial subject in the nation's diaspora. In *Imperialism*, Harry Magdoff suggests that fifty-five million Europeans moved to non-European spaces in the century between 1820 and 1920. The British Empire spanned the globe, from Canada to the Caribbean and from Africa and India to Australia and New Zealand. French territories ranged from Africa through to the South Pacific, and the Spanish and Portuguese empires extended through most of the Americas. It was not just European imperialism, but also a European diaspora, or what Alfred Crosby refers to as 'a Caucasian tsunami' (5), which overtook the world during the long nineteenth century.

In the years of the operation of the British East India Company, which predated India's formal entry into the Empire, 'factors' (agents or representatives), often as young as fifteen, left Britain to work in India, where they might live for the next two or three decades. Having left Britain during their formative years, they became more Indian than British in their attitudes, mores, and sense of aesthetics. Whether or not these young men used the term, India became their 'home', and they became Anglo-Indians. Then, in 1911, with a shift in its signification, the term Anglo-Indian was adopted for people of mixed descent with British origins on the patrilineal side. The old Anglo-Indians became British, as if unmarked by their close contact with India and apparently unaffected by their 300-year-old relationship with the subcontinent. In 1947, when India attained Independence, 350,000 people of purely British descent left the country. At the same time, the new Anglo-Indians of mixed descent numbered between 300,000 and 500,000, many of whom, unable to see India as home in the absence of Britain and the British, left for other countries that were still under the yoke of colonialism – Australia, New Zealand, Canada, and South Africa – or for Britain itself. Only about 150,000 mixed-race Anglo-Indians, with their uneasy relationship to the nation-state, remain in India today.

In 'Nation, Migration, Globalization', Jana Braziel and Anita Mannur suggest that diaspora theoretically functions as an internal critique of binarisms, such as colonizer/colonized, white/black, and West/East (4). In so doing, as they point out, diasporic subjects epitomize hybridity and heterogeneity. In the case of Anglo-India, the shift in nomenclature in 1911 from Anglo-Indian to British forecloses this critique of binarisms and, in fact, reinforces them. This shift is a denial of hybridity and a demand for an unproblematic continuum between centre and periphery (at least where British identity is concerned). It is a demand that also obscures the discourse of class and regional difference – English, Welsh, and Scottish – in the production of a white British identity. Even the Irish could be British in India, and all of the British were represented as belonging to a bourgeois aristocracy. The tens of thousands of British Other Ranks (BORs) in India were first subsumed and then erased in these representations. Thus, if diaspora is a hybridizing move, imperialism is a movement to homogenize.

This homogenization of whiteness that is a legacy of the British Empire has also led to a new narrative – that Britain started becoming multicultural only in the post-war period, with the arrival of waves of migrants from the Caribbean and the Indian subcontinent in the 1950s. Indeed, the historical fact that Britain (or, more accurately, the United Kingdom) was always already multicultural, with its Welsh, Scottish, and (Northern) Irish populations and its waves of economic and religious migrants from other European countries, is obscured in this new narrative of multiculturalism captured in Kobena Mercer's oft-quoted phrase: 'we are here because you were there' (7). This obscuring of the British diaspora and the genealogy of multiculturalism embedded in Mercer's phrase had earlier led to Enoch Powell's 'Rivers of Blood' speech in 1968 and a focus on race relations in the United Kingdom. Only such an obscuring of imperialism as diaspora would permit a reading of multiculturalism as code for multiracial, as if only the presence of a non-white makes a (white) society multicultural.

Furthermore, the equating of diasporic groups with less fortunate and less powerful minorities within the host nation allows for the perpetuation of a certain teleological narrative of the nation – that Britain (like the United States) supports freedoms, democracies, and capitalism. But it is an equation that obscures the hand of history. For Caribbean blacks, who came to Britain in search of employment in the 1950s, their migration is a repetition of the Middle Passage, which took them into the 'new world' in the eighteenth and nineteenth centuries. For the waves of migrants from the Punjab and Bengal in the 1950s, the flight to Britain was a repeat of the upheaval of partition and sense of homelessness that ensued. Indeed, to quote Arjun Appadurai, Britain is merely 'another diasporic switching point' (171), if we take the long historical view. Finally, the equation of diasporic groups as only coming from less powerful nations obscures the continued large-scale migration of Britons to other parts of the world. The *Migration Statistics Quarterly Report*, published in February 2012 by the Office for National Statistics in the United Kingdom, showed that long-term emigration by British nationals between June 2010 and June 2011 was 343,000. Will these people remain British or will they become diasporic?

Critics of diaspora studies suggest that the term 'diaspora' is sometimes used ahistorically and uncritically and that it conflates voluntary or economic migrants with those who are exiled or fleeing political and national trauma. In this conflation, historical, political, and cultural specificity is lost. While such arguments are valid, it is within the context of affect – the loss of home, loved ones, and familiar sites – that such differences become less clear. Despite the availability of cheap travel, the existence of Skype, ready access to texting with mobile phones, and the pervasive presence of social media that allow for instant contact with the place of origin and access to loved ones, the experiences of loneliness, the travails that they encounter, the frustrations and losses, the sharp memories of landscape, smell, and family of present-day migrants are not always dissimilar to that experienced by refugees fleeing political trauma. And it is especially within the context of affect that the diasporic sensibility of imperialism becomes visible. Notwithstanding the power that the Empire conferred on them, in India, the diaspora that imperial rule produced changed Anglo-Indians. Anglo-India caused them to lose their friends to the Mutiny and other hostilities, fear for their lives daily at the hands of millions of Indians that surrounded them, lose their children to heat and disease, and, crucially, the experience of being diasporic changed their tastes and their morality. It also made them love those whom they ruled over. They were diasporic.

Bibliography

Abbott, James. *Narrative of a Journey from Heraut to Khiva, Moscow, and St Petersburgh, during the late Russian Invasion of Khiva.* 2 vols. London: W.H. Allen, 1843.

Allen, Charles. *Soldier Sahibs: The Men Who Made the North-West Frontier.* 2000. London: Abacus, 2003.

'An Anglo-Indian Story.' Review of *Idolatry*, by Alice Perrin. *New York Times*, 6 March 1909: BR134.

Appadurai, Arjun. *Modernity at Large: Cultural Dimensions of Globalization.* Minneapolis: University of Minnesota Press, 1996.

Arnold, David. 'European Orphans and Vagrants in India in the Nineteenth Century.' *Journal of Imperial and Commonwealth History* 7.2 (1979): 104–27.

Arnold, David. 'White Colonization and Labour in Nineteenth-Century India.' *Journal of Imperial and Commonwealth History* 12.2 (1983): 133–58.

Atkinson, George Francklin. *'Curry and Rice,' on Forty Plates: Or The Ingredients of Social Life at 'Our Station' in India.* 1859. Chennai: Rupa, 2001.

Axel, Brian. 'The Diasporic Imaginary.' *Public Culture* 14.2 (2002): 411–28.

Ballhatchet, Kenneth. *Race, Sex, and Class Under the Raj: Imperial Attitudes and Policies and their Critics.* London: Macmillan, 1980.

Barr, Pat. *The Memsahibs: The Women of Victorian India.* London: Secker, 1976.

Baucom, Ian. *Out of Place: Englishness, Empire, and the Locations of Identity.* Princeton: Princeton University Press, 1999.

Bayly, C.A. *The Raj: India and the British 1600–1947.* London: National Portrait Gallery, 1990.

Beddoe, John. *The Races of Britain: A Contribution to the Anthropology of Western Europe.* 1862. Bristol: J.W. Arrowsmith, 1885.

Berlant, Lauren. 'Intimacy: A Special Issue.' *Intimacy.* Ed. Lauren Berlant. London and Chicago: University of Chicago Press, 2000. 1–8.

Berlant, Lauren. *The Queen of America Goes to Washington City: Essays on Sex and Citizenship.* Durham and London: Duke University Press, 1997.

Bernal, Martin. *Black Athena: The Afroasiatic Roots of Classical Civilization, Vol. 1: The Fabrication of Ancient Greece, 1785–1985.* London: Free Association Press, 1987.

Bhabha, Homi. 'Introduction.' *The Location of Culture*. London and New York: Routledge, 1994. 1–19.

Bhabha, Homi. 'The Commitment to Theory.' *The Location of Culture*. London and New York: Routledge, 1994. 19–39.

Bhabha, Homi. 'On Mimicry and Man: The Ambivalence of Colonial Discourse.' *The Location of Culture*. London and New York: Routledge, 1994. 85–92.

Bhabha, Homi. 'Signs Taken for Wonders: Questions of Ambivalence and Authority Under a Tree Outside Delhi, May 1817.' *The Location of Culture*. London and New York: Routledge, 1994. 102–22.

Blunt, Alison. 'Embodying War: British Women and Domestic Defilement in the Indian "Mutiny", 1857–8.' *Journal of Historical Geography* 26.3 (2000): 403–28.

Boehmer, Elleke. *Empire Writing: An Anthology of Colonial Literature 1870–1918*. Oxford: Oxford University Press, 1998.

Boyarin, Daniel, and Jonathan Boyarin. 'Diaspora: Generation and the Ground of Jewish Identity.' *Critical Inquiry* 19.4 (1993): 693–725.

Brah, Avtar. *Cartographies of Diaspora: Contesting Identities*. London: Routledge, 1996.

Brantlinger, Patrick. *Rule of Darkness: British Literature and Imperialism, 1830–1914*. Ithaca: Cornell University Press, 1988.

Braziel, Jana Evans, and Anita Mannur. 'Nation, Migration, Globalization: Points of Contention in Diaspora Studies.' *Theorizing Diaspora: A Reader*. Ed. Jana Evans Braziel and Anita Mannur. Malden: Blackwell, 2003. 1–22.

Brontë, Charlotte. *Jane Eyre*. 1847. New York, NY: Norton, 1987.

Buettner, Elizabeth. *Empire Families: Britain and Late Imperial India*. Oxford: Oxford University Press, 2004.

Burnes, Alexander. *Travels into Bokhara: Being an Account of a Journey from India to Cabool, Tartary and Persia; also Narrative of a Voyage on the Indus from the Sea to Lahore*. 3 vols. London: John Murray, 1834.

Burton, Antoinette. *Burdens of History: British Feminists, Indian Women, and Imperial Culture, 1865–1915*. London and Chapel Hill: University of North Carolina Press, 1994.

Butler, Judith. *The Psychic Life of Power: Theories in Subjugation*. Stanford: Stanford University Press, 1997.

Carens, Timothy L. 'Mapping India.' *Victorian Literature and Culture* 31 (2003): 613–23.

Carpenter, Mary. *Six Months in India*. 2 vols. London: Longmans, Green and Co., 1868.

Chakravarty, Gautam. *The Indian Mutiny and the British Imagination*. Cambridge: Cambridge University Press, 2005.

Chamberlain, J. Edward, and Sander L. Gilman. 'Degeneration: An Introduction.' *Degeneration: The Dark Side of Progress*. Ed. J. Edward Chamberlain and Sander L. Gilman. New York: Columbia University Press, 1985. ix–xiv.

Chambers, Iain. *Migrancy, Culture, Identity*. London: Routledge, 1994.

Chatterjee, Partha. 'The Nationalist Resolution of the Women's Question.' 1990. *Postcolonial Discourses: An Anthology*. Ed. Gregory Castle. Oxford: Blackwell, 2001. 152–66.

Chowdhry, Prem. *Colonial India and the Making of Empire Cinema*. Manchester: Manchester University Press, 2000.

Churchill, Winston S. *The Story of the Malakand Field Force: An Episode of Frontier War*. London: Thomas, Nelson & Sons, 1898.

Colley, Linda. *Britons: Forging the Nation 1707–1837*. London and New Haven: Yale University Press, 1992.

Collingham, E.M. *Imperial Bodies: The Physical Experience of the Raj.* Cambridge: Polity Press, 2001.

Conolly, Arthur. *Journey to the North of India through Russia, Persia and Afghanistan.* 2 vols. London: Bentley, 1834.

Cowasjee, Saros. Introduction. *A Raj Collection.* Ed. Saros Cowasjee. New Delhi: Oxford University Press, 2005. ix–l.

Crosby, Alfred. *Ecological Imperialism: The Biological Expansion of Europe, 900–1900.* Cambridge: Cambridge University Press, 1986.

Cross, Victoria. *Life of My Heart.* London and Felling-on-Tyne: Walter Scott, 1905.

Dalrymple, William. *City of Djinns: A Year in Delhi.* London: Harper Collins, 1993.

Dalrymple, William. *The Last Mughal: The Fall of a Dynasty, Delhi, 1857.* New Delhi: Viking, 2006.

Das, Veena. *Critical Events: An Anthropological Perspective on Contemporary India.* New Delhi: Oxford University Press, 1995.

David, Saul. *The Indian Mutiny 1857.* London: Viking, 2002.

Davidoff, Leonore, and Catherine Hall. *Family Fortunes: Men and Women of the English Middle Class 1780–1850.* 1987. Rev. ed. London: Routledge, 2002.

Dawson, Graham. *Soldier Heroes: British Adventure, Empire and the Imagining of Masculinity.* London and New York: Routledge, 1994.

Diver, Maud. *The Englishwoman in India.* Edinburgh: Blackwood, 1909.

Diver, Maud. *The Great Amulet.* Edinburgh and London: Blackwood, 1909.

Diver, Maud. *Lilamani: A Study in Possibilities.* 1911. Ed. Ralph Crane. New Delhi: Oxford University Press, 2004.

Diver, Maud. *Far to Seek: A Romance of England and India.* Edinburgh and London: Blackwood, 1921.

Diver, Maud. *The Dream Prevails.* 1938. London: John Murray, 1939.

Diver, Maud. 'Sunia: A Himalayan Idyll.' *Sunia: and Other Stories.* Edinburgh and London: Blackwood, 1913. 1–27.

Diver, Maud. 'Light Marching Order.' *Siege Perilous and Other Stories.* Boston and New York: Houghton Mifflin, 1924. 3–29.

Dyer, Richard. *White.* London: Routledge, 1997.

Eden, Emily. *Up the Country: Letters Written to Her Sister from the Upper Provinces of India.* 1866. London: Curzon Press, 1978.

Edwardes, Michael. *Raj: The Story of British India.* 1967. London: Pan, 1969.

Edwards, David B. 'Mad Mullahs and Englishmen: Discourse in the Colonial Encounter'. *Comparative Studies in Society and History,* 31.4 (1989): 649–70.

Edwards, Owen Dudley. 'Macaulay's Warren Hastings.' *The Impeachment Of Warren Hastings: Papers from a Bicentenary Commemoration.* Ed. Geoffrey Carnell and Colin Nicholson. Edinburgh: Edinburgh University Press, 1989. 109–44.

Enloe, Cynthia. *Bananas, Beaches, and Bases: Making Feminist Sense of International Politics.* 1989. Berkeley: University of California Press, 2000.

Farrell, J.G. *The Siege of Krishnapur.* 1973. London: Phoenix, 1993.

Forster, E.M. *A Passage to India.* 1924. Ed. Oliver Stallybrass. London: Penguin, 1989.

Forster, E.M. *Selected Letters of E.M. Forster: Vol. 1: 1879–1920.* Ed. Mary Lago and P.N. Furbank. London: Collins, 1983.

Gandhi, M.K. 'A Drain Inspector's Report.' *The Collected Works of Mahatma Gandhi.* Vol. 34. New Delhi: Publications Division, Government of India, 1969. 539–547.

Ganguly, Swagato. 'A Weakness of Reason: Idolatrous Subjects and Colonial Order in British India.' Dissertation, University of Pennsylvania, 1998.

George, Rosemary Marangoly. *The Politics of Home: Postcolonial Relocations and Twentieth Century Fictions*. Berkeley and Los Angeles: University of California Press, 1999.

Ghose, Indira. *Women Travellers in Colonial India*. New Delhi: Oxford University Press, 1998.

Ghosh, Amitav. 'The Imam and the Indian.' *The Imam and the Indian: Prose Pieces*. New Delhi: Ravi Dayal, 2002. 1–12.

Gibbes, Phebe. *Hartly House, Calcutta*. 1789. Ed. Michael J. Franklin. New Delhi: Oxford University Press, 2007.

Gray, Russell Ion. 'The Man Alone in British Colonial and Scientific Romance 1886–1904.' Dissertation, University of Edinburgh, 2007.

Gregg, Hilda. 'The Indian Mutiny in Fiction.' *Blackwood's Edinburgh Magazine* February 1897: 218–31.

Greenberger, Allen J. *The British Image of India: A Study of the Literature of Imperialism*. London: Oxford University Press, 1969.

Guha, Ranajit. 'The Prose of Counter-Insurgency.' 1988. *Postcolonial Discourses: An Anthology*. Ed. Gregory Castle. Oxford: Blackwell, 2001. 120–50.

Gupta, Brijen K. *India in English Fiction, 1800–1970: An Annotated Bibliography*. Metuchen: Scarecrow Press, 1973.

Heathorn, Stephen J. 'Angel of Empire: The Cawnpore Memorial Well as a British Site of Imperial Remembrance.' *Journal of Colonialism and Colonial History* 8.3 (2007).

Herbert, Christopher. *War of No Pity: The Indian Mutiny and Victorian Trauma*. Princeton: Princeton University Press, 2008.

Hibbert, Christopher. *The Great Mutiny, India 1857*. 1978. Harmondsworth: Penguin, 1980.

Hobsbawm, Eric. *The Age of Empire, 1875–1914*. London: Weidenfeld and Nicolson, 1987.

Hopkirk, Peter. *The Great Game: The Struggle for Empire in Central Asia*. London: John Murray, 1990.

Hopkirk, Peter. *Quest for Kim: In Search of Kipling's Great Game*. 1996. Oxford: Oxford University Press, 1997.

Hussain, Yasmin. *Writing Diaspora: South Asian Women, Culture and Ethnicity*. Aldershot: Ashgate, 2005.

Hutchins, Francis G. *The Illusion of Permanence: British Imperialism in India*. Princeton: Princeton University Press, 1967.

Hyam, Ronald. *Empire and Sexuality: The British Experience*. Manchester: Manchester University Press, 1990.

'Idolatry.' Review of *Idolatry*, by Alice Perrin. *Times Literary Supplement* 11 February 1909: 53.

Ignatiev, Noel. *How the Irish Became White*. London: Routledge, 1996.

James, Lawrence. *Raj: The Making and Unmaking of British India*. London: Little, Brown and Co., 1997.

Jasanoff, Maya. *Edge of Empire: Lives, Culture, and Conquest in the East, 1750–1850*. New York: Knopf, 2005.

Jenkyns, Richard. *The Victorians and Ancient Greece*. Oxford: Blackwell, 1980.

Johnston, Anna. *Missionary Writing and Empire, 1800–1860*. Cambridge: Cambridge University Press, 2003.

Joseph, Betty. *Reading the East India Company, 1720–1840: Colonial Currencies of Gender*. London and Chicago: Chicago University Press, 2004.

Judd, Denis. *The Lion and the Tiger: The Rise and Fall of the British Raj 1600–1947*. London: Oxford University Press, 2004.

Katrak, Ketu. 'Indian Nationalism, Gandhian Satyagraha, and Representations of Female Sexuality.' *Nationalisms and Sexualities*. Ed. Andrew Parker, Mary Russo, Doris Sommer, and Patricia Yaeger. New York: Routledge, 1991. 395–406.

Kipling, Rudyard. 'Lispeth.' *Plain Tales from the Hills*. 1888. Oxford: Oxford University Press, 1987. 7–11.

Kipling, Rudyard. 'Beyond the Pale.' *Plain Tales from the Hills*. 1888. Oxford: Oxford University Press, 1987. 127–32.

Kipling, Rudyard. 'Yoked to an Unbeliever.' *Plain Tales from the Hills*. 1888. Oxford: Oxford University Press, 1987. 30–34.

Kipling, Rudyard. 'The Ballad of East and West.' 1889. *A Choice of Kipling's Verse*. Ed. T.S. Eliot. London: Faber, 1941. 111–16.

Kipling, Rudyard. *Kim*. 1901. Oxford: Oxford University Press, 1998.

Kipnis, Laura. 'Adultery.' *Intimacy*. Ed. Lauren Berlant. London and Chicago: University of Chicago Press, 2000. 9–47.

Lawson, Philip. *The East India Company: A History*. London: Longman, 1993.

Le Mesurier, A. *From London to Bokhara and a Ride through Persia*. London: Bentley, 1889.

Lewis, Ivor. *Sahibs, Nabobs and Boxwallahs: A Dictionary of the Words of Anglo-India*. 1991. Delhi: Oxford University Press, 1997.

Low, Gail Ching-Liang. *White Skin, Black Masks: Representation and Colonialism*. London: Routledge, 1996.

Macaulay, Lord Thomas Babington. 'Minute on Indian Education.' *Archives of Empire, Volume 1: From the East India Company to the Suez Canal*. Ed. Barbara Harlow and Mia Carter. Durham and London: Duke University Press, 2003. 227–38.

Macaulay, Lord Thomas Babington. 'Government of India.' *Macaulay, Prose and Poetry*. Ed. G.M. Young. 1952. London: Rupert Hart-Davis, 1967. 688–718.

McClintock, Anne. *Imperial Leather: Race, Gender and Sexuality in the Colonial Contest*. London and New York: Routledge, 1995.

MacMillan, Margaret. *Women of the Raj*. 1988. London: Thames and Hudson, 1996.

Mahmood, Cynthia Keppley. *Faith and Nation: Dialogues with Sikh Militants*. Philadelphia: University of Pennsylvania Press, 1996.

Malgonkar, Manohar. *The Devil's Wind*. 1972. New Delhi: Penguin India, 1988.

Mangan, J.A., and James Walvin. 'Introduction.' *Manliness and Morality: Middle-Class Masculinity in Britain and America, 1800–1940*. Ed. J.A. Mangan and James Walvin. Manchester: Manchester University Press, 1987. 1–6.

Marshman, John Clark. *Memoirs of Major-General Sir Henry Havelock, K.C.B.* 1860. London: Longmans, Green and Co., 1909.

Marx, Karl, and Friedrich Engels. *The First Indian War of Independence 1857–1859*. 1959. Moscow: Progress Publishers, 1988.

Mason, A.E.W. *The Broken Road*. 1907. Ed. Ralph Crane. New Delhi: Oxford University Press, 2008.

Mason, Philip. *The Men Who Ruled India*. 2 vols. 1953 and 1954. Abridged ed. 1985. New Delhi: Rupa, 1992.

Mayo, Katherine. *Mother India*. London: Jonathan Cape, 1927.

Mercer, Kobena. *Welcome to the Jungle*. London: Routledge, 1994.

Metcalf, Barbara D., and Thomas R. Metcalf. *A Concise History of India*. Cambridge: Cambridge University Press, 2002.

Metcalf, Thomas R. *Ideologies of the Raj*. New Cambridge History of India 3.4. Cambridge: Cambridge University Press, 1995.

Mishra, Vijay. 'The Diasporic Imaginary: Theorizing the Indian Diaspora.' *Textual Practice* 10.3 (1996): 421–47.

Mohanram, Radhika. *Imperial White: Race, Diaspora, and the British Empire.* Minneapolis: University of Minnesota Press, 2007.

Mohanty, Chandra Talpade. 'Under Western Eyes: Feminist Scholarship and Colonial Discourses.' *Boundary 2* 12.3 (1984): 333–58.

Moorhouse, Geoffrey. *India Britannica.* London: Collins, 1983.

Morey, Peter. *Fictions of India: Narrative and Power.* Edinburgh: Edinburgh University Press, 2001.

Mukerji, Chandra. 'Visual Language in Science and the Exercise of Power: The Case of Cartography in Early Modern Europe.' *Studies in Visual Communications* 10.3 (1984): 30–45.

Mukherjee, Sujit. *Forster and Further: The Tradition of Anglo-Indian Fiction.* Hyderabad: Orient Longman, 1993.

Mullens, Joseph. *The Results of Missionary Labour in India.* London: London Missionary Society, 1852.

Mundy, Talbot. 'Hookum Hai.' *Told in the East.* New York: McKinlay, Stone and Mackenzie, 1920. 1–128.

Naik, M.K. *Mirror on the Wall: Images of India and the Englishman in Anglo-Indian Fiction.* New Delhi: Sterling, 1991.

Nayar, Pramod K., ed. *The Penguin 1857 Reader.* New Delhi: Penguin, 2007.

Newsome, David. *Godliness and Good Learning: Four Studies on a Victorian Ideal.* London: John Murray, 1961.

Oaten, Edward Farley. *A Sketch of Anglo-Indian Literature.* London: Kegan, 1908.

Office for National Statistics. 'Migration Statistics Quarterly Report, February 2012.' *Office for National Statistics.* Web. 23 October 2012.

Parkes, Fanny, *Begums, Thugs and Englishmen: The Journals of Fanny Parkes.* 1850. Ed. William Dalrymple. New Delhi: Penguin, 2003.

Parry, Benita. *Delusions and Discoveries: Studies on India in the British Imagination 1880–1930.* Berkeley and Los Angeles: University of California Press, 1972.

Paxton, Nancy L. *Writing Under the Raj: Gender, Race, and Rape in the British Colonial Imagination, 1830–1947.* New Brunswick: Rutgers University Press, 1999.

Pearce, Charles E. *Love Besieged: A Romance of the Defence of Lucknow.* 1909. Ed. Ralph Crane. New Delhi: Oxford University Press, 2003.

Pearce, Charles E. *Red Revenge: A Romance of Cawnpore.* 1911. Toronto: The Copp, Clark Co., 1912.

Penny, F.E. *The Outcaste.* London: Chatto & Windus, 1912.

Perrin, Alice. *Idolatry.* London: Chatto & Windus, 1909.

Radhakrishnan, R. 'Nationalism, Gender, and the Narrative of Identity.' *Nationalism and Sexualities.* Ed. Andrew Parker, Mary Russo, Doris Sommer, and Patricia Yaeger. New York: Routledge, 1991. 77–95.

Ray, Sangeeta. *En-Gendering India: Woman and Nation in Colonial and Postcolonial Narratives.* Durham: Duke University Press, 2000.

Richardson, Angelique. *Love and Eugenics in the Late Nineteenth Century: Rational Reproduction and the New Woman.* Oxford: Oxford University Press, 2003.

Riddick, John F. *The History of British India: A Chronology.* New York: Praeger, 2006.

Robinson, Jane. *Angels of Albion: Women of the Indian Mutiny.* London: Viking, 1996.

Rougement, Denis de. *Love in the Western World.* Trans. Montgomery Belgion. 1956. New York: Schocken, 1990.

Said, Edward W. *Culture and Imperialism*. London: Chatto & Windus, 1993.

Said, Edward W. 'Reflections on Exile.' *Reflections on Exile and Other Essays*. Cambridge: Harvard University Press, 2001. 173–86.

Sangari, Kumkum, and Sudesh Vaid, eds. *Recasting Women: Essays in Indian Colonial History*. New Delhi: Kali for Women, 1989.

Scott, Joan. 'Gender: A Useful Category of Historical Analysis.' *American Historical Review* 91 (1986): 1053–75.

Sen, Indrani. *Woman and Empire: Representations in the Writings of British India (1858–1900)*. New Delhi: Orient Longman, 2002.

Sharpe, Jenny. *Allegories of Empire*. London and Minneapolis: University of Minnesota Press, 1993.

Singh, Bhupal. *A Survey of Anglo-Indian Fiction*. London: Oxford University Press, 1934.

Singh, Shailendra Dhari. *Novels on the Indian Mutiny*. New Delhi: Arnold-Heinemann India, 1973.

Sinha, Mrinalini. *Colonial Masculinity: The 'Manly Englishman' and the 'Effeminate Bengali' in the Late Nineteenth Century*. Manchester: Manchester University Press, 1995.

Spivak, Gayatri Chakravorty. 'Three Women's Texts and a Critique of Imperialism.' *Critical Inquiry* 12.1 (1985): 235–61.

Spivak, Gayatri Chakravorty. 'Can the Subaltern Speak?' *Marxism and the Interpretation of Culture*. Ed. Cary Nelson and Lawrence Grossberg. Basingstoke: Macmillan, 1988. 271–313.

Spivak, Gayatri Chakravorty. *A Critique of Postcolonial Reason: Toward a History of the Vanishing Present*. Cambridge: Harvard University Press, 1999.

Steel, Flora Annie. *On the Face of the Waters*. 1896. *A Raj Collection*. Ed. Saros Cowasjee. New Delhi: Oxford University Press, 2005. 1–391.

Steel, Flora Annie, and Grace Gardiner. *The Complete Indian Housekeeper and Cook*. 1888. Ed. Ralph Crane and Anna Johnston. Oxford: Oxford University Press, 2010.

Stepan, Nancy. 'Biological Degeneration: Races and Proper Place.' *Degeneration: The Dark Side of Progress*. Ed. J. Edward Chamberlain and Sander L. Gilman. New York: Columbia University Press, 1985. 97–120.

Stoler, Ann Laura. *Carnal Knowledge and Imperial Power: Race and the Intimate in Colonial Rule*. Berkeley and Los Angeles: University of California Press, 2002.

Stoler, Ann Laura. 'Educating Desire in Colonial Southeast Asia: Foucault, Freud and Imperial Sexualities.' *Sites of Desire, Economies of Pleasure: Sexualities in Asia and the Pacific*. Ed. Leonore Manderson and Margaret Jolly. London and Chicago: University of Chicago Press, 1997. 27–47.

Stone, Lawrence. *The Family, Sex and Marriage in England. 1500–1800*. New York: Harper and Row, 1979.

Teltscher, Kate. *India Inscribed: European Writing on India 1600–1800*. Delhi: Oxford University Press, 1995.

Teo, Hsu-Ming. 'Romancing the Raj: Interracial Relations in Anglo-Indian Romance Novels.' *History of Intellectual Culture* 4.1 (2004): 1–16.

Thorne, Susan. 'Religion and Empire at Home.' *At Home with the Empire: Metropolitan Culture and the Imperial World*. Ed. Catherine Hall and Sonya O. Rose. Cambridge: Cambridge University Press, 2006. 143–65.

'The Mutinies in India'. *The Times* 17 September 1957: 9+.

Tobin, Beth Fowkes. *Picturing Imperial Power: Colonial Subjects in Eighteenth-Century British Painting*. Durham: Duke University Press, 1999.

Tololyan, Khachig. 'Elites and Institutions in the Armenian Transnation.' *Diaspora: A Journal of Transnational Studies* 9.1 (2000): 107–36.

Tosh, John. *Manliness and Masculinities in Nineteenth-Century Britain: Essays on Gender, Family and Empire*. Harlow: Pearson, 2005.

Trevelyan, E.J. 'Marriage Between English Women and Natives of British India.' *Journal of the Society of Comparative Legislation* NS 17.1–2 (1917): 223–26.

Van der Veer, Peter. *Imperial Encounters: Religion and Modernity in India and Britain*. Princeton: Princeton University Press, 2001.

Vertovec, Steven. 'Three Meanings of Diaspora, Exemplified among South Asian Religions.' *Diaspora: A Journal of Transnational Studies* 6.3 (1997): 277–99.

Viswanathan, Gauri. *Masks of Conquest: Literary Study and British Rule in India*. 1989. London: Faber, 1990.

Viswanathan, Gauri. *Outside the Fold: Conversion, Modernity, and Belief*. Princeton: Princeton University Press, 1998.

Vogt, Carl. *Lectures on Man: His Place in Creation and in the History of the Earth*. London: Green and Roberts, 1864.

Ward, Andrew. *Our Bones Are Scattered: The Cawnpore Massacres and the Indian Mutiny of 1857*. 1996. London: Murray, 2004.

Weeks, Jeffrey. *Sex, Politics and Society: The Regulation of Sexuality Since 1800*. London: Longman, 1981.

White, Paul. 'Geography, Literature and Migration.' *Writing Across Worlds: Literature and Migration*. Ed. Russell King, John Connell, and Paul White. London and New York: Routledge, 1995. 1–19.

Wilkie, Everett C., Jr. 'Margaret Wilson.' *Dictionary of Literary Biography, Volume 9: American Novelists, 1919–1945*. Ed. James J. Martine. Detroit: Gale, 1981. 159–66.

Wilson, Margaret. *Daughters of India*. 1928. Ed. Ralph Crane. New Delhi: Oxford University Press, 2007.

Index

Abbott, James 19–20, 59–60n5
Adams, J.H. 130
adventure fiction 55–9
Afghanistan 56–9
Age of Consent Act (1891) 43
Allen, Charles 60
Almond, Dr H.H. 38–9
American Baptist Foreign Mission
     Society 90
American Civil War 19
Amritsar 98
Anglo-Indian
     attacks on Indian culture and
        customs by British colonisers 8–9,
        22, 121–2
     binarisms 4, 53–4, 137
     definition of 5–6, 10
     fiction 2, 10–11, 16, 17, 17–19, 22–3,
        24, 36–7
     interracial marriage 108–20
     missionary imperative 20
     racial hierarchies 67–8, 80, 81–2
     rationialisation of imperialism 19–20,
        34–5
     sense of identity 2, 4–5, 12–13, 14,
        78–9, 105
     symbolism of British clothing 4–5,
        105, 111, 121
     see also diasporic status; racial
        hierarchies
Appadurai, Arjun 138

Ardis, Ann 118
Arnold, David 79, 103
Arnold, Matthew 17
Arnold, Thomas 38
Arnold, William Delafield 17
Atkinson, Captain George Francklin
        88–9
Axel, Brian 12, 16

Baden-Powell, Robert 113
Ballhatchet, Kenneth 109, 132
Baptist Missionary Society (Serampore)
        86
Barker, Thomas Jones 27–8
Barr, Pat 9–10
Battle of Plassey 7, 11–12
Baucom, Ian 59
Beddoe, John 78
Benares 75
Bengal 7–8, 23, 137–8
Bentham, Jeremy 8
Bentinck, Lord William 8–9, 49, 76
Berlant, Lauren 120–1, 135
Bernal, Martin 75
Bhabha, Homi 63, 66, 69–70, 72, 74, 77,
        126
Bhor, Marie 48
biracial relationships see racial
        hierarchies
Blunt, Alison 14, 15, 26, 30
Boehmer, Elleke 32n5

Bokhara 59
Bombay 7, 17
Boyarin, Daniel 3
Boyarin, Jonathan 3
Brah, Avtar 5, 53–4
Braziel, Jana 137
British
    colonization of India 2–3, 7–9
    Raj regime 9, 55, 93
Bromfield, Louis 11
Brontë, Charlotte 47, 96–8, 99–100, 104, 106
Bruce, Henry 89
Brunes, Alexander 19–20
Brydon, William 56–7n1
Buettner, Elizabeth 51–2, 103
Burke, Edmund 62
Burke, Thomas Henry 78
Burma 23
Burma Circular (1867) 20, 108–9
Burnes, Alexander 'Bokhara' 59–60
Burton, Antoinette 47, 48, 87, 129
Butler, Josephine 47, 129–30
Butler, Judith 125–6
Butler, Lady Elizabeth 56–7

Calcutta 17, 75
Campbell, Mary Jane 92
Campbell, Sir Colin 27
Candler, Edmund 17
Carey, Revd William 86
Carpenter, Mary 130
Cavendish, Lord Frederick 78
Cavignari, Louis 58
Cawnpore 1, 13–16, 24–6, 29, 33, 39, 43, 50
    see also massacre art memorials
Chakravarty, Gautam 18
Chamberlain, Edward 67
Chambers, Iain 3
Chatterjee, Partha 41, 130–1
Chesney, Sir George Tomkyns 17
Chinhut 40
Chowdhry, Prem 116
Chunder, Bholanauth 30
Church of England, establishment in India 8
Church Missionary Society 86
Clarke, G. Kitson 84

class systems
    degeneration 66–8, 73, 114
    working class Indians and ruling elite 117
Clive, Lord Robert 7, 59
Cobbold, Captain Ralph 61
Colley, Linda 12–13
Collingham, E.M. 4, 13, 52, 83, 121–2
Conolly, Arthur 19–20, 59–60
Contagious Diseases Acts 46–7, 52, 129
Cook, Thomas 13
Cotes, Mrs Everard *see* Duncan, Sara Jeanette
Cowasjee, Saros 17, 18
Crane, Ralph 18
Crew Circular (1909) 20, 108–9
Crocker, B.M. 101
Croker, Bithia M. 17
Cronin, Richard 18
Crosby, Alfred 136
Cross, Victoria 18–19, 20, 110, 114, 116, 134–5
    Life of My Heart 110, 116–17, 120–1, 123–6
cross-cultural relationships 108–10, 112–19
Cunningham, Henry Stuart 17
Cuvier, Georges 67

Dalhousie's Doctrine of Lapse 23
Dalrymple, William 110
Das, Veena 12
David, Saul 28–9, 39
Davidoff, Leonore 51
Dawson, Graham 40–1
de Boigne, Benoît 112, 114
de Moraine, Rene 24, 25
de Rougement, Denis 96
degeneration 66–8, 73, 114
Delhi 13, 15–16, 24, 25, 29, 75
diasporic status 136–8
    definition 138
    gender 2, 9–10, 11–12, 14–15, 53–4, 55–6
    importance of history 3, 14, 31
    reiteration of home 4–5, 21, 107
    sexuality 2, 20, 108–9, 135
    see also imperialism
Dick, G. 114

Dickens, Charles 30, 105, 106
Disraeli, Benjamin 31
Diver, Maud 17, 18–19, 20, 56, 61, 90–1,
    101, 102–3, 114
    Lilamani 110, 116, 126–35
Doyle, Arthur Conan 58
Duncan, Sara Jeannette 11, 17
Dutch East India Company 7
Dyer, Richard 19, 99

East India Company 5–6, 8, 9, 12, 31, 55,
    76, 77, 84, 85, 87, 101
Eden, Emily 9
Edmonstone, Neil 112
education
    British approach in India 9
    public school models 37–8, 40–1
    valorization of militaristic qualities
        37–8, 38–9, 42–4, 55–6
    see also Macauley, Sir Thomas
        Babington
Edwardes, Michael 60
Eliot, George 105, 106
Enloe, Cynthia 113
Eurasian *see* Anglo-Indian; racial
    hierarchies

Farrell, J.G. 18, 27, 28, 29, 60
Fay, Eliza 113
female infanticide 8
femininity *see* gender
feminism 128–9
    relationship to colonialism 95,
        116–18, 130
    white femininity 126–7
    zenana 86–7, 129, 132
    see also New Woman
fiction
    adventure fiction 55–9
    Anglo-Indian 2, 10–11, 16, 17, 17–19,
        22–3, 24, 36–7
    missionary genre 83–5, 87–8, 89–90,
        92
    mutiny fiction 19, 22–3, 24, 32–44
    romance plot 39–40, 55–6
    siege/military plot 39–40, 55–6
Forster, E.M. 17, 63, 90–1, 100, 116
Franklin, Michael J. 113
Fraser, Sir William 111–12

Freres, Bequet 24, 25
Freud, Sigmund 2, 96

Gardiner, Grace 93
gender 2, 9–10, 11–12, 14–15
    attributes of Indian sexuality 43–4,
        71–2, 113
    constructions of gender as metaphors
        for imperialism 33–4, 35, 49–50,
        109, 116
    definition of Indian and Anglo-Indian
        femininity 45, 46–7, 71–2, 126–7
    iconography of attacks on women
        and children 24–5, 27–8, 29–30,
        31, 33–4, 43, 50, 112–13
    public school models 37–8, 40–1
    redefining of masculinity 37–44, 53,
        55–6, 82, 132–3
    relationship between British
        feminists and Indians 46–8, 52–3
    structure of marriage in Anglo-Indian
        society 50–3
    valorization of militaristic qualities
        37–8, 38–9, 42–4, 55–6
General Service Enlistment Act (1856)
    23
George, Rosemary Marangoly 54
Ghosh, Amitav 3
Gibbes, Phebe 16, 113
Gibbon, Frederick P. 28
Gilman, Sander 67
Godden, Rumer 17
Goodall, Frederick 27–8
Grant, Charles 66, 77, 84
Grant, James 24
Great Game 59–62, 73, 74, 82
Greenberger, Allen J. 17, 18, 55–6, 64,
    134
Gregg, Hilda 22
Guha, Ranajit 36
Gupta, Brijen K. 18, 22
Gwalior 29

Habermas, Jürgen 121
Haggard, H. Rider 36
Hall, Catherine 51
Hamilton, Elizabeth 16
Harcourt, A.F.P. 24
Haskell 62

Hastings, Warren 8, 110
Havelock, General Sir Henry 13, 27, 37n7,
    39, 40
Heathorn, Stephen J. 13
Henty, G.A. 28, 36n6, 55–6
Herbert, Christopher 16, 22–3
Hickey, William 113
Hobsbawm, Eric 32n5
Hodges, William 113
Hopkirk, Peter 59–60
Horne, Amelia 25n2
Hunter, William W. 90
Hussain, Yasmin 3
Hutchins, Francis 31
Hyam, Ronald 51, 109
Hyatt, H.W. 62

identity, effect of diasporic status on
    sense of identity 1–2
Ignatiev, Noel 78, 99
Ilbert Bill (1883) 43, 45, 46, 47–8
imperialism 2, 11–13, 82
    notion of duty and trusteeship 62
    rationalisation 21, 31, 72
    relationship to feminism 116–17,
        129–30
    valorizing of masculine civilizers 56,
        64
India Act (1833) 8, 86
Indian, attacks on Indian culture and
    customs by British colonisers 8–9,
        22
Indian Mutiny (1857) 4, 9, 11–12, 23–8,
    31, 55, 71, 112–13
    iconography of attacks on women
        and children 24–5, 27–8, 29–30,
        31, 33–4, 43, 50, 112–13
    Mutiny fiction 19, 22–3, 24, 32–44
    see also Cawnpore; Delhi; Lucknow
International Council of Women (ICW)
    48
Irwin, H.C. 28
Islam, Shamsul 18

Jafar, Mir 7–8
Jalabahad 56–7
James, Lawrence 56, 59, 60–1
Jasanoff, Maya 112
Jenkyns, Richard 123

Jewish diaspora 3, 21
Jhabvala, Ruth Prawer 18
Johnston, Anna 86–7
Joseph, Betty 85, 110
Judd, Denis 55
Judson, Adoniram 90

Kabul 56–7, 60
Kashmir 59
Kavanagh, T. Henry 16
Kaye, M.M. 18, 60
Kincaid, Dennis 17
Kindersley, Jemima 113
Kipling, Rudyard 5, 17, 18–19, 20,
    59–60, 61–3, 89–90, 101, 113–14,
    127, 133
    Kim 73–80, 81–2
Kipnis, Laura 120
Kirkpatrick, Colonel James Achilles
    110–11, 113

Lacan, Jacques 96
Lambton, William 59
Laqueur 62
Laurence, Sir John 28–9
Lawrence, General Sir Henry 13, 27, 37,
    39, 60n5
Lawson, Philip 5
Le Mesurier, Colonel A. 61
Lewis, Ivor 10
Llewellyn-Jones, Rosie 13, 14
Lloyd, David 65
London Missionary Society 86
Low, Gail 80
Lucknow 13, 15–16, 27–8, 29, 30, 54,
    113

Macaulay, Sir Thomas Babington 9, 28,
    41–2, 66, 69–70, 72, 74–6, 77, 86
McClintock, Anne 66–7
Maclean, Colonel Charles 60–1
MacMillan, Margaret 46
Madras 7, 17
Magdoff, Harry 136
Mahmood, Cynthia Keppley 14
Malcolm, John 10
Malgonkar, Manohar 27, 29
Mannur, Anita 137
mapping of subcontinent 59, 76–7

Married Women's Property Act (1882) 118
Martin, Claude 112
Marx, Karl 31
masculinity *see* gender
Mason, A.E.W. 18–20, 61–2
    The Broken Road 60, 62–3, 66, 68–71, 72–3, 81–2
Mason, Philip 24
Masood, Syed Ross 100
massacre art memorials 14–15
Masters, John 18, 60
Matrimonial Causes Act (1857) 51
Mayo, Katherine 94, 130
Meerut 23–4
Mercer, Kobena 137
Metcalf, Barbara 23–4
Metcalf, Thomas 8, 23–4
Mill, James 8
Mill, John Stuart 8
mimicry
    postcolonial 63–6
    The Broken Road 68–73, 81–2
    see also Bhabha, Homi; degeneration
miscegenation 15, 113, 122–3, 128, 132
Mishra, Vijay 5
missionaries
    conversion imperative 87, 90–1
    fiction genre 83–5, 87–8, 89–90, 92
    relationship to imperialism 84, 85, 98
    societal position 83, 102–3
    zenana work 86–7
    see also diasporic status
Mohanram, Radhika 10
Mohanty, Chandra Talpade 94–5
Money, Edward 27
Montgomerie, Thomas 59
Moorhouse, Geoffrey 7, 8, 9, 30, 58–9, 60n5
Morant Bay Rebellion 19
Morrow, Honoré 90
Mukherjee, Chandra 77, 117
Mukherjee, Sujit 18
Mundy, Talbot 56, 61

Nabobs *see* Anglo-Indians
Naik, M.K. 11, 18–19
Naipaul, V.S. 63
National Ladies Association 47

Neill, General 30, 40
New Woman 116–17, 118–20, 122–3, 134–5
Newsome, David 37–8, 55
Nicholson, General 28, 40
Nicholson, Lt. John 60n5
Nightingale, Florence 129
Nisbet, Hume 28

Oaten, Edward Farley 17, 18
Ochterlony, Sir David 111–12
O'Malley, L.S.S. 18
Orientalism 86
Orwell, George 63
Oudh (Awadh) 23, 37
Outram, General Sir James 27
Owenson, Sydney 87

Palmer, William 110–11, 113
Parkes, Fanny 9
Parry, Benita 18, 114, 133
Paton, Sir Joseph Noel 32–3, 34
Paxton, Nancy 55–6, 86, 88, 116–17, 124–5, 127
Pearce, Charles E. 18–19, 24, 26–7, 28, 35
    Love Besieged 32–44, 49, 50–1
Penny, F.E. 87, 101, 115, 116
Penny, Frank 88
Perrin, Alice 17, 18–19, 20, 87–8
    Idolatry 85, 100–6
Perrin, Charles 101
Peshawar 28–9
Polier, Antoine 112
postcolonialism 2
Punjab 57, 137–8

racial hierarchies 67–8, 80, 81–2
    attitudes to race-mixing 108–15, 119, 128, 132–3
    miscegenation 15, 113, 122–3, 128, 132
Ray, Sangeeta 46
Reinhard, Walter 112
Renaldi, Francesco 110
Rennell, James 59
Richardson, Angelique 118
Roberts, General 58
Robinson, Jane 24–5

romance plot 39–40, 55–6
Rose, General Sir Hugh 13
Ross, Robert 77
Rubin, David 18
Russia
    threat to British Empire 56–9, 73

Sahib, Nana 24, 25, 29, 37
Said, Edward 2, 80, 109
sati 49–50, 129
Savi, E.W. 131
Scott, Joan 33
Scott, Paul 18, 63
Scott, Sir Walter 17
Sen, Indrani 9, 84, 109n1, 118–19
sepoys 23–4, 25–6, 30, 85
    see also Indian Mutiny (1857)
Serampore 86
sexuality 2, 20, 108–9, 135
    attributes of Indian sexuality 43–4,
        71–2, 113
    miscegenation 15, 113, 122–3, 128,
        132
    structure of marriage in Anglo-Indian
        society 50–3
Sharpe, Jenny 15, 26–7, 45, 46, 113
Shelley, Percy Bysshe 87
Sherratt, Thomas H. 24
Sherwood, Mary Martha 90
siege/military plot 39–40, 55–6
Sind 57
Sinderby, Donald 114
Singh, Bhupal 10–11, 18, 23, 88, 100,
    114–16
Singh, Rashna B. 18
Singh, Shailendra Dhari 23
Sinha, Mrinalini 15, 42, 45
Skinner, James 114
social structures, effect of geographical
    movement of subjects 1–2
Solomon, Abraham 27–8
Sorabji, Cornelia 115
sowars 23
Spivak, Gayatri 4, 41, 46, 47, 49–50, 77,
    94n2
Steel, Flora Annie 17, 18–19, 24, 87, 93,
    101, 105, 114, 116
    On the Face of the Waters 32, 35,
        44–53, 50–1

Stepan, Nancy 73
Stevens, Fr Thomas 85
Stoler, Ann 15, 109
Storrow, Revd Edward 87
Surat 6
Survey of India 59
suttee 8

Taylor, Meadows 17
Teltscher, Kate 16
Tenniel, Sir John 26, 32–3
Tennyson, Alfred Lord 28
Teo, Hsu-Ming 84
Thackery, William Makepeace 17
Thomas, George 112
Thompson, Edward 17
Thorne, Susan 84, 105
thuggee 8
Tololyan, Khachig 4, 107
Tope, Tantia 29
Tosh, John 33, 38, 55
Tracy, Louis 27
Treaty of Gandamak 58
Trevelyan, G.O. 31
Trevelyan, Sir E.J. 115
Tupper, Martin 30

Vagrancy Act (1869) 79
van der Veer, Peter 13
Vellore 85
Vertovec, Steven 21
Viswanathan, Gauri 86, 99
Vogt, Carl 42

Ward, Andrew 26, 39
Weeks, Jeffrey 38
Wellesley, Richard (Earl of Mornington)
    8
Wesleyan Missionary Society 86
Weston, Christine 17
Wheeler, General Sir Hugh 13–14, 25
Wheeler, Judith 15, 25–6n2
white female diaspora 9–10
White, Paul 4
Wilkie, Everett 92
Wilson, Margaret 11, 18–19, 20, 90, 91,
    94
    Daughters of India 85, 91–100, 105,
        106